What People Are Saying About
Be On Your Best Cultural Behavior

Today, all of us interact in a global milieu, running the gamut from international business interchange to worldwide leisure travel. Often, unfamiliarity with the basic cultural nuances of a particular country can mean the difference between business success or failure. Colleen's book, a no-nonsense compendium dealing with cultural basics on a country-by-country basis, is a must-read for everyone from the highest corporate level executive to the vacation traveler. A wealth of timely and useful information.

—J. William Boyd, CMP, CMM, CITE
President & CEO
Sunbelt Motivation & Travel, Inc.

With so much relationship-building communication done digitally these days, you have to be well-prepared for every personal connection. Effective use of protocol, etiquette, even the subtleties of "small talk," in an increasingly globalized marketplace can literally make or break your business and personal success. Be On Your Best Cultural Behavior provides answers and insights that will take the potential uncertainty out of new cultural encounters and turn them into foundations for long-term relationship building. In a competitive, multicultural marketplace, this in one resource you cannot be without.

—Bruce M. MacMillan, CA
President & CEO
Meeting Professionals International

The most brilliant strategic business plan can be undone in a moment by the commission of a serious breach of international etiquette. As more and more organizations expand their operations globally, the chances of a serious derailment occurring increase dramatically—except for those who are wise enough to recognize the international communications, cultural, and etiquette challenges. This book is an incredibly rich resource that contains valuable information that every traveling business person should read and study.

—Steven Hacker, CAE
President
International Association of Exhibitions & Events

As someone who travels the world addressing issues of cultural diversity, I can testify to the usefulness of such a handy guidebook to different countries' customs. Colleen knows how to keep it simple. She gives you the basics of what you need to know to prevent embarrassment, whether you're traveling for business or pleasure. Put this book in your carry-on and give yourself a refresher course as you head to your next destination.

— Hattie Hill
Chief Executive Officer
Hattie Hill Enterprises, Inc.

It is critical to be able to see other countries through the eyes of a global citizen rather than as a citizen of your own country. Only then will you be open to other ways of living and be able to see the colors, sounds, smiles, and nuances. Understanding the culture and protocol of each country is essential for business success, but understanding their beliefs and values will make the difference in you as a human being.

—Morton H. Meyerson
Chief Executive Officer and Chairman
2M Companies, Inc.

Business today is global, whether conducted in London, Singapore, or Omaha, Nebraska. Be On Your Best Cultural Behavior touches on various cultures and beliefs in more than 30 countries that affect how you do business in those countries or how you conduct business with someone from another country in your own backyard. The book is a perfect complement to the critical business skills needed today to forge effective relationships and engage in business on a global scale. For anyone who has ever wished they knew just a little more about someone's culture before the big business meeting, Colleen's book is the answer. It is a fabulous guide to help maneuver the protocol, from introductions and gift giving to business card exchange and toasts. Approach your next meeting with confidence knowing you best cultural behavior is "by the book."

—Mary E. Power, CAE
Executive Director
Human Resource Certification Institute

A rare, brilliant find! A must in every university library, an essential tool for every briefcase. In today's global business environment, success requires knowledge of cultural and business differences, protocol, etiquette, and more. This is a must-have, must-read tool for the mainstay of your success. Having traveled to more than 110 countries with senior U.S. government officials, including the President of the United States, I would have chosen this as my first reference book.

—Michael D. Lynn CEM, CME, CMM, CMP, CPC
Director Marketing Communications, Exhibitions, Events & Protocol
Major Defense Contractor

BE ON YOUR BEST
CULTURAL
BEHAVIOR

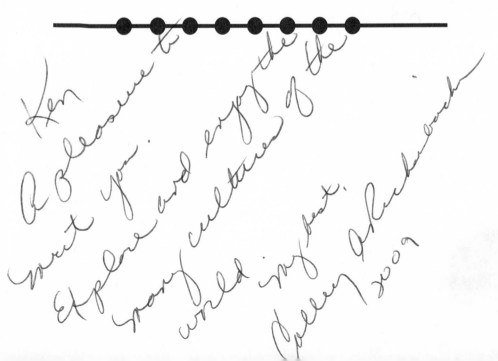

Ken

A Pleasure to
meet you.
Explore and enjoy the
many cultures of the
world. my best.
Colleen A Richardson 2009

BE ON YOUR BEST
CULTURAL
BEHAVIOR

HOW TO AVOID SOCIAL
AND PROFESSIONAL FAUX PAS
WHEN DINING, TRAVELING, CONVERSING
AND ENTERTAINING

Colleen A. Rickenbacher, CMP, CSEP, CPC

BE ON YOUR BEST CULTURAL BEHAVIOR
© 2008 Colleen Rickenbacher

Cover Design: Tim Cocklin/ Worlds of Wonder

Manufactured in the United States of America

For Information, please contact:
www.colleenrickenbacher.com

ISBN 97809787642-2-7

Dedication

To my Mom . . .
She has always been my foundation and my solid rock.
She was the best role model anyone could ever hope for
and the most gracious lady of all.

She is my angel watching over me.

Contents

Dedication VII

Acknowledgements XI

1 - Argentina 2

2 - Australia 14

3 - Austria 24

4 - Brazil 34

5 - Canada 46

6 - Chile 56

7 - China 68

8 - Egypt 84

9 - France 94

10 - Germany 106

11 - Greece 118

12 - India 128

13 - Ireland 142

14 - Israel 152

15 - Italy 162

16 - Japan 174

17 - Mexico 188

18 - Netherlands 200

19 - New Zealand 210

20 - Portugal 220

21 - Russia 230

22 - Singapore 242

23 - South Africa 256

24 - South Korea 268

25 - Spain 282

26 - Sweden 294

27 - Switzerland 306

28 - Thailand 316

29 - Turkey 330

30 - United Arab Emirates 340

31 - United Kingdom 350

32 - United States 360

33 - Vietnam 372

References 384

More Areas You May Want To Explore 386

Acknowledgments

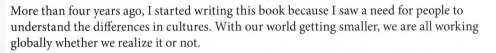

More than four years ago, I started writing this book because I saw a need for people to understand the differences in cultures. With our world getting smaller, we are all working globally whether we realize it or not.

Over the past four years, various stops and starts occurred, as they often do, but finally, I am happy to present a quick and easy reference for the business or leisure traveler. I want everyone to be comfortable, explore, make better deals, and discover something new about these 33 countries—how business deals are handled, what gifts are appropriate, or what gestures should you avoid.

Many people helped me along the way and I will forever be grateful to them. The first two people that I met in the beginning of this journey were Thomas "Tom" A. O'Brien and Carmen Mihelich. They were both so dedicated in the early creation, meeting with me numerous times for discussion. After I had to put the book on the back burner, our paths haven't crossed anymore, but their efforts were so appreciated and I hope they will be happy with the end result.

A big thanks to Hattie Hill and Bill Boyd. They proofed chapters, helped me select the countries to cover, and are always there for me when I ask them for "one more favor." Never have they ever refused.

To my other dedicated friends for being so generous with their time to read, proof, suggest, evaluate, and provide their knowledge for each country. My special thanks to Ali Alsaloom, Brenda Anderson, Belinda and Alan Barnes, Gary Drabczuk, Terry Tidwell, Betty Garrett, Sandro Jensen, Loic Le Gall, Yuri Matsuo, Danelle O'Donnell (who I literally met on a plane and asked to review a chapter), Bob Page, Sheri Pizitz, Deborah King, and Michael D. Lynn. You are all just absolutely wonderful and I truly appreciate your help.

My editor Linda C. Chandler and graphic designer Tim Cocklin helped put this all together for me. They made sure I said it properly and made it look good. They were devoted, valuable, understanding, patient, fabulous team players, and I couldn't have done this without them!

Also a kind thanks to Yolanda Hall and Natalie Mozingo at Lightning Source for her guidance and reassurance throughout the printing process.

My entire family has been so tolerant of my being in my office at all hours and promising them I only had one more chapter to go. Thank you so much for helping me make this possible. I love you all from the bottom of my heart and soul.

BE ON YOUR BEST
CULTURAL
BEHAVIOR

Chapter 1: ARGENTINA

LOCATION/GEOGRAPHY

Situated in the southern half of South America, Argentina borders Bolivia and Paraguay on the north, Uruguay and Brazil on the northeast, Chile to west and south, and the Atlantic Ocean on the southeast.

 DID YOU KNOW?

- Argentina is the second-largest country in South America (after Brazil) and eighth largest in the world.
- Mount Aconcagua 22,834 feet (6,960 m) is the highest point in Argentina and all of South America.
- The Iguazu waterfalls in Argentina are one of the largest waterfalls in the world.
- Dinosaur fossils that have been found in Argentina are some of the oldest known in the world.
- In 1816, Argentina declared independence from Spain.
- President Juan Domingo Peron was elected President in 1946. His wife, Evita, who gained notoriety for developing labor relations, died of cancer in 1952 at the age of 33.
- The Strait of Magellan, named after the famous Portuguese explorer Ferdinand Magellan, separates Tierra del Fuego from the rest of Argentina.
- Argentina hosted the World Cup soccer matches in 1978 and won. They also won in Mexico City in 1986.
- From 1991 to 2001, the Argentine peso was tied to the U.S. dollar 1:1. After this ended, Argentina plunged into major inflation.
- The name Argentina comes from the Latin word *argentum*, which means silver.
- The city of Mendoza is one of the eight wine capitals of the world.
- Argentines have the highest consumption of red meat in the world.
- Five Argentines have won Nobel Prizes in categories ranging from chemistry and medicine to peace.
- Buenos Aires has the largest number of Jews in Latin America and is commonly referred to as *Los Rusos* (the Russians) because most of the early Jewish settlers emigrated from Czarist Russia.
- Argentina is known for the tango.
- Castellian Spanish is a romance language and widely used in Latin America. Some consider Castellano more a generic term with no political or ideological link. Some will use it to differentiate their own variety of Spanish as opposed to the variety of Spanish spoken in their region.

Catellano will use "*vos*" instead of "*tu*." The pronunciation and rhythm is considerably different from that of other Latin American countries.

BUSINESS ETIQUETTE

Punctuality

- You are expected to be punctual for your business meetings, but be prepared to wait 30 minutes or more for your associate to arrive.
- The more important the person, the longer they may keep you waiting.
- Argentines put in long days. It is not unlikely to be scheduled for 8 p.m. (2000) appointments.

Meeting Manners

- Personal relationships are more critical than business ones. Be consistent with your business dealings. Do not change representatives in the middle of negotiations. It could curtail your relationship.
- Appointments are recommended. Confirm at least one week in advance.
- Women in Argentina are respected but more for the role they play as the center of the family. Currently, 41.3 percent of all Argentine women work, which is a tremendous increase over the past. A lot of this movement goes back to the efforts of Eva Peron, who helped by removing some of the formal obstacles facing women in the workplace. Legally, the women of Argentina have equal rights at all levels but still fall behind in their advancement and upper government positions. Foreign businesswomen, however, are generally not met with the level of resistance that they might encounter in other Latin American countries.
- The pace of your meeting will be slow and a meeting may last longer than anticipated.
- Argentines usually enjoy a warm and friendly atmosphere, so enjoy social conversation before starting business.
- Remain relaxed; do not push the meeting ahead or move into a hard-sell approach.
- Maintain good eye contact throughout the meeting.
- Refrain from using gestures.
- Seating is critical, and all participants usually will be escorted to their seats. The visiting senior executive is seated opposite the Argentine senior executive.
- Negotiations can be lengthy. Several meetings and discussions may be required before a deal can be made.
- Each segment of a contract or negotiation is reviewed carefully until the

contract is signed. Argentines are tough negotiators. They may go back to renegotiate, so make sure everything is in writing and signed.

- Decisions are made at the top, so try to meet with the higher ranking people in the organization.
- Observe the country's holidays and festivals when scheduling travel and appointments.

 ## Business Cards

- Cards are commonly exchanged after initial introductions.
- Print your cards in English on one side, Spanish on the other. It is not absolutely necessary but is a nice gesture.
- Remember the protocol steps of standing to present your card, having your name face the recipient as you present, and not placing cards in your back pocket.

 ## Meals/Toasts

- Eat European style with fork in left hand and knife in right and the implements never leaving your hands unless you're resting or finished with the meal.
- To indicate your meal is complete, cross the knife and fork (tines down) in the middle of your plate, or at 5:25 or at the right side of the plate.
- Rest your hands and wrists on the table, never on your lap. Never put your elbows on the table.
- Guests should wait for the host to sit down before sitting.
- Never begin eating until everyone is served.
- Offer food or drink to others before helping yourself.
- Taste everything that is served.
- Never lick your fingers.
- Never touch food with your hands.
- Your bill will not be presented until you request it.
- The host is expected to make the first toast. The guest can then follow with a toast.
- Make your toast in their language if you can. Keep toasts short—to health and happiness, for instance, or just simply raise your glass, say *salud* (sah-LOOD), which means health, and sip.
- It is acceptable for women to give toasts.
- Prepare to remain at least one to one-and-a-half hours after the dessert. Dinners may last several hours, so be prepared for a long evening.

- Dinners never start before 9 p.m. (2100) and may begin at 10 p.m. (2200) or later on weekends.
- Food and drink are served abundantly, so be ready to enjoy both. Parties usually include music and dancing.
- Argentines will frequently put soda water in their wine at dinner.
- Birthdays are a big production, involving caterers and musicians. A girl's 15th birthday, *cumpleanos de quince*, is a huge celebration.
- Tea or coffee and pastries are served between 4 p.m. and 6 p.m. (1600 and1800). If you are in a meeting, refreshments will be offered. Argentines do not put milk in their coffee, so it may not be available. In the morning, they may drink *café con leche* or *café con crema*, but after lunch or for dinner, milk is not served with coffee.
- *Yerba mate* is a drink that is prepared by steeping dry leaves of an herb called *yerba mate* in hot water. It's a little weaker stimulant than coffee and a lot gentler on the stomach. *Yerba mate* is also sold in tea bags and drunk with breakfast or as part of *menenda* (roughly afternoon tea) with *facturas* (sweet pastries). You will see people drinking this while driving. It is a very important to the culture and identity of the nation.
- To summon a waiter, just raise your hand with you index finger extended. A waiter is addressed as *Senor*, and a waitress as *Senorita*.
- Barbecues of beef and lamb are very popular. Beef is preferred over fish, chicken, or lamb. Chicken is becoming more popular and acceptable, along with pasta and fresh vegetables.
- Follow up the next day with a thank-you note to the host.

Entertainment

- Business meals, usually held in restaurants, are very popular. On the other hand, business luncheons are uncommon except in Buenos Aires. Most residents go home for lunch.
- Do not initiate business talk at a dinner. Allow your Argentine associate to start this conversation. Argentines usually do not discuss business over meals.
- A guest should always wait for the host to sit down before sitting. They should also open the door for the host before leaving.
- If you are the host, arrange payment in advance. If you cannot do this, insist on paying, no matter how many times you need to insist.
- Imported liquor is very expensive, so don't order it unless you are paying the bill. Try the local favorites.
- Argentines are serious and more formal.
- Social entertaining takes on a different tone. Do not arrive for dinners or social occasions, such as parties, exactly on time. You are expected

to be 30 to 60 minutes late. To show up on time would be impolite. But do arrive on time for a luncheon, the theater, or any scheduled events, especially soccer.

- Tender beef and red wine are common staples. Argentines love, and are very proud of, their beef and red wines.
- It is common to have long conversations with meals. Good topics of conversation include soccer, automobile racing (a well-known and beloved sport), history, culture, home, children, and the tango, which originated in Argentina.
- Argentines welcome compliments about their children, the meal, and their homes.

Forms of Address/Introductions/Greetings

- Titles are very important. Use the title and surname, which comes first on the business card.
- Using titles among the elderly is critical. When addressing them, you can use their title only. If a person does not have a professional title, then he or she should be addressed as Mr. or *Senor*, Mrs. or *Senora*, or Miss or *Senorita*, plus the surname in Spanish. Titles could include Doctor for a physician or a Ph.D., Professor is used for teachers, engineers use *Ingeniero*, and lawyers are *Abogado*.
- Hispanics will generally have two surnames. One from their father, which is listed first and then followed by one from their mother. But when addressing them, only the father's surname is used.
- Even though business greetings are becoming more relaxed, be prepared and use proper greetings. Using a first name without being invited to do so can create an uncomfortable situation. Either ask which name someone prefers, or follow suit if someone uses your first name repeatedly.
- Ask for a business card so you have the correct spelling and title.
- If you are not sure how to pronounce a name, ask them again, and if possible write it phonetically so you can pronounce it correctly.
- Say your own name slowly.
- Many women will keep their own names for business, so be correct when addressing them.
- Argentines converse at a close distance, sometimes closer than U.S. citizens, Canadians, Asians, or some Europeans are comfortable with or used to. Do not back away; they will just come closer and close the

gap. It is not unusual for a business associate to hold your elbow during conversation or to walk arm-in-arm with you down the street.

- Maintain good eye contact. It is very important and sometimes difficult at such close quarters.
- It is traditional to shake hands and nod. Greetings may last a little longer than you are accustomed to and may be followed by a squeeze of the arm, a hug, and a nod. It is customary for an Argentine to put a hand on the other person's shoulder or lapel.
- Greeting close friends may include one kiss, a full embrace, or an *abrazo*, which is a hug, handshakes and, for men, several hearty pats on the shoulder or back. Some older people might kiss twice.
- Women friends kiss each other on the cheek and shake hands with both hands. Women will not usually talk to strangers without first being properly introduced. It is very common for women to walk in the street arm-in-arm.
- Smiles are welcomed and returned.
- Avoid using overly demonstrative gestures.

 ## Appearance/Attire

- Argentines are very fashion conscious. First impressions are critical and are based on appearance and clothing.
- Avoid wearing excessive jewelry.
- Neat hair, shoes, and nails are important.
- Never wear socks with sandals. Select good quality, and always have well-polished shoes.
- If you are not sure what to wear, check with a knowledgeable person. It's better to be overdressed than underdressed.
- Jeans are worn, but they are typically fashionable designer styles.
- Women dress professionally but with considerable style and flair.
- Business dress for men consists of dark suits, light-colored or white shirts, and good quality ties. This works for both evening events and business meetings. Casual dress or informal dress will include wearing a blazer, nice dress pants, and a stylish shirt.

 ## Gift Giving

- Avoid giving knives because they represent severing a friendship.
- Avoid personal gifts such as ties and shirts.
- If you are invited to an Argentine home, bring a gift of imported chocolates, flowers, or imported liquor. Bird-of-paradise is a favorite

flower. You could also arrange to send flowers or candy to the hostess when invited to a home.

- Do not bring wine; they have an abundance of quality wine.
- When given a gift, open it immediately and show appreciation.
- Business gifts are not expected until a fairly close relationship has been established. Gifts are not necessarily reciprocal.
- High-quality gifts are appreciated but may be interpreted as a bribe attempt, especially if given too early in the relationship.
- High-quality Scotch, books, and gifts with your company logo are appropriate.
- Small gifts to secretaries or assistants are appreciated and appropriate.
- Avoid leather gifts because Argentina is a major cattle producer and manufactures an abundance of leather products.

 Tipping

- Tipping is not required but is becoming customary in restaurants. Tip 10 percent if there is not a service charge, five percent if there is one.
- Tip hotel porters and doormen 3.03 Argentine pesos (US$1).
- Tipping taxi drivers is optional, but recommended.

Gesture Awareness

- Rotating the forefinger around the ear or temple in the United States may denote "crazy," but in Argentina it means "You have a telephone call."
- Standing with your hands on your hips suggests anger or challenge.
- Slapping the inside of the thighs near the groin is considered an obscene gesture.
- Brushing the backs of the fingers under the chin, and then outward means "I don't care" or "I don't know."
- Holding the index and pinky finger up with the middle fingers down can be interpreted as "Your spouse is cheating on you."
- To indicate "so-so," Argentines will extend the hand and fingers and waggle the thumb up and down several times.
- The OK sign of making a circle by connecting your index finger to the thumb with your other three fingers extended, is considered very rude in Brazil, so many Argentines will be aware of this gesture and its meaning in its neighboring country rather than its meaning in the United States.
- A pat on the shoulder is a sign of friendship.
- Touching your thumb and finger, like holding a pinch of salt, and tapping with the index finger indicates "a lot" or "hurry up."

Faux Pas

- Avoid pouring wine with your left hand or back-handed.
- Avoid discussing the Peron years, religion, and the Malvinas War/ Falkland Island conflicts. If Argentines speak about them, do not add your comments or opinions.
- Remember Argentines are "Americans" also. Refer to "North Americans" and the United States.
- It is inappropriate to refer to South Americans as Hispanic.
- Do not sit on a table or ledge or prop your feet up on a table, chair, or desk.
- Do not eat in the street or on public transportation.
- Do not rush people or ask them to meet early.

 ## USEFUL FACTS

President	Dr. Cristina Fernandez (2007) Wife of Former President Nestor Kirchner
Vice President	Julio Cobos (2007)
National Name	Argentine Republic Republica Argentina
Size	1,056,636 square miles (2,736,690 square km)
Population	40,677,348 (2008)
Capital	Buenos Aires
Government	Republic
Currency	Argentine peso
Religions	Roman Catholic 92%, Protestant 2%, Jewish 2%, other 4%
Languages	Official: Spanish English, Italian, German, French
Ethnicity	Mostly Spanish and Italian 97%, mestizo (mixed Amerindian and Spanish ancestry), and Amerindian

Industry	Motor vehicles, textiles, food processing, farming, chemical and petrochemicals, metallurgy, and steel
Time Zone	Argentina is three hours behind Greenwich Mean Time (GMT -3) or two hours ahead of U.S. Eastern Standard Time (EST +2). Argentina does not observe daylight saving time.
Telephone Code	Country Code: +54 City Code: +11 (Buenos Aires)
Weather	Because Argentina is such a long country, the climate varies from the north to the south. The northern region is a tropical climate and can be extremely uncomfortable in the summer due to the heat and humidity. The winters are mild and can also have warm weather. The western area is a dry region, with minimal rain and hot summer months.

In the Pampas area, there are mild winters and rainy summers. The weather stays pretty neutral, with no excessive hot or cold.

Since Argentina is south of the Equator, the seasons are the reverse of Europe, North America, and most of Asia. Climate is similar to the seasons of Australia and Africa. So just make sure you check the areas you will travel and come prepared with proper clothing because you could travel from excessive heat to colder temperatures. |
| **Voltage/Frequency** | 220 V; 50 Hz |

HOLIDAYS/FESTIVALS

1 January	New Year's Day
6 January	Three Kings Day (This is the day for gift giving, not Christmas.)
February/March	Carnival (Be prepared for major public celebrations)
6 February	Memorial Day (Anniversary of the *coup d'etat* that started the dictatorial rule of the *Proceso* in 1976)
March/April	Holy Week and Easter
2 April	Malvinas Day (Tribute to the fallen in the Falklands/ Malvinas War)
1 May	Labor Day
25 May	Anniversary of the First Independent Government in Buenos Aires (In May 1810, a small revolution took place in Buenos Aires. This was the first step toward independence.)
20 June	Flag Day (Commemorates the death of Manuel Belgrano, who created the current flag)
9 July	Independence Day
17 August	Commemoration of the Death of General Jose de San Martin (The most important founding father, who liberated not only a part of Argentina but also, along with O'Higgins and Bolivar, helped liberate Chile and Peru)
21 September	Student Day
12 October	Columbus Day
8 December	Immaculate Conception Day
25 December	Christmas Day

Regional saint days and fiestas throughout the year may close down areas for a day or two. Make sure you check before scheduling your business trip and meetings. If the holiday falls on a Tuesday or Thursday, most offices will close on Monday or Friday as well as on the holiday.

LANGUAGE TIPS

Spanish	Phonetics	English
Buenos dias	bway-nohs dee-ahs	Good morning/day
Buenas tardes	bway-nahs tard-ays	Good afternoon
Buenas noches	bway-nahs noh-chays	Good evening/night

Argentina

Hola!	oh-lah	Hello!
Ciao!/Adios	Chow/ah-dee-ohs	Bye/Good-bye
Como esta usted?	koh-moh ay-stah oo-sted	How are you? (more formal)
Bien/Muy bien	bee-ehn/moy bee-ehn	Good/Very well
Por favor/gracias	pohr fah-vohr/grah-syahs	Please/thank you
De nada or por nada	day nah dah/poor nah dah	You're welcome
Bienvenidos	Byen-veh-nee-dos	Welcome

Please see chapters about other Spanish-speaking countries for additional words and phrases.

Chapter 2: AUSTRALIA

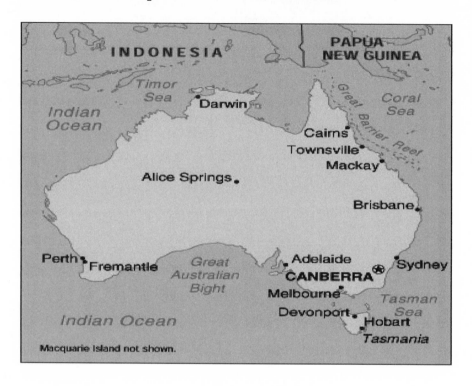

LOCATION/GEOGRAPHY

Australia lies in the Southern Hemisphere between the South Pacific
Ocean on the east and the Indian Ocean on the west. Its northern
border is just south of New Guinea and Indonesia

 DID YOU KNOW?

- The largest coral reef in the world, the Great Barrier Reef, is located on the northeastern coast of Australia.
- Australia is the world's smallest continent and biggest island. It is also the flattest and driest of the continents. It is the only continent that is an entire country.
- The Australian government is a democracy, with symbolic executive power vested in the British monarch and represented throughout Australia by the governor-general.
- Driving is on the left, and seat belts are mandatory.
- Australia produces 95 percent of the world's opals.
- The first inhabitants were the Aborigines that migrated from Southeast Asia more than 40,000 years ago. At one time there were up to one million Aborigines but today only approximately 350,000 still live in Australia.
- A British penal colony was set up at Port Jackson (now Sydney) in 1788. Approximately 161,000 English convicts were settled there until 1839, when the system was suspended.
- Free settlers and former prisoners established six colonies: New South Wales (1786); Tasmania, then Van Diemen's Land, (1825); Western Australia (1829); South Australia (1834); Victoria (1851); and Queensland (1859).
- Numerous gold rushes attracted settlers. Other inhabitants came to the area because of the mining of other minerals.
- The 3-1-1 (3 ounces—actually 3.5 fluid ounces or 100 mls—one-quart bag, one person) travel policy applies to international flights to and from Australia but not to domestic travel.
- The iconic Sydney Opera House at Bennelong Point on the harbor front took 14 years to complete and was designed by the Danish architect Joern Utzon. He resigned midway through the project and was not present when Queen Elizabeth II presided over the official opening in 1973. Despite this turmoil, the Sydney Opera House is now recognized as the symbol and true focal point of the city, and even the entire country.

BUSINESS ETIQUETTE

 Punctuality

- Arrive on time for meetings and make your appointments in advance. It's much better to arrive a few minutes early than to keep someone waiting.
- Make appointments one month in advance or with as much lead time as possible.
- If invited to a dinner party, arrive on time. Arrive no more than 15 minutes late to a *barbie* (barbeque) or a large party.
- Do not keep anyone waiting. Tardiness shows a careless attitude

 Meeting Manners

- Australians are more interested in the bottom line than in flashy presentations and wasting their time. Profit is important. Emotions and feelings are not as important in their business climate.
- Australians are easy to approach and have a friendly and open culture.
- Set up your meetings in advance. Do not make cold calls.
- They appreciate directness, but high-pressure sales and negotiations are discouraged.
- Be patient for a final decision. The decision can be collaborative. Top management generally will consult their team members and value their input before making a final decision. It takes time, so do not rush them.
- You will be taken at your word, so deliver what you promise.
- Decisions must comply with company policy.
  Saying no does not bother Australians. They value directness and brevity.
- Australians love to tease and banter, but with no insult intended. Take it in stride, and tease back. They enjoy opinionated discussions.
- Brief small talk should start your business meetings.
- Refrain from talking about your personal life during business negotiations.
- Australians frown on authority or those that consider themselves better. Be modest in your transactions and you will create a long-term, productive relationship.
- Australians are analytical and conceptual thinkers, and are open to new ideas.
- Pay attention and be a good and active listener. If you do not understand a statement or discussion, be sure to ask for explanation.
- Watch over-praising, since it can create suspicion and embarrassment.

Business Cards

- It's common to exchange business cards, and no formal ritual accompanies the exchange of cards.
- If you do not receive a card in exchange, don't consider it an insult; your counterpart possibly may not have a card.

Meals/Toasts

- It's common to be invited to an Australian home for casual barbecues. You may need to bring your own wine or beer, and you might even be asked to bring your own meat.
- Ask the hosts in advance if you could bring a dish or what they may need for the dinner.
- You can also offer your help in setting up for the dinner or cleaning up at the end.
- Table manners are Continental, with the fork in the left hand and the knife in the right hand while eating.
- To show that you are finished with your meal, place the knife and fork parallel on your plate with the handles facing to the right.
- Keep your elbows off the table but show both your hands while you are eating.
- Toasts are generally simple but some may even include parts from rhymes, poems, or songs. If you are not up on these different lyrics, then a simple "cheers" will do.

Entertainment

- Do not assume that Australian associates will pick up the tab during a social setting, even if they invited you out to dinner. Going "Dutch" is more customary for casual dining. Unless arrangements have been made and announced, be prepared to pay your own way. Of course, if you extend the invitation, you should plan to pay for everyone.
- Business and drinking generally do not mix. Enjoy your evening unless the host brings up business. If not, save business for the office or meetings.
- Many smaller restaurants, do not serve alcohol but allow you to bring your own bottle of wine, so be prepared.
- Kangaroo meat is a delicacy, but most Australians have never eaten it.
- If you are invited to a home, it is usually a very relaxed setting and you will be encouraged to help yourself. A bottle of good quality wine, a box of chocolates, or flowers would be appreciated and a nice gesture. Gifts are opened when they are received.

- Barbecues are very popular and are a relaxed atmosphere with casual dress.
- When at the pub an Australian tradition is to buy a round for everyone in your group, which collectively is called a "shout." Everyone takes a turn paying for a round, or shout, for everyone in the group. Pace yourself and get ready to "shout for a round" before the glasses are empty.

Forms of Address/Introductions/Greetings

- "*G'day*" is not the normal greeting and tourists tend to overuse the phase. A nice "hello" is better.
- A firm handshake is customary at the beginning and end of meetings.
- Women may greet each other with a kiss on the cheek.
- Eye contact is important.
- Personal space is also important, and it's good to maintain an arm's length distance from another person. It's considered pushy or rude to invade their space.
- Personal contact, such as men touching or hugging other men in public, is not acceptable.
- The full name should be used for introductions and initial meetings. "Sir" is used to express respect. Initially "Mr.," "Mrs.," or "Ms." should also be used.
- Australians generally revert to a first-name basis immediately. Wait for them to initiate first names, and then you can follow.
- You will hear "*mate*" more so than "sir." *Mate* is used to refer to one's own sex. Women also will refer to other women as *mate*. "My *mates*" refers to one's friends.
- Business titles do not impress and are not important in the Australian business culture and are rarely used. If in doubt, follow the lead of your Australian associate or counterpart.
- A friendly, modest, and relaxed approach is the best.

Appearance/Attire

- For initial meetings, business dress is still appropriate. Depending on the situation and environment, the dress could become a little more relaxed.
- Fashions follow North American trends.
- Some cities, like Brisbane, are a little more casual, with lightweight suits and clothing. Dress is more informal in tropical locations.
- Shorts are acceptable and common. In tropical areas, it is not uncommon to see a man wearing a shirt, tie, and Bermuda shorts.

- Lightweight clothes with a jacket or sweater work most of the time. Keep the rain gear handy in some areas. Dress for mild winters and warm summers.
- Jackets usually are not worn in the summer months.
- Remember when packing that Australian winter and summer seasons are opposite those of the United States and Europe. The hot months are November through March, and winter is from June to August.

Gift Giving

- If invited to a home, you can bring a modest gift, but it is not expected. Flowers, chocolates, wine or whiskey, or gifts from your home country would be appropriate for a home invitation.
- Keep gifts simple and modest.
- Gifts generally are not exchanged or given in business situations.
- Be careful about bringing gifts through customs. Check in advance to be certain that items can be brought into the country. Do not wrap gifts before arriving. Preserved food products must be in cans or bottles.
- Gifts are opened when they are presented.

Tipping

- In most instances, tipping is not expected, but it is appreciated. It is acceptable to leave a small amount if you think the service you received was exceptional. Since tipping is not common practice, many of the locals don't appreciate tourists' tipping.
- Taxi tipping is not expected but is generally practiced by tourists and is appreciated.
- Tipping in a restaurant is more common but generally not more then 10 percent of the entire bill.
- The hospitality industry is compensated well, so tips are not expected or needed as much as they are in the United States.

Gesture Awareness

- The thumbs up sign to signify OK is considered rude.
- Winking by a man to a woman is considered inappropriate.
- "V for victory" sign with palm facing inward is an obscene gesture.
- Raising one or two fingers up in the air is considered rude.
- Do not place your arm around a man's shoulder or be overly friendly man-to-man, unless you are a close friend.
- Personal contact between a man and woman, such as a man touching a woman's arm during a conversation, is not appropriate in a business setting.

Faux Pas

- Be careful if discussing politics, religion, or the Aborigines. Australians take these topics very seriously and have strong opinions. Stay away from these conversations until you get to know someone well.
- Do not criticize Australians or their country. They may do it themselves, but it is not appreciated from you.
- If you do discuss any topics that Australians find confrontational, be prepared for an argumentative discussion. This is truly enjoyable to them.
- The term "stuffed" as used in the United States to mean full after a meal is considered vulgar.
- If you are cheering for one of their sporting teams, do not state you are "*rooting*" for their team. In Australia, "*rooting*" refers to a sexual act. You want to join them and "*barrack*" for their team.
- Don't be a "*tall poppy.*" This expression is based on the notion that poppies that grow taller than their neighbors will have their heads chopped off when it is time to pick them. Australia is an egalitarian culture, where you need to be as good as your neighbor, not a class above.
- Don't overuse the term of "*G'day.*" A simple "hello" is fine.
- Never try to shop for a "fanny pack." In Australia "fanny" refers to women's genitals.
- Don't be overly talkative about kangaroos. Other topics could include the weather, sports (particularly Australian Football AFL in Victoria, and National Rugby League NRL in New South Wales and Queensland). Anything related in a positive way to Australia is an OK topic.
- A single, male rider in a taxi could sit in the front seat. A woman traveling alone should always sit in the back left passenger seat of the car. The taxi driver will be on the right.

USEFUL FACTS

Sovereign	Queen Elizabeth II (1952)
Governor-General	Quentin Bryce (2008)
Prime Minister	Kevin Rudd (2007)
National Name	Commonwealth of Australia
Size	2,941,283 square miles (7,617,931 square km)
Population	20,600,856 (2008)
Capital	Canberra
Government	Democracy
Currency	Australian dollar
Religion	Roman Catholic 26%, Anglican 21%, Uniting Church in Australia 7%, Presbyterian/Reformed 3%, other Christian 21%, Buddhists 2%, Islam 2%, 18% none.
Language	English. Largest English-speaking country in the Southern Hemisphere. School children learn Japanese as their first foreign language.
Ethnicity	Caucasian 92%, Asian 7%, Aboriginal and Other 1%
Industry	Mining, industrial and transportation equipment, food processing, chemicals, steel

Time Zone

Australia: Three time zones
Eastern Standard Time (EST) which
includes Sydney, Melbourne, Canberra
(capital), New South Wales, Australian
Capital Territory, Victoria, Tasmania and
Queensland is 10 hours ahead of Greenwich
Mean Time (GMT +10) or 15 hours ahead of
U.S. Eastern Standard Time (EST +15).
Daylight saving time is practiced in
all of Australia except Queensland and
Western Australia, which remain on
standard time throughout the entire year.

Telephone Code

International Code: +61
City Code: +2 (Canberra)

Weather

Australia is south of the equator, and due to
its large size, experiences varying weather
from region to region. Northern tropical
areas have high temperatures and humidity
with very distinct wet and dry seasons.
The central areas have drier desert regions.
The climate in the south ranges from hot to
cold, with moderate rainfall.

Voltage/Frequency

240 V; 50 Hz

HOLIDAYS/FESTIVALS

1 January	New Year's Day
26 January	Australia Day (Celebrates the establishment of white, English settlement at Port Jackson by Captain Arthur Phillip in 1788.)
March-April	Easter (Good Friday to Easter Monday)
25 April	ANZAC Day (Remembers the citizens who fell fighting or serving the country in wars. The tradition originally began to remember the Australian and New Zealand Army Corps (ANZAC) soldiers that landed at Gallipoli in Turkey during World War I.)
14 June	Queen's Birthday
25 December	Christmas
26 December	Boxing Day (This occurs on the day after Christmas except in South Australia. In South Australia, the first working day after Christmas is a public holiday called Proclamation Day. Boxing Day also is the start of the post-Christmas sales season. It has also become a major sporting day.)

LANGUAGE TIPS

Australian Terms	English Terms
Mate	Friend
Bloke/Sheila	A man/a woman
Digger	Australian
Full bottle	Knowledgeable
To be crook	To be sick or ill
Loo or dunny	Toilet
Ripper	Terrific, fantastic
Tucker	Food
Fortnight	Two weeks
Fair dinkum	Honest, truth

Chapter 3: AUSTRIA

LOCATION/GEOGRAPHY

Austria is located in central Europe, bordering the Czech Republic, Germany, Hungary, Slovakia, Slovenia, Italy, Liechtenstein, and Switzerland.

DID YOU KNOW?

- You could be fined if you do not display a valid sticker to drive in Austria. You need to purchase an Autobahn-Vignette, which is available at the border crossings and from most petrol stations and tobacconists.
- Come ready with change to visit a public bathroom. You may need this change to pay an attendant or to insert a coin in the door to unlock it. If looking for the bathroom, ask for the WC (pronounced *vay-tsay*) or *die Toilette*.
- *Tiergarten Schonbrunn* in Vienna is the oldest zoological garden in the world and was founded in 1752.
- The Austrian Alps cover 62 percent of Austria's total land area.
- The Krimmi Falls (*Krimmler Wasserfalle*), which are Europe's tallest waterfalls, are located in the state of Salzburg and are 380 meters high (1,246 Feet).
- Approximately one fourth of Austria's population lives in the capital of Vienna.
- Austria is not a member of NATO and is the only continental EU country that is not a member.
- Many famous composers of classical music, including Haydn, Mozart, Liszt, Strauss, Mahler, Bruckner, and Schubert, were of Austrian descent.
- Salzburg was the setting for *The Sound of Music*.
- Graz, Austria, is the birthplace of actor and California Governor Arnold Schwarzenegger.
- Sigmund Freud, the father of psychoanalysis, was Austrian.
- The Austrian Ferdinand Porsche was the founder of the German sports car company Porsche and also designed the Volkswagen.
- In 1818, Josef Madersperger, an Austrian, invented the sewing machine.
- There are 2.5 million tombs in Vienna's Central Cemetery (Zentralfriedhof), which is more than the city's living population. Tombs include those of Beethoven, Brahms, Gluck, Schubert, Strauss, and Schoenberg.
- The world's largest emerald, which is 2,860 carats, is displayed in the Imperial Treasury of the Hofburg (Imperial Palace) in Vienna.

BUSINESS ETIQUETTE

 Punctuality

- It's extremely important to be on time. Arriving late is seen as wasting time. If you see you will be delayed, then a telephone call is necessary to explain the delay.
- Even worse than being late for a meeting is to cancel one at the last minute. This could definitely affect your working business relationship.

 Meeting Manners

- Third-party introductions are preferred.
- Appointments should be made weeks or, at times, months in advance. Avoid August meetings—most people are on vacation the entire month— the two weeks around Christmas, and the week before Easter.
- Meetings are set in a more formal format, with definitive agendas and starting and ending times. Usually no business will be discussed if it is not on the agenda.
- Wait to be told where to sit. This is an important step in their protocol.
- Little chitchat is conducted before the start of the meeting.
- All presentations and back-up materials should be accurate and detailed.
- Keep a record of all your letters, faxes, and e-mails.
- At the conclusion of the meeting, a follow-up report or letter is important to outline all the details and further steps that will need to be taken.
- Importance is placed on long-term relationships and not on short and rushed business deals.
- Hierarchy is important. Pay attention to rank and position and the decision maker.
- Take your time in business dealings with Austrians. They want to know all the details and understand each step of the process. Be patient. Trying to force pressure or confrontational tactics will work against you and affect the outcome of your business dealings.
- Austrians may seem blunt, but they are just trying to move the discussions forward.
- Women doing business in Austria are respected as decision makers, but be prepared for the old-fashioned courtesies that will be displayed at every step along the way.

Business Cards

- There is no formal ritual during the exchange of business cards.
- Even though it is not necessary, it would be considered great attention to detail to have one side of your card translated into German.
- Always include your title and advanced academic degrees or honors on your business card. These advanced degrees and the amount of time your company has been in business are important in your business dealings. The founding date of your company (if in business for a long time) should also be stated on your card.
- Always come with plenty of business cards. You will exchange them with everyone, including the receptionist and administrative staff.

 ## Meals/Toasts

- A particular seat will be shown to you. Do not sit until shown this seat or invited.
- The style of eating is Continental, with the fork in your left hand and the knife held in the right.
- As soon as you are seated, place the napkin on your lap.
- Your host will signal the start of the meal by saying, "*mahlzeit*" or "*Guten Appetit.*"
- At less formal occasions, you may receive the food in bowls or on platters. These are placed on the table, and everyone will serve themselves. If there is a host, then wait for him to tell you to help yourself and wait for the host to take the first bite.
- To compliment the cook, try to use your fork to cut or separate the food to show its tenderness.
- Finish all food on your plate. If serving yourself, do not take large portions because it is perceived wasteful not to eat everything.
- To indicate you have finished your meal, place the knife and fork parallel on your plate with the handles facing to the right.
- At meals it is common to have Austrian beers and/or wines. A fine wine is reserved for a more formal occasion.
- Drinks and appetizers usually precede the meal. After the meal, conversation continues with coffee, brandy, or liquors. Plan to leave within an hour of the conclusion of the meal.
- Lunch is the largest meal of the day. Allow the host to bring up business first, so be prepared with chitchat leading up to the business.
- The host will give the first toast, so do not raise your glass until this takes place. The tradition is to lift your glass, clink glasses, and look the person making the toast in the eye and say, "*Prost!*" The host will make eye contact with the most senior guest.

- At the end of the meal, the honored guest will extend thanks to the host by offering a toast.

Entertainment

- More formal invitations are generally extended far in advance of an event to ensure that it does not compete with other engagements.
- It's an honor to be invited to an Austrian home. Dress conservatively, arrive on time, and come with gifts for everyone in the family.
- If the spouse of the host is included for a dinner or event, then your spouse will also receive an invitation. The seating is at the host's discretion, but traditionally the guest of honor will sit to the right of the host.
- You may be asked to remove your shoes upon entering a home. This custom is fading, but be respectful and ready just in case.
- In a restaurant you will generally seat yourself. But be careful in bars or pubs where you see a "*Stammtisch*" sign. This area or table is reserved for the "regulars" and as an outsider you should never sit there even if all other seats are taken.
- Good topics of conversation include classical music, opera, Austrian art and architecture, and winter sports.
- Topics to avoid include money, separation and divorce, religion, anti-Semitism, and the role of Austria in World War II.

Forms of Address/Introductions/Greetings

- The traditional greeting is a firm but quick handshake. Good eye contact is maintained throughout the greeting.
- Always shake hands with everyone when you enter a room.
- If you enter a meeting and you know the people, extend your hand to the most senior person first.
- Many men will still wait for a woman to extend her hand. It is still a tradition of some older Austrian men to kiss the hand of a female. But a male from another country should not follow suit and try to kiss an Austrian woman's hand. Generally they do not really kiss the hand but it's more a symbolic gesture.
- A handshake is also given at the end of the discussions.
- Titles convey respect and should be used along with surnames. Until advised to move to a more informal status with first names, continue to use surnames. First names are usually reserved for family and friends.
- As a courtesy, use *herr* (Mr.), *frau* (Mrs. or for all women regardless of her marital status), or *fraulein* (girls and young women).

- Avoid using *fraulein* to address a waitress. This old-fashioned phrase is becoming less acceptable, but you will still hear it from elderly Austrians.
- It is impolite to leave a room, building, or meeting with out saying *fuf wiedersehen* or *auf wiederschauen t*o everyone present.

Appearance/Attire

- Dress and appearance are important to Austrians. Even for a more informal occasion, they dress conservatively and never ostentatiously.
- Formal dress is the norm for the theater and special occasions. Some upscale events will even suggest a dress code.
- Men generally wear dark and conservative business suits with white shirts.
- Women wear business suits or dresses and appropriate accessories and always convey elegance.
- During the winter, you may find both men and women in the *loden* overcoat. It is heavy, wool, and usually green. Both men and women also wear hats.

Gift Giving

- Generally gifts are not exchanged for business. However, if you are presented with a gift from your Austrian associate, you should be prepared to present one immediately.
- Gifts should always be appropriately wrapped and are opened in front of one another.
- Best gifts are products from your home country or something that cannot be found in Austria.
- If invited to a home, make sure you bring gifts for the host, spouse, and children.
- Gifts for your host could include a vintage wine, brandies, chocolates, flowers, or a gift that your recipient would enjoy and appreciate.
- Avoid chrysanthemums, white lilies, red roses, or red carnations. Flowers should be presented in odd numbers. Except for 12, even numbers convey bad luck.
- Gifts for children could be candy, electronic devices, or something from your country appropriate for their age group. Children are given gifts on the feast of St. Nicholas, 6 December.

Tipping

- A service charge is usually included in the bill. If the tip is not included, then an additional 10 percent to 15 percent should be provided for the service rendered. If the tip is included, you should still add an additional amount by at least rounding up your bill.
- Tips are not left on the table. When you give your credit card or pay cash, tell the server the total amount you want to pay.
- Taxi drivers are usually given 10 percent of the fare. If the driver helps you with your luggage, a little extra should be added to the tip.

 Gesture Awareness

- To get another person's attention, raise your index finger with your palm open and facing outward.
- Putting your hands in your pockets is seen as offensively bad manners, especially among older Austrians. Keep your hands out of your pockets when talking with other people or even standing alone.
- When dining, keep your hands above the table.

 Faux Pas

- Do not flag down or hail a taxi on the street. There are designed taxi ranks or areas to secure a taxi. You can also ask the concierge of your hotel to call a taxi company for you.
- Even though they speak German, never refer to an Austrian as being a German, as Austrians are very proud of their separate national identity.
- Be careful if presenting red roses to a host in Austria, as it will give the impression that you have a romantic interest.

 USEFUL FACTS

President	Heinz Fischer (2004)
Chancellor	Alfred Gusenbauer (2007)
National Name	Republik Osterreich
Size	31,942 square miles (82,730 square km)

Population	8,205,533 (2008)
Capital	Vienna
Government	Federal Republic
Currency	Euro (formerly schilling)
Religion	Roman Catholic 74%, Protestant 5%, Islam 4%, other 5%, non-affiliated 12%
Language	German (official language), Slovene, Croatian, Hungarian
Ethnicity	Austrians 91%, former Yugoslavs 4% (includes Croatians, Slovenes, Serbs, Bosniaks), Turks 2%, Germans 1%, other 2%
Industry	Textile production, machinery production, metals, chemicals, electronics, iron, and steel
Time Zone	Austria is one hour ahead of Greenwich Mean Time (GMT +1) or six hours ahead of U.S. Eastern Standard Time (EST +6). Austria observes daylight saving time.
Telephone Code	International Code: +43 City Code: +1 (Vienna)
Weather	Cold winters with rain and some snow in the mountains and in the lowlands. Moderate summers with occasional rainfall.
Voltage/Frequency	230 V; 50 Hz

HOLIDAYS/FESTIVALS

1 January	New Year
6 January	Epiphany
1 May	Labor Day
15 August	Assumption
26 October	National Day (commemorates the State Treaty of 1955)
1 November	All Saints Day
8 December	Immaculate Conception
25 December	Christmas
26 December	Boxing Day (Also known as Feast of Saint Stephen) Over time, the meaning of Boxing Day has changed. Once celebrated by giving presents to people that have helped you throughout the year (including doormen, mail carriers, porters, and tradesmen), it is now also a day of sporting activities, like football and horse racing, and a day when stores sell their excess Christmas inventory at much reduced prices. Some stores have had such success that it has turned "Boxing Day" into "Boxing Week."

 LANGUAGE TIPS

German	Phonetics	English
Guten tag/morgen	Goo-ten tahk/morgen	Good day/morning
Guten abend	Goo-ten a-bin	Good evening
Auf wiedersehen	Auf vee-der-zane	Good-bye
Tschuss	choohs	Bye
Zahlen, bitte	TSAH-len bit-uh	The bill please
Guten Appetit	Goo-ten ah-peh-teet	Enjoy your meal.
Die Speisekarte bitte.	Dee shpy-zuh-kar-teh bit-eh	The menu, please.
Bitte	bit-uh	Please
Danke (schon) /vielen dank	Dahn-kuh	Thank you (very much)
Entschuldigung soe	Ent-shool-de-gen-zee	Excuse me
Ja/nein	Yah/nine	Yes/No

See chapters about other German-speaking countries for additional words and phrases.

Chapter 4: BRAZIL

LOCATION/GEOGRAPHY

Brazil covers half of South America and is about the size of the United States. It borders every nation on the continent except Chile and Ecuador. Forests cover 65 percent of the land area and include the world's largest tropical rain forest, the Amazon River Basin. The majority of the country lies below the Equator and its eastern coast is on the South Atlantic Ocean.

 DID YOU KNOW?

- Brazil is the only Latin American nation that derives its language and culture from Portugal.
- Early explorers found a wood that produced a red dye, pau-brasil, which gave the country its name.
- The first seedless oranges came from Brazil. Brazil produces the most oranges in the world.
- Right in the heart of downtown Brazilia, 16 cars can drive side by side on the Monumental Axis (also known as the Ministries Esplanade), which is the world's widest road.
- The most popular auto fuel in Brazil is ethanol, and it sells for considerably less than gasoline. Ethanol makers are consuming a large share of the U.S. corn crop, and this is adding to higher food prices around the world.
- Of the 15,000 known orchids, 3,000 are found in Brazil.
- More than 50 percent of Brazil's foreign trade income from the mid-1800s until the 1970s was from growing coffee beans. Brazil is still the second largest supplier of coffee in the world (behind Columbia), with 30 percent of the total and employing more than five million people in the coffee trade.
- Portuguese is the main language, but English is the language for business culture.
- Before 1960, Brazil had two capitals, Rio de Janeiro and Salvador da Bahia. The capital, Brasilia, was built to help populate the interior of the country. If seen from above, the city resembles the shape of a bird in flight, butterfly, or airplane.

BUSINESS ETIQUETTE

 ## Punctuality

- Arriving late is a fact of life in Brazil. Anticipate waiting for your Brazilian associates.
- Make appointments at least two weeks in advance, and then follow up.
- Brazilians will arrive late for work but will stay later in the evening.
- Brazilians do observe protocol when it comes to punctuality for a business meal or a meeting at a restaurant.
- Allow additional time for arrival because of the heavy traffic.
- At social dinners, arrive no more than 30 minutes late. Business dinners require on-time arrival, and parties at a club will give you a 15-minute grace period from the arranged starting time.

 ## Meeting Manners

- Be patient. It may take time to bring negotiations to a satisfactory conclusion for both sides.
- Allow them time to know you before immediately going into the business meeting. They hold long-term relationships above all. Business in Brazil is conducted mainly through personal connections.
- Women will have little trouble being accepted by their male colleagues in Brazil.
- Be prepared to discuss all aspects of the contract simultaneously rather than sequentially.
- Keep your entire team during your negotiations and until the contract is signed. The person is more important than the company.
- Use a local accountant, *condator*, and a notary, *notario*, who are familiar with the local laws and regulations instead of bringing in your own.
- Hire a contact, *despachante*, to help you work your way through all the paperwork.
- Business hours are generally 8:30 a.m. to 5:30 p.m. (0830 to 1730), Monday through Friday. The best times to schedule your meetings are from 10 a.m. to 12 p.m. (1000 to 1200) and 3 p.m. to 5 p.m. (1500 to 1700).
- Lunch and dinner are the best times to combine a meeting with a meal, but the breakfast meeting is becoming more popular.
- Banks are usually open from 10 a.m. to 4:30 p.m. (1000 to 1630)
- Expect interruptions during a meeting. Private offices are not the norm. People may walk in and out freely during your meeting.
- Always knock on office doors before you enter. Even though the formality of this act is decreasing, wait to be invited into an office.

Brazil

- Use charts, good visual handouts, or presentations for your meeting.
- Avoid any confrontations or obvious frustrations during your business meeting.
- Decisions are hierarchical, with the highest person making final decisions.
- Do not immediately leave at the end of the meeting. It will give the impression that you have more important things to do. It's wise not to schedule meetings too close together or even any other appointments on the same day. If time is a restriction, then announce this at the beginning of your meeting.

Business Cards

- It's common to exchange business cards after initial introductions.
- Printing your cards in English or your country's language on one side, Portuguese on the other, is not absolutely necessary but is a nice gesture. Your cards can easily be printed within 24 hours in Brazil.
- Bring lots. Brazilians love to exchange cards.

Meals/Toasts

- Breakfast (*pequeno almoco*) can consist of coffee, rolls, marmalade, butter, and possibly fruit. The coffee is strong and black or with hot milk ·(*café com leite*). Breakfast is usually served 7:30 a.m. to 9 a.m. (0730 to 0900)
- Their main meal of the day is traditionally lunch (*almoco*). It is a massive affair, served between noon and 2 p.m., (1200 and 1400) and an important business luncheon can take up to several hours. But don't worry; you can still get a quick lunch if your schedule or appetite requires something smaller, lighter, or quicker. On Sunday, which is saved for the family, their main meal is served at the lunch hour, but can extend into the evening hours.
- Dinner generally starts at 7:30 p.m. (1930) and is lighter than the luncheon meal or their main meal. Usually dinner consists of similar food as that served at lunch—soup; meat, chicken, or fish; rice; beans; a small salad; and ending with fruit or a sweet dessert. Business dinners at restaurants usually start at 9 p.m. (2100) Wine or beer may accompany these meals.
- A late afternoon snack (*lanche*) will consist of coffee, tea, fruit juice, and cookies.

- Be careful of dairy products that may lack refrigeration. Avoid raw shellfish and fish and uncooked vegetables or fruits (unless you can peel them). Be very careful about eating the food from street stalls or vendors. Do not drink the tap water unless there are specific signs stating it is safe. This includes avoiding ice cubes and brushing your teeth with tap water.
- People always wash their hands before eating and never touch food with their hands. Use a knife and fork for everything, including fruit and sandwiches.
- To call a waiter, hold up the index finger of your right hand.
- You will need to request your check, "*A conta, por favor.*" It will not be automatically brought to you.
- Meals are more about socializing than food. Expect to stay one hour to one-and-a-half hours after dessert.
- When inviting Brazilian friends for dinner or a party, do not suggest that your guests bring food or drink. Do not expect them to arrive on time, and never have an ending time to your dinner or party.
- Coffee is very strong, and it's their chief drink. *Mate* is a kind of tea served all the time. Cold *mate* is common in Rio and on the beaches.
- Barbecues (*churrasco*) are very popular, but the meat is not served with sauce.
- The national dish is *Feijoada*, which is black beans with beef, pork, sausage, and tongue.
- If you are toasted, raise your glass and return a toast. Make sure you drink after the toast is made before returning your glass to the table. At least give the impression you are drinking, so it is not perceived that you do not care for the sentiment of the toast.

Entertainment

- Select a well known, upscale restaurant to host your guests.
- Select a first-class hotel that can accommodate your business meetings and meals.
- Try to wait to the end of the meal and dessert before talking business. Allow your Brazilian associate to mention business first.
- Dinners usually start at 7 p.m. (1900), but it's very common for business dinners to begin at 9 p.m. (2100). Dinner parties could be all-night events, literally ending anywhere from 2 a.m. to even 7 a.m. (0200 to 0700), so be prepared.
- Good topics for discussion and small talk could include soccer, family, their country, and industry.
- Ask about their children.
- It is an honor to be invited to a Brazilian home.

Forms of Address/Introductions/Greetings

- Handshakes are common during first meetings; embraces are established early in a friendship.
- Follow the lead of your host and shake hands with everyone in the group upon arrival and departure.
- Men normally wait until the woman extends her hand.
- Men should remove their gloves when they shake hands with a woman, but it is not necessary for the woman to remove her gloves when shaking hands with a man.
- Women will kiss each other on alternating cheeks—twice if they are married, three times if single. The third kiss is to indicate good luck for finding a spouse.
- Brazilians converse in very close proximity, less than 12 inches. Do not try to back away; they will just follow you.
- Touching arms, elbows, and backs is very acceptable and common, but there is not a lot of kissing in business. Again, allow your Brazilian associate to initiate.
- In Brazil, a person's given name is followed by the mother's surname, then the father's surname. Generally in conversation, a person is addressed by his or her father's surname. Juan Herrero Hernandez is addressed in conversation as *Senhor* Hernandez.
- If you are not sure how to pronounce a person's name or the correct order, then ask. Don't guess. Use titles when appropriate.
- Brazilians will go to a first name instantly, but wait to be invited before calling them by their first name.
- Expect to be interrupted while talking with Brazilians. This conveys their excitement, not rudeness. Their conversation is fast-paced and animated.
- Brazilians are expressive and passionate when they speak. They are not arguing their points, just showing their style of communicating.
- They may directly ask your religious or political preferences, your income, and your marital status. They will reveal little of their own personal information. If you don't want to share details with them, you can be vague but polite.
- Good topics of discussion include their food, travels, their industry, arts, and definitely their sports of soccer (which is called football there), basketball, horse racing, tennis, volleyball, and fishing.

Appearance/Attire

- Brazilians tend to be very fashion-conscious and trendy even at work.
- Women dress stylishly and elegantly in all situations.

Be On Your Best Cultural Behavior

- Shoes are important and must be stylish, polished, and well kept.
- Nails and hands are important. Manicures are critical.
- The Brazilian flag is green and yellow, so avoid wearing those colors together.
- Men should wear a dark suit, shirt, and tie.
- Casual dress is nice slacks and shirt for men, and nice slacks or skirt and blouse for women.
- Parts of Brazil are hot, so clothing needs to be cooler and more comfortable. Remember their seasons are opposite of the United States and Europe, with warmer weather in January and winter in July.

 ## Gift Giving

- How the gift is wrapped is very important.
- Always open the gift in front of the giver. It's considered impolite and insulting not to do so.
- Send flowers before or after a dinner at someone's home. Include a thank-you note the following day.
- Purple and black are the colors of mourning, so avoid these colors for gifts or wrapping paper.
- Avoid giving knives, which symbolize cutting off a friendship.
- Handkerchiefs denote grief.
- Buying lunch or dinner is appropriate for a first meeting. Once you get to know the person, you can determine future gifts.
- For business, gifts are not important in establishing a relationship and not expected on the first few contacts. For business gifts, give good quality whiskey, wine, coffee table books, name brand pens, and small electronic items. Gifts of candy and Copenhagen chocolate (good quality which is made and sold in Brazil) are safe.
- Be careful to avoid a gift that could be perceived as too personal, such as a wallet, tie, jewelry, or perfume.
- An expensive gift could look like a business bribe. Present a gift at a social meeting and during a formal business meeting.
- Bring gifts for children if invited to a home. A t-shirt from your home university or sports team or a DVD of a popular and well known entertainer would be appropriate. Just make sure they have the equipment needed to enjoy your gift.

 ## Tipping

- Ten percent is generally included in a restaurant bill. Add 10 percent to 15 percent if not included. Leave extra change if a service charge is included.

- You can tip more in an upscale restaurant.
- Taxis are typically tipped 10 percent in Rio. Tipping is not expected elsewhere.
- Tip porters US$1 per bag.

Gesture Awareness

- The sign for OK in the United States, made with a circle of index finger and thumb, is considered totally unacceptable and vulgar.
- Flicking the fingertips under the chin shows that you don't understand or know the answers to the question.
- The thumbs-up gesture is used for approval.
- Clicking your tongue and shaking your head back and forth indicates your disapproval.
- Wiping your hands together indicates "it doesn't matter."
- The "fig" gesture of tucking your thumb between your index and middle finger signifies good luck.
- A finger snap means "Do it quickly."
- Yawning or stretching in public is frowned upon.
- To signal "come here," extend your hand palm down and wave your fingers toward your body.
- Snapping fingers while whipping hand up and down adds emphasis to a statement, or can indicate "long ago."
- Keep steady eye contact at all times. To break eye contact is considered impolite.

Faux Pas

- Brazilians do not consider themselves Hispanic, and they do not like being addressed in Spanish.
- Brazilians are also "Americans." Do not use "in America" when referring to the United States.
- Don't tell ethnic jokes about Portuguese, even though Brazilians may do so.
- Do not talk about politics, poverty, religion, or Argentina.
- Refer to their soccer as football (*futebol*), never as "soccer." The United States plays American football.
- Wearing the colors of their flag, green and yellow, together is disrespectful.
- Do not burp in public.

- Do not attempt to control or monopolize the conversation.
- It's considered rude to touch food with your fingers.
- Don't cut meat with your fork even if it is tender or easy enough to pull away. Use your knife.
- Do not move away during a conversation. Brazilians will stand very close.
- Smoking is illegal in most public areas.
- Do not eat on the street or while using public transportation.
- Avoid pushing or shoving people while in lines or queuing.

 ## USEFUL FACTS

President	Luiz Inacio Lula da Silva (2003)
Vice President	Jose Alencar Gomes da Silva (2003)
National Name	Republica Federativa do Brasil
Size	3,265,059 square miles (8,456,511 square km)
Population	191,908,598 (2008)
Capital	Brasilia
Government	Federal Republic
Currency	Real
Religion	Roman Catholic 77%, Protestant 15%, spiritualist 1% none 7%
Language	Official: Portuguese Spanish, English, French
Ethnicity	White 54%, mulatto (mixed) 39%, black 6%, other 1%
Industry	Major industries include coffee, sugar, iron and steel production, tourism, gold mining, automobile assembly, textiles, and petroleum
Time Zone	Brazil has four time zones, but the one most visited is three hours behind Greenwich Mean Time (–3)

or two hours ahead of Eastern Standard Time (EST +2). Brazil observes daylight saving time.

Telephone Code	Country Code: +55 City Code: +61 (Brasilia)
Weather	Ninety percent of Brazil is within the tropical zone. The climate ranges from mostly tropical in the north to temperate zones below the Tropic of Capricorn. There are five climate regions. Frosts in the southern regions and snow in the mountainous areas are not uncommon during winter.
Voltage/Frequency	110-220 V; 60 Hz

 # HOLIDAYS/FESTIVALS

1 January	New Year's Day
February/March	Carnival (the week before Ash Wednesday) Shrove Tuesday (the day before Ash Wednesday)
March/April	Good Friday to Easter
21 April	Tiradentes Day (Joaquim Jose da Silva Xavier was known as Tiradentes (Tooth Puller). He was a physician and dentist but also a leader of the first organized movement against Portugal's rule in Brazil (in 1789). After his torture and death, Tiradentes became a national hero.)
1 May	Labor Day
June	Corpus Christi (Celebrated on Thursday after Trinity Sunday to commemorate the institution of the Holy Eucharist)
7 September	Independence Day
12 October	Day of the Patroness of Brazil, Our Lady of Aparecida
2 November	All Soul's Day
15 November	Proclamation of the Republic
25 December	Christmas

LANGUAGE TIPS

Portuguese	Phonetics	English
Boa tarde	Bow-a tahr-je	Good afternoon
Boa noite	Bow-a noy-che	Good evening/night
Oi!	Oy!	Hi
Por favor	Poor fa-voor	Please
Nao falo portugues	Now fah-lo pohr-too-gase	I don't speak Portuguese
Onde esta...?	Ohn-gee-estah...	Where is...?
O banheiro	ooh bahn-yay-roo	the bathroom
O banco	ooh bahnco	the bank
Quanto que e...?	Quantoo ki eh...	How much is...?
Estou com fome	Estoh cohm foam-y	I'm hungry

Chapter 5: CANADA

LOCATION/GEOGRAPHY

Twice the area of the United States, Canada covers most of the northern part of North America. Many of Canada's geographic features are similar to those of the United States, since they share the Rocky Mountains, the Interior Plains, four of the Great Lakes, the Appalachian Highlands, and many rivers. The Atlantic, Pacific and Artic oceans touch Canada.

DID YOU KNOW?

- Canada is the second largest country in the world. (The Russian Federation is the largest.) Almost one fourth of the world's fresh water is in Canada.
- Canada is composed of 10 provinces and three territories. Canada stretches from the Atlantic Ocean to the Pacific Ocean, and the country's motto is "from sea to sea."
- The Mackenzie River is the longest river.
- Wood Buffalo National Park in Alberta is the largest park in Canada. It is home to the world's largest bison herd and the only nesting site of the endangered whooping crane.
- The Trans-Canada highway is the longest national highway in the world.
- The first snowmobile was invented in 1937 by Joseph-Armand Bombardier in Valcourt, Quebec. His dream was to build a vehicle that could "float on snow."
- Even though Canadians participate in many sports, hockey and lacrosse are their national sports.
- Canada is a bilingual country with two official languages—English and French. Although most citizens are not bilingual, the government produces information and signs in both languages. In the province of Quebec, there are stringent French-language requirements for all commercial endeavors.
- Canadians whose first language is French are commonly referred to as "Francophones." Canadians whose language is primarily English are referred to as "Anglophones." Many English-speaking Canadians are not of British descent, so the term "British Canadian" is reserved for immigrants to Canada from the United Kingdom.
- According to the Employment Standards Act, a newborn can have a parent home for approximately one year. This is unpaid time, but eligible workers can receive parental benefit payments.

- Settlers and explorers from Western Europe arrived in the 1500s. In 1535, the French explorer Jacques Cartier named Canada. The name was derived from the Iroquois and Huron word *kanata* meaning "village."
- On 1 July 1867, Canada became a country, separate from the United Kingdom.
- Pedestrians and bicycles have the right-of-way on Canadian roads.
- A passport is required to enter Canada. No longer is a driver's license, birth certificate, or social security card sufficient.
- Canadian coins are similar to U.S. coins in size and shape, except that Canadian coins are magnetic and U.S. coins are not. U.S. coins will not work in Canadian vending machines. Canadians also have $1 and $2 coins (*loonies and toonies*).

BUSINESS ETIQUETTE

 ## Punctuality

- Punctuality is considered important, expected, appreciated, and a priority.
- French-speaking areas of Canada may have a more casual attitude toward time, but individual businesspeople vary.
- As a visitor, you should arrive on time even if your Canadian counterpart does not. As a general rule, it is acceptable to be 15 minutes late for evening social occasions. Never be more than 30 minutes late for an evening function.

 ## Meeting Manners

- An open and friendly manner is necessary when dealing with Canadian businesspeople.
- In the province of Quebec, provide a French translation for promotional materials and documents.
- Refrain from religious discussion or controversial issues.
- Canadians will avoid arguing or creating a scene in public.
- It is considered rude for people to speak in a foreign language in the presence of others who do not understand what is being said.
- Rank and title are important, and you should be conscious of them in your dealings.
- The pace for negotiating is similar to that in the United States but might move slightly slower.
- Businesspeople are well informed and generally open to new ideas and discussions.

- Canadians are polite listeners and will rarely interrupt a good presentation.
- Canadians may see U.S. businesspeople as self-promoting and crass. Refrain from exaggerated or unsubstantiated claims in presentations or promotional material. Boasting and bragging have little acceptance in Canadian society.
- If there is a change of personnel, negotiations will continue without a disruption.
- Stay away from discussing family or personal affairs in the course of negotiations.
- Experts are relied upon at all levels of negotiation.
- Even though decision making can be very individualistic, company policy must be followed at all times.

Business Cards

- Business cards are exchanged but not usually in the initial meeting.
- It is to your advantage to include both French and English on your business cards, especially if doing business in the province of Quebec. Also include your academic degree(s) and/or title.

Meals/Toasts

- Business meals are popular.
- Business lunches are generally short (60 to 90 minutes), with lighter foods and often no alcohol.
- When invited to dinner, wait until your Canadian host brings up the subject of business.
- Both American and Continental styles of eating are used and acceptable. Either the fork is held in the right hand switched to the left or put down when the knife is used for cutting or spreading, or the knife and fork remain in right and left hands, respectively.
- Follow the lead of your Canadian host or hostess. Let them set the pace at the meal and then follow.
- Offer main dishes to others at the table before you serve yourself.
- Refusing food is acceptable and will not cause offense.
- The Royal Toast is given as the toast to Her Majesty the Queen, Canada's Head of State. This toast will not occur before the meal but after the main course. They will all stand and raise their glasses. The toast of "The Queen, la Reine" is said and all respond back with the same phrase. Guests should not clink glasses and should not toast with alcohol but with either wine or water.

Entertainment

- It is an honor and an infrequent occurrence to be invited to a Canadian home for business, but if you are, flowers, candy, wine, or liquor will make a nice gift. You may want to check your host's preference.
- White lilies are generally associated with funerals and red roses are saved for romantic occasions, so be careful giving flowers.

Forms of Address/Introductions/Greetings

- Handshakes are appropriate. Generally, men will wait for a woman to extend her hand before shaking hands.
- Using first names is acceptable, but it is always better to wait until the Canadian instructs or invites you to do so.
- Be concerned with the proper pronunciation. You can ask people to repeat their names to ensure you say them properly or ask their coworkers the correct pronunciation.
- Good eye contact is acceptable, but it should not be too intense. Some ethnic groups will look away to show respect.
- Two feet is the general distance of personal space. French Canadians may stand a little closer.
- English expressions are used the same as in the United States: "Good morning," "Good afternoon," "Good evening," "Goodnight," "Hi," and "Hello." "How are you?" is a standard greeting.
- Titles are respected, as in "Dr." or "Ms.," *"Monsieur,"* or *"Madame,"* followed by the last name.
- If you are not sure of the woman's marital status, use "Ms."
- Follow their lead. If they refer to you as "Mr." or "Mrs." or "Ms.," then out of respect and hierarchy, you should do the same.

Appearance/Attire

- Business dress is a little less formal than in the United States but dressier for evening functions.
- Good quality is important, especially in shoes.
- A well-dressed, conservative look is appropriate. Suits and ties are still the norm for men in business, and business suits, dresses, or pantsuits are common for women.
- Casual clothes of jeans, t-shirts, sweatpants, and shorts are acceptable for activities outside the workplace.

- Removing your shoes when visiting someone's home in Canada is customary.
- The winters in Canada can be very cold, so dress appropriately when traveling.
- Scents are not worn in business settings. Aftershave, perfume, cologne, or heavily scented shampoos and hairspray should be avoided. An old custom is that perfume is worn to cover up poor hygiene. Because scents can be a health hazard for people with asthma, some Canadian hospitals and doctors' offices forbid them.

Gift Giving

- A small gift of candy, flowers, wine, or liquor is appropriate when visiting a home. If your hosts have children, also bring the children an appropriate gift.
- Remember that white lilies are associated with funerals and red roses are saved for romance.
- If you receive a gift, open it immediately, show it to everyone, and express your appreciation.
- Business gifts are usually given at the close of a deal, but they may also be presented upon arrival. Give a gift from your own country. Business gifts should be quality items but should not be too extravagant.
- It is inappropriate to give women personal items like perfume or clothing.
- Taking a client or customer out to dinner or to a concert or other form of entertainment works well as a gift.
- Gift giving in the office or to a business associate is common. These gifts could be office items or possibly a bottle of wine or liquor. Make sure that the gift is appropriately wrapped and presented.

% Tipping

- A five percent Goods and Services Tax is included on the bill in restaurants. A tip would be in addition to this. Check whether a service charge has been included in a restaurant bill. If so, this is the tip. Additional gratuity can be given for exceptional service.
- A 15 percent tip is customary and 20 percent for exceptional service is fine, but do not feel obligated if the service does not merit it.
- Tipping at hotels could include the person who handles your bags, valet service, housekeeping, and concierge for special services.

Be On Your Best Cultural Behavior

- Some tourist destinations may provide a tip jar on the counter. If you think the service they provided is worth it, then you can add a tip to their jar.
- Tips for taxi drivers can range from 10 percent to 20 percent depending on the service and whether they provide assistance with your luggage or offer information about the city.
- Do not tip the police, especially the Royal Canadian Mountain Police.

Gesture Awareness

- Pointing at other people is considered unacceptable.
- To get a person's attention or to call to them, make sure that your fingers are curled toward you and that your palm is facing up.
- The OK sign and thumbs-up are popular gestures used for expressing approval.
- To wave good-bye, move your entire hand facing outward.
- To give the "V for victory" sign with the first two fingers, have the palm facing out. This gesture with the palm inward may cause offense.

Faux Pas

- Respect "first come, first served" for lines and waiting to be served. Canadians resent people who push ahead in line.
- People using automated teller machines (ATMs) expect the next person to give them their privacy and stand a few feet behind them.
- Smoking is restricted in most public places.
- Placing your hands in your pockets while you are talking is considered rude.
- In visiting a home, do not wander from room to room. Wait to be given permission.
- Do not eat food on the move. If you buy take-out food, stand or sit down to eat.

USEFUL FACTS

Sovereign	Queen Elizabeth II (1952)
Governor-General	Michaelle Jean (2005)
Prime Minister	Stephen Harper (2006)

National Name	Canada
Size	3,511,003 square miles (9,093,507 square km)
Population	33,212,969 (2008)
Capital	Ottawa, Ontario
Government	Federation with Parliamentary Democracy
Currency	Canadian dollar
Religions	Roman Catholic 46%, Protestant 36%, other 18%
Languages	English 59%, French 23% (both official languages), other 18% Ethnicity British Isles origin 28%, French origin 23%, other European 15%, indigenous Indian and Inuit 2%, other (mostly Asian, African, Arab) 6%, mixed background 26%
Industry	Transportation equipment, chemicals, processed and unprocessed minerals, food products, wood and paper products, fish products, petroleum, and natural gas. Also financial, high-tech, health care, research and development, and tourism.
Time Zone	There are six primary time zones in Canada including Newfoundland Time Zone, Atlantic, Eastern, Central, Mountain, and Pacific Time zones. A few areas, including Saskatchewan, do not use daylight saving time.
	The capital city of Ottawa is located in the Eastern time zone and is five hours behind Greenwich Mean Time (GMT –5) and is the same as the U.S. Eastern Standard Time (GMT –5).
Telephone Code	International Code: +1 City Code: +613 (Ottawa)

Weather	In the winter months, the temperatures can fall below freezing in most of Canada. The southwestern area climate is mild, but the Arctic Circle will be below freezing for seven months of the year. You will find high humidity during the summer months in the southern provinces, along with temperatures of 86 F (30 C) on a regular basis.
	The western and southeastern areas of Canada have high rainfall but the prairies are dry, with minimal rain each year.
Voltage/Frequency	110 V; 60 Hz

Like the United States, residential Canada uses 110 volt electrical. Small electronics and razors can operate on a 50-watt converter. Hair dryers, irons, coffee makers, and other high-power electrical appliances need a 1600-watt converter.

HOLIDAYS/FESTIVALS

1 January	New Year's Day
15 February	National Flag of Canada Day
March/April	Good Friday to Easter
May	Victoria Day (Monday preceding May 25)
1 July	Canada Day (July 2 is Canada Day when 1 July is a Sunday)
September	Labor Day (first Monday)
October	Thanksgiving Day (second Monday)
11 November	Remembrance Day (commemorates Canadians that died in World War I and II and the Korean War)
25 December	Christmas
26 December	Boxing Day (Also known as the Feast of Saint Stephen, it originated in England for the merchant class to give boxes containing food, fruit, money, and/ or clothing to tradespeople or servants. Still celebrated today in Canada, United Kingdom, Australia, New Zealand, and other Commonwealth nations.)

LANGUAGE TIPS

French	Phonetics	English
De rien	duh re-ahn	You're welcome
Parlez-vous anglais?	Parleh voo angleh	Do you speak English?
Pouvez-vous m'aider?	Pooveh voo mehdeh	Can you help me?
A bientot	ah bee-ahn-toh	See you soon
Pardonnez-moi!	Pahr-dohn-nay-mwah	Excuse me
Comment allez-vous?	Koh-mawn tahl-ay-voo	How are you? (formal)
Je vais bien	zhuh vay bee-ahn	I'm fine
Enchante(e)	awn-shawn-tay	Nice to meet you.
Je (ne) comprends (pas)	zhuh nuh kohm-prawn pah	I (don't) understand
Pouvez-vous m'alder?	poo-vay voo meh-day	Can you help me? (formal)

See the chapter about France for additional words and phrases.

Chapter 6: CHILE

LOCATION/GEOGRAPHY

Chile is located in southern South America, bordering the South Pacific Ocean, west of Bolivia and Argentina, and south of Peru.

DID YOU KNOW?

- Bargaining is not practiced in the street markets or in stores. It is illegal to sell anything and not issue a receipt. The failure to issue a receipt implies that the merchant is not declaring the sale on tax reports. Only in smaller villages may you see bargaining as the norm.
- All males 18 to 45 years old are required to serve in the military.
- Peru and Chile are disputing their boundary in the maritime zones of the two countries, and Peru possesses exclusive sovereign rights in this maritime area.
- Divorce was illegal until 2004.
- Older Chileans still celebrate their saint's day just as much as they do their own birthday.
- The family still plays the central role in the lives of Chileans. Nepotism is seen as a positive concept in businesses. Many of the smaller companies and firms will be 100 percent family owned and operated.
- Class in Chile is drawn along financial lines and it is possible to move upward or downward, depending on your salary. The middle class accounts for nearly half the population.
- The country is 4,000 miles (6,000 km) long and only approximately 100 miles (150 Km) wide. Chile is the longest country in the world. The Andes Mountains run along the entire length of Chile.
- Almost half of Chile's population lives in or around the capital city, Santiago. It was founded in 1541 by Spanish conquistador Pedro de Valdivia.
- Chile's number one export is copper. Chile is the second largest producer of salmon in the world. Chile provides North America with almost 15 percent of its fruit sales from November through April.
- The island of Tierra del Fuego, which is separated from the rest of the country by the Strait of Magellan, is divided between Chile and Argentina.
- Before the Spanish arrived, the Incan Empire stretched from Ecuador, through Peru and Bolivia, to northern Chile.
- The northern part of Chile is the driest place on earth. Areas of the Altacama desert have not had rainfall in recorded history.

- Easter Island, which is known for its famous giant stone statues that were carved from the rock of an extinct volcano, is owned by Chile.
- There are more than 200 volcanoes in Chile and 50 are active.
- Chile is known for having some of the finest wines in the world.
- Two Chileans, Gabriela Mistral and Pablo Neruda, have won the Nobel Prize in literature. Gabriela Mistral is also the first Latin American woman to win the Nobel Prize for Literature.
- Smoking is prohibited inside public vehicles, including buses, subways, and trains.
- Renting a car and driving in Chile is easy and convenient. Most car rentals and police control checks will accept the driver's license from your country, but it's advisable to secure an international license.
- Smoking, using a cell phone, or using headphones are prohibited while driving. Driving under the influence and speeding are both severe offenses resulting in fines or arrest.
- Chile claims as its territory about 1,250,000 square kilometers (482,627 square miles) of Antarctica, roughly nine percent of its total size.

BUSINESS ETIQUETTE

 ## Punctuality

- If you're invited to a home, arrive 15 minutes late. This is considered good manners.
- For a dinner party, 30 minutes late is the norm and still very polite and acceptable.
- For business occasions, punctuality is appreciated and expected from visitors. But your Chilean associates may be 15 to 30 minutes late.

 ## Meeting Manners

- Schedule appointments at least two or three weeks in advance and always confirm the appointment before your visit and upon your arrival.
- Best times for meetings are generally 10 a.m. to 12:30 p.m. (1000 to 1230) and 3 p.m. to 5 p.m. (1500 to 1700). Some will meet from 11 a.m. to 3 p.m. (1100 to 1500) and combine their appointment with a business lunch.
- Initial meetings will be used to build a relationship and establish trust. Time will be spent on non-business discussions. Wait for the Chileans to initiate the change to business.

- Third-party introductions may be necessary to prepare for a meeting or to develop special personal relationships.
- Fitting in is extremely important, and these cordial relations can be more important than your actual business and professional competence. Rapport and friendship are key to conducting business.
- There is a definite hierarchical order. You should understand and observe this chain of command from the beginning of your business dealings.
- Initial meetings should include your upper-level management, accompanied by mid-level executives. Once you move into further discussions, the mid-level executives will continue with the negotiations.
- Be prepared for interruptions. It's common practice to interrupt people while they are talking.
- Meetings can be a lesson in multitasking. The schedules are not necessarily very well structured and various topics and issues may be handled at the same time.
- You must be patient because time is not a factor. It may take several trips before a contract or transaction is completed. But once the contracts are agreed upon, the final process, including payment, will be handled promptly and within deadline.
- Get to know the secretary or assistant well. This person will play a major role in determining who gets access to the manager or gets appointments.
- Most Chileans speak English, but you will need to determine the language of the meetings and if interrupters will be needed.
- Chileans will tend to be serious and straightforward negotiators, but hard-selling or other aggressive tactics will not work. Let them know your priorities, terms, and conditions.
- Chileans are extremely courteous and may say what they think you want to hear as opposed to a candid response.
- Constant contact and service no matter the difference of travel and time is always appreciated.
- Do not bribe your Chilean business associates. Although it's a common practice in other Latin American countries, it is illegal in Chile.
- Decisions and thinking can be influenced by their Catholic or Protestant beliefs.
- Women in Chile are professionally advanced, so the female business person will be accepted and can find success. But the machismo is still a very strong influence, and women should exercise caution and restraint in their social and professional lives.

Business Cards

- Business cards are exchanged in the very beginning of the initial meeting and generally right after the initial handshake.
- Smiling and eye contact are also part of the exchange of the cards.
- It's advisable to have one side of your card translated into Spanish.
- Always take the time to look at and read the business card being presented to you.
- Cards should always be in good condition with the most up-to-date information listed. An outdated or poorly kept card will reflect badly on you and your business.
- Also show respect for the card that you receive by placing it in a special business card case or holder. Do not quickly put it in your back pocket or just set it aside. They will notice and it will make a difference to them.

 Meals/Toasts

- There is more formality with dining in Chile, so follow and observe when you are not sure of the protocol.
- Always wait to be shown to your seat. Do not automatically come in and sit down.
- The women will sit before the men.
- The host or the most senior man present will customarily be seated at the head of the table, with the guest of honor at his immediate right. The next seat of honor will be to the immediate right of either the hostess or the second-highest ranking Chilean.
- Wait until the host invites everyone to start to eat.
- Always keep your hands visible during the meal. Your wrists should rest on the edge of the table. It is bad form to keep hands concealed or rest your hands on your lap during a meal.
- Continental style of eating is a must, with the knife staying in your right hand and the fork in the left. Never switch your utensils.
- You will always use your utensils to eat. Finger food is not a part of their formal meals.
- Place your utensils down before you begin to speak.
- You may eat everything on your plate and it's considered polite to do so. If you don't like something on your plate, at least take a small bite or two just to be polite.
- A toast will be made by the host before you take the first sip of your drink. The most common toast is "*Salud!*"
- During the toast, when you lift your glass, look at the person being toasted. If a toast is proposed to you, propose one in return.
- Use your right hand to pour wine.

Entertainment

- Thank-you notes or gifts are not common practice. After an event or dinner party, a phone call expressing thanks will be sufficient.
- Lunch is the biggest meal of the day and generally occurs between 12 p.m. and 3 p.m. (1200 and 1500) and will last two hours.
- *Onces,* or a small break, will take place between 5 p.m. and 6 p.m. (1700 and 1800). You will be served bite-sized sandwiches, tea, pastries, and other snacks.
- Dinner will take place between 8 p.m. and 10 p.m. (2000 and 2200). If you are invited to a Chilean home for drinks, you will probably also be invited to dinner.
- To make a good impression as a visitor, stay at a nicer international hotel.
- Most business entertaining will take place in a major hotel or restaurant.
- Always handle the payment in advance of the meal if you are the host. This will avoid the guests' insisting on picking up the tab. If you are the guest, then reciprocate this hospitality at a later time.
- During a business social event, always allow the host to initiate business discussion. It is important that your Chilean host or guest knows that the relationship is more important than business.
- Topics to avoid include criticizing any aspect of Chile; the surrounding countries of Argentina, Bolivia, and Peru; politics, war, human rights violations; the Araucanian Indians; ethnic and social classes; and religion.
- Sports (soccer, polo, skiing and fishing), cultural life, arts, and places of interest for tourists are good starting topics for discussion.

Forms of Address/Introductions/Greetings

- There is a formality during introductions and greetings for business.
- In business settings, the handshake and smile is the normal greeting, with direct eye contact. Shake hands with everyone present.
- The group hello could be perceived as impersonal and rude.
- Most women will now shake hands with men. This was not the case in the past but is becoming more common.
- Be prepared for Chileans to stand very close when they are talking with you. Do not move away or step back and always maintain good eye contact to assure them you are genuinely interested.
- The appropriate greeting that accompanies the handshake or pat will be *buenos dias* (good morning), *buenas tardes* (good afternoon) or *buenas noches* (good evening).

- Between friends and family, men will embrace and enthusiastically pat one another on the back. The women will kiss once on the right cheek. Women will usually pat one another on the right forearm or shoulder.
- Generally Chileans are a very affectionate and warm people, so expect touching once they get to know you on a more personal level.
- Follow the lead of the formality that your Chilean counterpart displays.
- Chileans will use both their maternal and paternal surnames. The father's surname is always listed first and is the one used in conversation.
- When a woman marries, she generally takes her husband's surname but she may keep her father's surname for her professional identity.
- Always use titles such as professor or doctor. If no other title, then use *Senor* for males or *Senora* for females followed by their surname.
- Older people with whom you have a personal relationship may be referred to as *don* for male and *dona* for female, followed by their first name.
- Continue to use surnames and titles until invited to use first names.

 ## Appearance/Attire

- Dress plays a major role in relationship to the class structures in Chile. People will try to deduce another's position from their external appearance and dress.
- As a visitor, dress conservatively and formally. Dressing well is of high importance and is perceived as a sign of respect.
- Business casual dress of sports coat, khakis, and casual shoes will not be well received.
- Men should wear blue or gray suits, white shirts, and conservative ties.
- Women will wear a similar look with blue or gray business suits and low heels.
- Jewelry should be conservative and tasteful. You don't want to come across as vain and self-absorbed, with expensive or excessive accessories.
- If invited to a home, men should wear coat and tie and women should wear an elegant, yet conservative, dress.
- Summer dress is a little more casual, with short-sleeved shirts and slacks for men and more casual dresses for women.

 ## Gift Giving

- Gifts are not expected initially in business until the relationship grows and becomes close.
- Be careful selecting gifts so they are not perceived as expensive or bribes.
- Make sure your gift is always wrapped properly and a card is enclosed.

- If you are invited to a Chilean's home, then you should take sweets, chocolates, or wine for the hostess.
- Send flowers in advance but be very careful of the type and color. Yellow roses mean contempt, while purple or black flowers symbolize death.
- Scissors or knives indicate you want to sever the relationship.
- When invited to a Chilean home, you should also bring gifts for the children. Suggestions are candy, games, a university t-shirt, or something from your own country that they may not be able to get in Chile.
- As a young girl celebrates her 15th birthday, the normal gift is gold.
- Gifts are opened when they are received.

Tipping

- The gratuity is generally included in the bill. If service is exceptional, an additional 5 percent left on the table would be appropriate.
- If gratuity is not included automatically in the bill, a 10 percent to 15 percent tip is in order.
- A porter/bellhop should receive Ch$500-$1,000 (US$1 – US$2) for each piece of luggage.
- A few pesos will be expected for each piece of mail delivered, so be prepared to tip the postal carrier.
- In general, tipping small amounts is customary for all services rendered.
- It isn't necessary to tip taxi drivers, but you can leave them change from the fare.

Gesture Awareness

- Slapping your right fist into your left open palm is perceived as obscene.
- An open palm with fingers separated indicates "stupid."
- Avoid raising your right fist to head level because this is a Communist sign.
- Point with your entire hand instead of just your index finger.
- Chew slowly and take small bites during a meal. Clanging silverware, scraping the plate, lip-smacking, and finger-licking are all considered vulgar.

Faux Pas

- Before smoking, you should offer cigarettes to your companions.
- Refrain from publicly criticizing others. Doing so could create embarrassment.
- Chileans are very patriotic and would take offense at any negative comments about their country.
- It's a mistake to compare Chile to Argentina. They are very distinct nations, and there has been a great deal of conflict between them.
- Do not ask personal questions. When they are ready, they will offer this information.
- Do not take interruptions as rude. It is quite the opposite because they perceive interruptions as a way of participating in conversations and displaying interest in what is being said.

USEFUL FACTS

President	Michelle Bachelet (2006)
National Name	Republica de Chile
Size	289,112 square miles (748,800 square km)
Population	16,454,143 (2008)
Capital	Santiago
Government	Republic
Currency	Chilean peso
Religion	Roman Catholic 89%, Protestant 11%
Language	Spanish is the official language, but there are indigenous languages, including Mapudungun and Aymara.
Ethnicity	White and White-Amerindian 95%, Amerindian 3%, other 2%

Industry	Petroleum, chemicals, electrical and telecommunications equipment, industrial machinery, vehicles and natural gas
Time Zone	Chile is four hours behind Greenwich Mean Time (GMT –4) or one hour ahead of Eastern Standard Time (EST +1). Chile does observe daylight savings time.
Telephone Code	Country Code: +56 City Code: +2 (Santiago)
Weather	Santiago and Middle Chile are best in the spring (September through November) or fall (late February into April). Southern Chile is best in the summer (December through March). You can visit the very dry Atacama Desert year-round, but be prepared for extremely hot days and bitterly cold nights in the higher altitudes. Winter in Chile can be great for skiers from July through September. Remember their seasons are reversed from the northern hemisphere.
Voltage/Frequency	220 V; 50 Hz

HOLIDAYS/FESTIVALS

1 January	New Year's Day
March/April	Easter and Holy Week
1 May	Labor Day or Day of the Worker
21 May	Navy Day (commemorates the great naval battle of Iquique and other naval victories)
29 June	Saint Peter and Saint Paul
17 July	Fiesta de la Virgin del Carmen (celebrated by Catholics)
15 August	Assumption of Mary
18 September	Independence Day (Independence from Spain 12 February 1818, but Chileans celebrate their independence 18 September with the Fiestas Patrias.)

19 September	Armed Forces Day
12 October	Columbus Day (Day of the Race)
	(Day Columbus arrived in the Americas)
1 November	All Saints Day
8 December	Immaculate Conception
25 December	Christmas Day

LANGUAGE TIPS

Spanish	Phonetics	English
Hablo un poco	ah-bloh oon poh-koh	I speak it a little.
No entiendo	no en-tee-en-do	I do not understand.
Me gusta la comida.	Meh-goo-stah lah Koh-mee-dah	The meal is good.
Podrias ayudarme por favor?	poh-dree-yahs ah-yoo-Dahr-meh pohr fah-bohr	Could you help me please?
Donde esta…?	Dohn-deh eh-stah…	Where is the…?
Cuanto cuesta?	Kuahn-toh Kwehs-tah	How much is it?
Lo siento	loh see-ehn-toh	I'm sorry.
Con permiso/Perdon	kohn pehr-mee-soh/ pehr-dohn	Excuse me/Pardon
Como estas?	Koh-moh ay-stahs	How are you? (informal)
Hasta la vista	Ah-stah lah vees-tah/	See you/See you
Hasta luego	Ah-stah loo-ay-go	later.

Please see other chapters of Spanish-speaking countries for additional words and phrases.

Chapter 7: CHINA

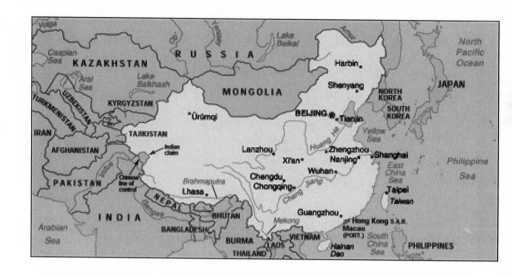

LOCATION/GEOGRAPHY

China is surrounded by Vietnam, Myanmar (Burma), India, Afghanistan, Kazakhstan, Kyrgyzstan, Tajikistan, Russia, Mongolia, and North Korea. It borders the East China Sea, Yellow Sea, and South China Sea.

DID YOU KNOW?

- Fourteen of the highest peaks in the world are found in China.
- The nation's largest river and the third longest in the world (after the Nile and the Amazon), the Yangtze River, originates on the Qinghai-Tibet Plateau.
- The Grand Canal passes through Beijing and Tianjin and the provinces of Hebei, Shandong, Jiangsu, and Zhejiiag. It is the longest artificial canal in the world, covering approximately 1,100 miles (1,770 km).
- In 1557, the world's deadliest recorded earthquake occurred in China, killing 830,000 people.
- Seventy percent of the world's silk is produced in China. It was actually developed in China and kept a secret for more than 2,000 years.
- Outside North America, you will rarely find "Chinese" fortune cookies. San Francisco is actually given the credit for creating these crescent-shaped cookies.
- One of the greatest wonders of the world, the Great Wall of China, stretches 4,163 miles (approximately 6,700 km) from east to west. It was built as a defensive fortification and underwent numerous expansions, actually becoming the "Great Wall" during the Qin Dynasty. Today only 30 percent of the wall still exists.
- Ketchup was actually started in China as a fish sauce called ketsiap.
- Tea was discovered in China more than 5,000 years ago.
- In 1950 China annexed Tibet.
- Close to 2 trillion cigarettes are sold in China every year; China is the home to 350 million smokers, which is a third of smokers globally. The government is trying to ban smoking in all restaurants, offices, and schools. More than 150 Chinese cities already have smoking restrictions.
- Pekingese dogs were sacred to the emperors of China for more than 2,000 years.
- Disney produced a version of the story of Mulan, who according to tradition in China, was a heroic woman who disguised herself as a man to take the place of her aging father in the army on the battlefields almost 1,300 years ago.

Be On Your Best Cultural Behavior

- Even though Mao Tse-Tung could be compared to Stalin or Hitler, he is honored for raising China to a united world force. His body is embalmed in a mausoleum on Tiananmen Square; a huge poster of him hangs in the main gate of the square; his portrait is on every Chinese bank note; and you will find a statue of Mao in every town and city. In 1976, millions of people in China stood still for three minutes to remember this leader.
- Today the great panda bear exists in nature only in six small areas in inland China.
- English is the second language taught in China, but not necessarily the second language spoken. Most will speak in their own regional dialect. Their language is not more difficult to learn, but the rules are different from Latin-based languages. Older Chinese speak no English or just a little, but younger Chinese do speak English. There are no past or future tenses in the Chinese language, only the present tense, so other parts of the sentence indicate speaking of the past or the future.
- Beijing hosted the 2008 Summer Olympic Games.

BUSINESS ETIQUETTE

 Punctuality

- To be on time is expected in China.
- It isn't necessary to be extremely early, five to 10 minutes is perfect.

 Meeting Manners

- It is not uncommon to have a "host organization" for your meetings. It is changing slightly, but a host organization or middleman can assist with moving your meeting situation a little faster by making appointments and facilitating applications for a business visa.
- Most meetings will take place in conference or meeting rooms instead of the official's office.
- The meetings will be more formal, including seating following protocol. This includes the senior Chinese host placing the senior foreign guest to his right, with members of the foreign party placed along one side of the room with the Chinese delegation on the other side.
- Keeping with their protocol, punctuality is expected, and the group will enter the room in protocol order led by the senior guest, and will be greeted by the senior Chinese host.

- A business meeting would begin with a brief welcome, purpose of meeting, and introductions, first of the Chinese and then of the guests.
- It is important to have the most senior member of your organization lead the negotiations. The Chinese will do the same on their behalf.
- It is highly recommended to have your own interpreters for your business meetings.
- Agendas and itineraries are preferred and efficient. Follow these agendas. Make sure your written material is translated properly. The dialects within China are totally different.
- Be careful of any colors you may use in your presentations or displays. The colors you have used may denote negativism or have a different meaning than you are trying to express. Even though the color red denotes joy and happiness, in ancient times it was reserved for the dead, including placing their names on the gravestones and plaques in red. Be careful not to write a person's name or your own in red on your notes, presentations, or the contract.
- The Chinese will review all proposals carefully, so be patient and show little emotion throughout the process. Even as the final discussions are reviewed, the Chinese may try to renegotiate. Avoid mentioning any deadlines or timelines you must follow.
- Use short sentences and eliminate all jargon and slang. Pause appropriately.
- Negative replies seem impolite to the Chinese, so the responses "may," "perhaps," "I'm not sure," or "I'll think about it" actually mean "no." This exchange is common when one's Chinese counterpart is helping to save face. You can discuss the true meaning of the response with your interpreter or escort after the meeting. Chinese may say "yes" but it could actually mean they are just listening, they do not understand, or they are not in agreement.
- Chinese often work in teams, and tasks may be handled by groups instead of individuals. Even in negotiation, collective thinking still prevails. Group consensus is important.
- "Saving face" is important to understand. Chinese reputation and social standing centers on this concept. To cause a person embarrassment will alter or completely eliminate your business negotiations.
- At the end of the meeting, the Chinese may not see you out of the room. They may want to discuss without you, so just lead yourself out of the room. You are expected to leave before your Chinese associates.
- Many Chinese still adhere to their old beliefs from astrology and geomancy. So don't be surprised if they wait for a "lucky" day to make their final decision.

Be On Your Best Cultural Behavior

Business Cards

- Business card exchange is a respected process and an important part of doing business in China. Business cards are exchanged the first time you meet at a business meeting.
- If you visit China regularly, print your card with one side in your country's language and the other in Chinese characters. Present to your Chinese associates with the Chinese side up so they can read it. If they have translated their cards to your home language on one side, they should present this side to you.
- Cards are exchanged while standing. Pass and receive cards with two hands with the lettering facing the recipient and a slight bow of the head.
- Allow the recipients enough time to read your card before expecting them to give you one in return.
- Failure to do these small courtesies shows disrespect. The bow while exchanging cards is not as dramatic as it was in the past, but smiling and eye contact is appropriate when you first meet someone.
- When you begin the exchange, drop your eyes to the ground to show respect for the other person.
- Include your title on your card. The main purpose of the exchange of cards to a Chinese business person is to determine the key decision maker.
- Also state on your card any distinction your company may have in regard to being the oldest or largest in your country.
- Gold in the Chinese culture is a sign of prosperity and prestige. It's to your advantage to have cards printed in gold ink.
- Never write a person's name in red. Red and gold are good selections for your cards, but without using red for the name. Gold ink on the Chinese side will show respect.
- Business cards should never be bent, written on, or dirty.
- Never take a person's business card and place it in your wallet, and then put it in your back pocket.

Meals/Toasts

- Business lunches are increasing for meetings but evening banquets, generally in a restaurant, are the most popular. They usually begin between 5:30 and 6 p.m. (1730 and 1800) and last for several hours. Arrive on time. Even if you arrive early, your hosts will be ready.
- Seating is important, with the middle of the table facing the door generally reserved for the guest of honor directly across from the host. The next most senior guest of honor sits directly to the left of the guest of honor. There can be discussion on the order of importance but remain

standing and allow your hosts to place you in the correct order. It may even get down to the basis of age. This procedure is followed for hosting a meal in your home. The host will sit near the door so he is close to the kitchen and able to bring each dish quickly to the table. He will also serve his guests because they will be too polite to serve themselves.

- The host will be the first to eat and will also offer the first toast. The host will also take the first piece of the most valued food and place it on the guest of honor's plate after the first toast. This is the sign to start eating and also a gesture of friendship.
- Business is not generally discussed during meals.
- Eat only cooked food. Do not drink the tap water. Municipal water is not suitable for drinking. Stick with bottled water for drinking and brushing teeth, even in up-scale restaurants and hotels. Be extremely careful at street-side stands and night markets.
- "Banqueting" is their most common form of business entertaining. This is a more formal gathering, with several main dishes and individual bowls of rice.
- Chopsticks are used for all meals, but there are some rules regarding chopsticks. (See section on chopsticks.) Throughout the meal, your host will continue to replenish your dish. This dates back to the periods of famine in China. When you have completed your meal, always leave a little food on your plate to show that the meal was plentiful and delicious but that you cannot eat any more. The same applies to your teacup. It will constantly be refilled. You may be served a plain bowl of white rice as the second to last course, but do not eat it. You should refuse it because eating it shows that you are still hungry and this will insult the host.
- In more relaxed atmospheres, table etiquette becomes a little more relaxed. They enjoy the food, and that is their main concern. It is not considered impolite to place your elbows on the table, nor do they wait until all at the table have been served.
- Dishes are placed in the center of the table, not passed around. So feel free to even stand up to reach with your chopsticks for the food you want to eat. But watch your host for guidance. Even though it might be a more comfortable and relaxed atmosphere, take your cues from the host.
- There could be almost double the amount of food to feed the people at the table. The reason is so the host will not lose face if there are not a lot of leftovers at the end of the meal. There also will be many courses, so taste each one but do so lightly. Rice will not be served until the end of the meal, but you can ask for it to be served early if you would like it to accompany the rest of your meal. Rice is considered a "filler."

- *Yum cha*, the ritual of tea drinking, is an important part of the Chinese business entertainment. This ritual will establish rapport before a meeting or during meals.
- Toasting is an important part of the Chinese business protocol. It is usually done with beer, wine, or Chinese white liquors but is still acceptable with a soft drink, juice, or mineral water.
- Often three glasses will be placed on the table. One glass is for your drink of choice (to be used for the toast), a wine glass, and a shot glass for a liquor called *maotai* or *wu liang ye*.
- The host will offer the first toast. Two popular toasts are *ganbei,* or bottoms up, and *kai wei,* meaning starting the appetite.
- Be very careful of strong, potent drinks you might be served during a business meal. Eat something before you start on these drinks.
- The serving of fruit indicates the end of the meal. This may be the only time you will see a knife at a Chinese table. The purpose is for peeling the fruit. (The Chinese consider knifes weapons, so they are not appropriate at a dining table, where you share with friends or family. Most chopping is a part of the Chinese chef's craft, so cutting is typically handled in the preparation before the food is cooked in the kitchen.) When fruit is served and you are presented with a hot towel, this is your cue to prepare to leave. According to Chinese customs and protocol, the host will not initiate your departure.

Rice and Chopsticks Guidelines

- Chinese chopsticks are generally round and do not come attached together in paper wrappers.
- Do not point with or wave chopsticks aimlessly for any reason (talking, searching for food).
- It is customary to hold the bowl close to your mouth.
- Try to use chopsticks. Practice before you get to an important business meal. Your host would appreciate the effort of using chopsticks. If you're at a restaurant and you must absolutely use a fork to eat, ask and you may be given one, but a fork may not be found. If all else fails, you could use the porcelain spoon to scoop up your food. It's a little tacky but not against etiquette.
- When you have completed using your chopsticks, place them on the chopstick-rest if one is provided, or just rest them on the rim of a dish. Placing them in a parallel position on the top of your bowl is a sign of bad luck. They should not touch the table, so place the food end on your plate so it is not resting on the table.

- Placing your chopsticks straight up in your bowl relates to the process used in the incense burned to pay reverence to the dead. This would be considered disrespectful.
- Dropping chopsticks is considered bad luck.
- Reach for your food with your chopsticks. It is rare that food is passed around. Don't pick or sort out the exact piece of food you want from a common dish.
- Do not tap on your bowl with your chopsticks. It is insulting.
- Do not spear your food with your chopsticks. Try to seize your food between the tips of your chopsticks.
- Do not put bones or seeds back in your bowl. Place them on the table or a separate dish used for these pieces.
- At a banquet, the rice will be served individually in a bowl, but in a home, your hostess may serve the rice.
- Toothpicks are common practice, but cover your mouth with the other hand.
- Toothpicks are also used to pick up meal items that are too difficult or slippery to be retrieved with chopsticks.

Entertainment

- China offers an abundance of entertainment, including the symphony, operas, acrobatics, theater, and sporting events. Tickets to these events can be a challenge, so allow enough lead time.
- You can and should reciprocate with a banquet of the same value. Do not overdo your host with a more extravagant event or gathering. When you do host a banquet, always arrive at least 30 minutes before your guests.
- Be careful with the food you select for your entertainment. Chinese do not experiment a lot with food. Stick to a good, established Chinese restaurant.
- Entertaining in a Chinese home is very popular. Plan to arrive on time and expect to remove your shoes.
- To get a taste of the variety of Chinese food, tell the restaurant the number of dishes you want, the number of diners, and the time you want to be served.
- Reservations are recommended in the finer restaurants. But to enjoy an inexpensive meal with a lot of variety, join a table where there is a set price per person. The food will be placed in the center of the table for everyone to share. Rice is the staple, along with fish, chicken, pork, potatoes, and fresh vegetables. Dairy products are minimal, and bear's paw soup is a delicacy.

Be On Your Best Cultural Behavior

- Remember if you invite your Chinese guests to a meal, then you pay. Chinese do not observe the Western custom of splitting the bill.

Forms of Address/Introductions/Greetings

- Handshakes are the accepted form of greeting. A slight nod is more customary and appropriate when meeting someone. Follow the lead of your host.
- You might even be welcomed with applause if you enter a workplace. Reciprocate with applause back to them.
- Avoid using a lot of hand gestures while talking. The Chinese do not use their hands while speaking and can become annoyed or distracted by expansive movements.
- The Chinese do not like being touched by strangers. But you will see members of the same sex walking hand-in-hand in public as a sign of their friendship.
- Full titles are used for introductions. Address people by their full names or by title and family name.
- A married Chinese woman may chose to retain her maiden name and occasionally use her husband's last name for more formal situations.
- Many Chinese may take an English first name to help Westerners address them.
- Stand for all introductions. Introductions still follow a formal process.

Appearance/Attire

- Dress is generally conservative, with neutral colors. Business dress for men consists of conservative suits, shirts, and ties. Bright colors are considered inappropriate.
- Women also wear conservative suits, with low-heeled shoes, and higher-necked blouses or tops. Flat shoes or low heels should be worn by businesswomen if they are considerably taller than the hosts.
- Black-tie dress is not a part of Chinese culture.
- Schoolchildren wear uniforms, and business dress has a look of conformity.
- Traditional dress is rarely seen in China today but is saved for special occasions, rituals, or entertaining.
- Casual wear is still conservative, but jeans are acceptable for both men and women.
- Make-up, hairstyle, and accessories are important for women but are never worn excessively. Perfume and cologne are not popular.

- Red is a lucky color, so clothing in red is appropriate. A red tie is a good selection. The color white is worn for mourning, so you want to make sure you don't look like you are going to a funeral. Men should avoid white ties.
- Warm clothing, boots, heavy coat, and gloves are recommended for winter. Synthetic fabrics are uncomfortable because the dryness of the winter causes static electricity. Bring lots of moisturizer (lotion, lip balm) for the winter weather.

Gift Giving

- Technically gift giving is forbidden, but it is becoming a more common practice.
- Avoid making giving a gift a production. When presenting a gift from your company, make sure they understand it is from your company to their company as a whole. You can present a collective gift such as an illustrated coffee table style book or handicrafts from your country or company to the head of the delegation, but do it in the presence of all the delegation members.
- If you are going to give an individual a gift, do it privately to show friendship and not business.
- A gift could be refused three times so they do not appear greedy. But if it is accepted, do not expect one in return. If one is presented, go through the same process of not accepting initially.
- When accepting or presenting the gift, offer it with both hands and always make sure it is wrapped. It will not be opened in front of you because of the fear of that person showing any signs of disappointment.
- Make sure a gift is not presented until all negotiations have been completed.
- Writing instruments are always appreciated. Do not give a pen with red ink because writing in red ink symbolizes severing ties with this person or company.
- Do not give a clock because the sound of the word is very similar to the word for death in Chinese. Other gifts associated with funerals include straw sandals, a stork or crane (even though Westerners consider this related to birth), and handkerchiefs (since they symbolize weeping).
- Gifts are sometimes wrapped in ordinary paper, and then wrapped in either red or gold indicating the royal colors or bright, happy colors of yellow or pink. Green, white, and black should be avoided because they are funeral colors. Blue is a color of mourning. Check with a store, hotel,

or a person who offers these services. They will guide you in the correct selections for gifts, wrapping, and presentation.

- If shipping gifts, allow enough time for them to arrive so they may be presented while you are there. If carrying gifts with you, do not wrap them because of security in the airports.
- If you are invited to a Chinese home, it's customary to bring a gift. This could include fruit, imported cookies, chocolate, brandy, or cognac. A nice candy and fruit basket could be sent as a thank-you gift immediately after the event. Your choice will depend on the relationship and the occasion.
- Numbers play a major role in the Chinese culture. Eight is considered a lucky number, so if you receive eight of any item that is considered a gesture of good will. Six is also a good sign and a blessing of smoothness and problem-free advances. The number four is taboo and means "death" and numbers such as "73" meaning "the funeral" and "84" meaning "having accidents" should definitely be avoided. Knives, scissors, or any sharp object can be misunderstood as wanting to sever your relationship.
- It is virtually impossible to completely understand all of China's traditions and history on gift giving. Check with the appropriate people to make sure that gifts are given at the appropriate time, to the correct people, and are wrapped properly in the right color.

 Tipping

- In the past, tipping was frowned on and considered an insult in China. Western tourists have basically created the standard of tipping in high-end hotels, and it is spreading to all service providers and becoming more commonplace. Tips might be given to tour guides, drivers, skycaps, and waiters.
- In Beijing, taxi drivers are required by law to give a receipt to every passenger.
- A personalized gift to a tour guide is more appropriate than a tip. This could be wine, candies, hats, t-shirts, or even cigarettes from a foreign country.
- Tipping is still a personal matter and not a must in China.
- Your bill may include a tip of 5 percent to 15 percent service charge, so always check before adding additional gratuities. Generally, 10 percent to 15 percent of the bill is appropriate.
- Your tips or gratuities may improve the service from tour guides, bellmen, or waiters. US$1 to US$10 may be appropriate.

Gesture Awareness

- It's insulting to motion to a person with your forefinger. Turn your hand palm down and motion inward with all four fingers at the same time as in a scratching motion.
- To point, use your open hand instead of your index finger.
- Avoid finger snapping. To call a waiter, just raise your hand.
- Avoid hand gestures and exciting or dramatic facial expressions. Chinese do not use their hands while they are speaking and feel distracted by a speaker who is using overly emphatic hand or facial gestures.
- It is considered disgusting to put your hands in your mouth. This would include biting your nails or removing food from your teeth or mouth.
- Counting is done slightly in reverse of the Western culture. The number one is shown with the pinkie or small finger, and number five is shown with the thumb. When starting to count, open your entire hand, and then depress as you count. The fist represents ten.
- Whistling, winking, and other similar displays are considered vulgar.
- It's appropriate to bow slightly when passing or coming between people.
- Chinese people will stand farther apart than North Americans and Europeans. Do not try to get any closer. Remember they enjoy their space and non-touching.
- Do not do the double handshake with both hands resting on their hand. Avoid touching their shoulder or attempting to hug or kiss in the beginning of your relationship. It is considered very inappropriate.
- Do not feel that Chinese people are trying to cut or push their way in line at stores, public transportation, or any other areas that involve waiting in line. They are not cutting in front of you; they are just getting in position because of the large volume of passengers trying to get onto the train or into a building. This is not rude, just a part of their customs.

 ## Faux Pas

- If you drop a piece of food on the floor or on the table, do not pick it up.
- Do not pour your own drink.
- Do not give a gift of a green-colored hat to a married man. The saying "wearing a green hat" means that his wife is being unfaithful. This gift would then be an insult to the couple.
- Do not touch Chinese people that you do not know. This is especially important with older people or people in important positions. Do not touch the head of a Chinese person.
- Never point the sole of your foot in another person's direction.
- Avoid public displays of hugs and kisses, even among friends.

- When drinking tea or coffee, do not allow the spout of the teapot to point in the direction of another person.
- Translating names phonetically may result in an undesirable meaning.

 ## USEFUL FACTS

President	Hu Jintao (2003)
Vice President	Xi Jinping (2008)
National Name	People's Republic of China Zhonghua Renmin Gongheguo
Size	3,600,927 square miles (9,326,411 square km)
Population	1,330,044,605 (2008)
Capital	Beijing
Government	Communist State
Currency	Renminbi (RMB), also know as yuan
Religions	Officially atheist; Christian 3%-4%; Daoist (Taoist), Buddhist, Muslim 1%-2%
Languages	Standard Chinese (Mandarin/Putonghua), Yue (Cantonese), Wu (Shanghaiese), Minbei (Fuzhou), Minnan (Hokkien-Taiwanese), Xiang, Gan, Hakka dialects, minority languages
Ethnicity	Han Chinese 92%; Zhuang, Uygur, Hui, Yi, Tibetan, Miao, Manchu, Mongol, Buyi, Korean, and others 8%
Industry	Agriculture, industry, services, machinery, electronic products, toys, clothing, and textiles.
Time Zone	China is eight hours ahead of Greenwich Mean Time (GMT +8) or 13 hours ahead of Eastern Standard Time (EST +13). China does not observe daylight saving time.

China

| **Telephone Code** | Country Code: +86 |
| | City Code: +10 (Beijing) |

Weather   The weather in China is diverse, ranging from extremely cold to extremely hot. The monsoon winds affect climate and the amount of rainfall received throughout the country. Some parts of China in the winter can be -30C (-22F) but this is extreme. While summer weather in other parts can exceed 35C (95F). The capital city of Beijing can be very pleasant in the spring but can be sprinkled with chilly weather, wind and dust, and then followed with hot weather during summer.Because of the vastness of the country, you should check the weather of your destination(s) before you pack and travel.

Voltage/Frequency   220 V; 50 Hz

 # HOLIDAYS/FESTIVALS

1 January	New Year
Early February	Chinese Spring Festival (Lunar New Year)
8 March	Women's Day
15 March	Feast of the Ancestors
1 May	International Labor Day
4 May	Youth Day
15 May	Dragon Boat Festival
1 June	Children's Day
15 August	Mid-Autumn Festival
1 October	Chinese National Day
25 December	Christmas Day

LANGUAGE TIPS

China does not have an alphabet but a system of symbols that represent concepts rather than sounds, as in traditional phonetic alphabet systems. The letters in the different phonetic alphabets do not exceed 50. The Chinese need to know at least 3,000 characters to even understand a newspaper and a minimum of 6,000 characters for a small dictionary and everyday use. Here are the phonetic versions of some common phrases:

Chinese Phonetics	English
Ni hao ma	How are you?
Wo hen hao. Xie xie ni.	I am very well. Thank you.
Ni hao	Hello/Hi
Nar qu ya	Where are you going?
Chi le ma	Have you eaten yet?
Mafan ni	Excuse me
Zao shang hao	Good morning
Wan shang hao	Good evening
Huan ying	Welcome
Zai jian	Good-bye

Chapter 8: EGYPT

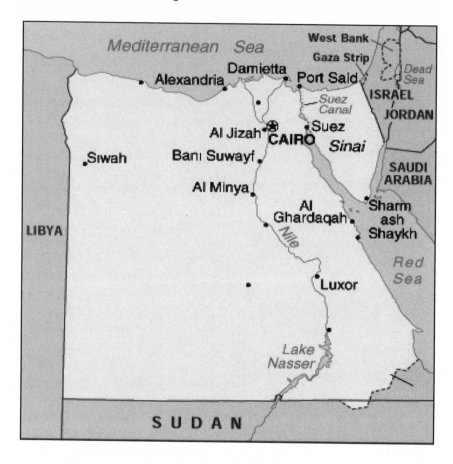

LOCATION/GEOGRAPHY

Located in the northeast corner of Africa, Egypt is bordered on the south by Sudan, on the west by Libya, on the north by the Mediterranean Sea, and on the east by Israel and the Red Sea.

DID YOU KNOW?

- Egyptians consider themselves to be the bridge between the European West and the Arab East, so business practices may look like European or Arab practices or anything in between.
- Muslims pray five times a day, asking God for his love at dawn, noon, afternoon, sunset, and evening. Exact times for prayers can be found daily in the local newspapers.
- Arabic is read from right to left, and books and magazines start at what would be the last page in the United States and many other countries. Printed literature should have a very impressive back cover, even if it is printed in English.
- The most historic mosque is in Alexandria, Egypt, and it was built in 1775 above the Tomb of the Spanish scholar and Saint Abu El Abbas El Mursi (1219-1286). Women cannot enter the mosque but can visit the mausoleum.
- There are three social classes in Egypt—upper, middle, and lower—with little social mobility. Status is defined more by family background than by wealth.
- Most of the Muslims in Egypt do not drink alcohol, but they do not object to others drinking in reasonable amounts. Most people do not eat pork, so don't expect it on many menus in Egypt.
- Friday is the Muslim holy day. Mostly weekends will be celebrated Thursday and Friday.
- The Nile River is the longest river in the world and flows into the Mediterranean Sea. It is 4,160 miles (6,695 kilometers) long.
- The pyramids of Egypt were built over a period of 200 years. The pyramids are three miles south of their original location. The earth's surface has shifted this much in the last 4,500 years.
- The Great Pyramid at Giza is 30 times larger in mass than the Empire State Building in New York, and its features can even be seen from the moon. This structure was started approximately 4,620 years ago and is the sole remaining structure of the Seven Wonders of the Ancient World.

- Two of the Seven Wonders of the Ancient World were in Egypt—the Great Pyramid at Giza and the Lighthouse at Alexandria, which was built around 290 BC from white marble and stone and stood for more than 1,500 years. The Lighthouse was damaged over the years by earthquakes, and it finally collapsed in 1326.
- The god Thoth is credited for inventing the Egyptian 365-day calendar in approximately 4241 BC.
- St. Catherine's in Sinai is the oldest operating monastery in the world and houses the second largest collection of religious manuscripts, after the Vatican.

BUSINESS ETIQUETTE

 ## Punctuality

- Egyptian business people will be late, but you are expected to be on time.
- Always expect to be kept waiting, so schedule only one appointment per day.

 ## Meeting Manners

- Appointments are necessary and always should be made in advance. Your meeting should be confirmed one week in advance in writing or by telephone. Then reconfirm again a day or two before the meeting.
- Egyptian agents are required for doing business in their country.
- Meetings are very open with, literally, an open-door policy. There could be frequent interruptions or just people wandering in and out with completely different agendas. You can join in this new discussion, but do not try to bring the topic back to your discussion until that new person leaves.
- If you do need to discuss business matters in private, then you must stress the need for confidentially and the closing temporarily of the open door. High-level government officials do understand the practice of more western-style business meetings that are held without interruptions.
- Business meetings do have a lot of chitchat before the meeting begins, inquiring about health, family, and other general topics.
- Egyptians believe that the social side is critical and must respect, know, and like you before they will conduct business with you. These personal relationships are very important to create long-term business.
- Follow the lead of the Egyptian in the meeting. Hierarchy and rank play a major role; the most senior person is respected and will be the

spokesperson for the group. Decisions will be made by the highest-ranking person after discussing and coming to a group decision.

- Who you know is much more important than what you know. It's critical to network and create a number of contacts.
- Coffee or tea will be offered to show hospitality. Even if you do not drink it, accept it. If you decline the drink, it is viewed as rejecting the person.
- Agendas or materials sent in advance of the meeting should be in both English and Egyptian Arabic translation.
- Documents should carry both the Gregorian (Western) date and the date by the Hijrah (Arabic) calendar.
- To support your claims, show your research and documentation.
- Direct eye contact is viewed as being honest and sincere, but don't be intimated or uncomfortable with what may seem to be intense stares.
- Egyptians are very emotional and expressive with hand gestures. Even shouting, pounding on the table, or showing anger are not uncommon, but just a way to demonstrate a point.
- A man's word is still considered his bond, so for them to go back on their word is to bring dishonor to their family.
- Do not rush or use high-pressure approaches. Decisions will be made after much discussion and deliberation.
- If the government is involved in your business deals, then expect a longer decision time because approval must be given by the ministers of several departments.
- Since Egyptians are respectful of age and experience, it is smart to include older and more experienced people with higher, impressive titles in your meetings.
- Offers are not viewed as final, so expect to negotiate. Egyptians are tough negotiators, so be prepared.
- Egyptians do not like to say "no," and they do not like confrontations. If they do not respond, it is generally a negative sign.

 ## Business Cards

- There is no formal business card protocol.
- Do not present with your left hand.
- It is important to have one side of your card translated into Egyptian Arabic. Present this side of the card to the recipient.
- Read over another person's card before you put it away.

 **Meals/Toasts**

- Your host/hostess will tell you where to sit, so wait for this invitation.
- Generally, the male guest of honor is seated to the right of the host.
- Use only your right hand to eat.
- Help yourself to seconds because it is considered a nice compliment.
- Show respect and appreciation for the meal.
- Avoid salting your food because it is considered an insult.
- When you have completed your meal, always leave a small amount of food on your plate. If you clean your plate, they will give you more.
- Even though Egypt is trying to reduce smoking in public with new laws, with 76 million smokers in Egypt, it could be difficult. Be prepared to see many smokers during meals or while sipping a cup of tea.
- Toasts generally involve no protocol, so just follow your host or hostess.

 Entertainment

- Shoes are normally removed before entering an Egyptian's home.
- Since appearance is very important to Egyptians, you want to dress well and conservatively if invited to a home.
- Be sure to compliment the hosts on their home.
- Families are critical and play an important role in all social relationships.
- Strict Muslims will not eat pork or drink alcohol. Plan ahead if you invite an Egyptian to a social event, and if you're not sure whether they drink alcohol, have plenty of nonalcoholic drinks available.
- You can find hard liquor in international hotels. Most Egyptian restaurants serve only beer and wine.
- Good topics for discussion are history, antiquity, and sports including soccer, boxing, and horse racing. Avoid discussing Middle East politics.

 Forms of Address/Introductions/Greetings

- Handshakes are customary for greetings of individuals of the same sex.
- Their handshake could be somewhat limp and prolonged, which can make the situation uncomfortable, but their handshakes are given with a big smile and direct eye contact.
- You may feel uncomfortable with the direct and intense stares you may receive. Egyptians believe direct eye contact is a sign of sincerity and honesty.
- After a relationship has been created, it's common to kiss on one cheek and then the other while shaking hands, men with men and women with women.

- When greeting occurs between men and women, the woman must extend her hand first. If the woman does not extend her hand, then the man will bow his head in greeting.
- Space between the same sexes is much closer than observed by North Americans and Europeans. Space between the opposite sexes is much greater.
- Men will be seen holding hands or in close contact as they greet or walk down the street. This is common. Make no assumptions of sexual preference. Men are simply physical with one another.
- But if a man physically expresses himself to a woman in public, even if it is his wife, then the woman is viewed as "loose," so be careful of any public display of affection.
- When Muslims greet one another, they say *Assalamo Alaikum* (as-salamu alaykum) instead of good morning or hello. This phrase means, "May peace be upon you and may God's blessings be with you."
- Names can be very confusing. Try to get the names in advance in English so you can find out both their full names and how they are to be addressed in person.

Appearance/Attire

- Dress is formal and conservative.
- Men wear dark, lightweight, conservative business suits, at least to the first meeting. Men should avoid wearing visible jewelry, especially around the face and neck.
- Women should cover themselves appropriately. The knees should be covered with skirts or dresses and the sleeves should cover most of your arms, at least to the elbows. Modest dress is suggested and is the safest choice.
- Women should have a scarf or something handy to cover their heads, especially if entering a mosque. Most women entering a mosque will show only their face, hands, and feet.
- Western-style dress is very common and accepted in more modern nightclubs, restaurants, hotels, and bars in tourist destinations.
- Official or more social functions usually require more formal dress.
- Do not wear native clothing. Visiting women are not expected to wear a *higab* (headscarf) or robe in public.
- Closed shoes are highly recommended for tours or visits to tourist attractions and the city.

Gift Giving

- If invited to an Egyptian home for dinner, then you should bring a gift of good quality chocolates, sweets, or pastries to present to the hostess.
- Because they are reserved for weddings or the sick, avoid flowers unless you know that the hosts would enjoy and appreciate them.
- Presenting a small gift to a child shows affection.
- Always present your gifts with the right hand or use both hands if the gift is heavy or big.
- If you give a gift or receive one, it will be opened in private.

Tipping

- Tipping is a way of life in Egypt and is expected. If someone does something you would consider as an extra effort, they expect to be tipped.
- Many Egyptians survive on very little, so tips for good service are appreciated.
- Generally the guidelines are 5 percent to 10 percent in restaurants, plus the service charge, and 20 percent in restaurants that do not include the service charge.
- Porters would be tipped equivalent to US$1 or Canada $1 per bag for hotels or Nile cruises.
- Tipping will help you get things done effectively and efficiently.
- Tip taxi drivers by rounding up the bill. An additional tip could be given if they help with your bags.

Gesture Awareness

- Egyptians may use exaggerated hand gestures when they are excited just to express their point of view, but generally hand gestures are kept to a minimum. Placing your right hand over your heart expresses gratitude and humility. This gesture can also be used as a polite way of saying no. To show that you do not want to accept a gift or even to refuse a cup of coffee, this gesture can be an easy way to say, "no, thank you."
- To show "so-so" or "a little bit," hold your hand in mid air with palm down and tip it back and forth.
- To ward off evil, stretch your hand out with your palm facing out. It is offensive to make this gesture in someone's face.
- To make the number five, turn your palm to face you.
- If you cross your legs, be very concerned that your soles are always down. It's impolite to show others the soles of your feet or shoes.
- The thumbs-up sign is considered offensive.

Faux Pas

- It's impolite to eat everything on your plate. Leaving a little food on your plate shows abundance and is considered a compliment to the host or hostess.
- Do not salt your food; it is considered an insult.
- Do not wear traditional native clothing.
- Do not move away, even if you feel someone is standing too close.
- Use only the right hand for eating. Most Middle Easterners use the left hand for bodily hygiene.
- Tapping the two index fingers together is a rude gesture meaning, "Would you sleep with me?"
- Smoking in public is still common. Be considerate of others by presenting and offering your cigarettes.

USEFUL FACTS

President	Hosni Mubarak (1981)
Prime Minister	Dr. Ahmed Nazif (2004)
National Name	Jumhuriyat Misr al-Arabiyah Arab Republic of Egypt
Size	384,344 square miles (995,451 square km)
Population	81,713,517 (2008)
Capital	Cairo
Government	Republic
Currency	Pound
Religions	Muslim (mostly Sunni) 94%, Coptic Christian and other 6%
Language	Arabic is the official language, but English and French are widely understood by the educated classes.

Ethnicity	Egyptian 98%; Berber, Nubian, Bedouin, and Beja 1%; Greek, Armenian, and other European (mostly Italian and French) 1%
Industry	Tourism, chemicals, crude oil and petroleum products, cotton and textiles, pharmaceuticals, hydrocarbons, construction cement, metals, light manufacturing, and food processing
Time Zone	Egypt is two hours ahead of Greenwich Mean Time (GMT +2) or seven hours ahead of Eastern Standard Time (EST +7). Egypt observes daylight saving time.
Telephone Code	Country Code: +20 City Code: +2 (Cairo)
Weather	Desert with hot and dry summers and moderate winters
Voltage/Frequency	220 V; 50 Hz Certain rural areas still use 100 to 380 V

HOLIDAYS/FESTIVALS

1 January	New Year's Day
7 January	Christmas (Celebrates the nativity of Jesus Christ according to the Oriental Coptic Orthodox Church)
22 February	Unity Day
21 March	Sham al-Naseem (First day of spring celebration Coptic Easter Monday)
25 April	Sinai Liberation Day
1 May	Labor Day
17 June	Leylet en-Nuktah (The Coptic calendar date of Payne 11. This is the fixed date for the rise of the Nile.)
23 July	Revolution Day (End of the Egyptian royal government and the establishment of the republic in 1952)
18 June	Evacuation Day (Commemorates the withdrawal of foreign troops in 1956 and the proclamation of the Republic in 1953)

6 October	Armed Forces Day (The Egyptian forces crossed the Suez Canal in 1973 during the war against Israel.)
24 October	Suez Day (The Egyptian/Israeli cease-fire on Suez Day in 1973 restored control of the Suez Canal to Egypt. Also called Popular Resistance Day)
23 December	Victory Day

LANGUAGE TIPS

<u>Arabic Phonetics</u>	<u>English</u>
Marhaba	Hello
Shukran	Thank you
afwan	You are welcome
Salam	Hello/good-bye
Fursa Sa'eeda	Nice to meet you
Ma a el salama	Good-bye
Aiwa	Yes
La	No
Bi-kam	How much?
Mumkin el-Hisab, Min fadlak	May I have the bill please?

Chapter 9: FRANCE

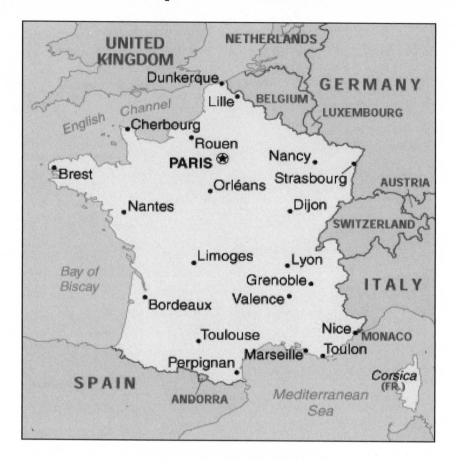

LOCATION/GEOGRAPHY

In Western Europe, France borders Belgium, Germany, Luxembourg, Switzerland, Italy, and Monaco on the north and east and Spain on the south. The English Channel, the Atlantic Ocean, and the Bay of Biscay are on the north and northwest, and the Mediterranean Sea is to the southeast.

 DID YOU KNOW?

- Under the law, French citizens are entitled to five weeks of vacation annually. July and August are the high vacation months for the French.
- Holidays are in abundance in the month of May and generally occur every week. Be prepared for museums, banks, restaurants, hotels, and stores to close their doors for several days. It's smart to call in advance to make sure the establishment is open.
- You could burn 123,900 calories if you were a rider in the Tour de France. But you'd need to bicycle 2,241 miles over a three-week period to accomplish this.
- The most famous painting in the Louvre and in the world is the Mona Lisa. But did you ever notice that she has no eyebrows? At the time of the painting, it was the fashion statement in Florence to shave them off.
- The Statue of Liberty was made in France and then given to the United States as a gift.
- Champagne was actually believed to be a serious mistake. Dom Perignon and his Benedictine monk colleagues thought that the bubbles were a defect until they tasted it.
- Jeans actually started in France and Levi Strauss imported them to the United States (California) to make work trousers for gold diggers. Denim is short for "*de Nimes*." Nimes is the birthplace of jeans.
- The modern bikini was invented in Paris in1946. It was actually named after Bikini Atoll, which was the site of a nuclear weapon test called Operation Crossroads, in the Marshall Islands. It took until the 1960s to become popular. Spain, Portugal, and Italy initially banned the bikini.
- The world's tallest bridge is Millau Viaduct over the River Tarn. It is higher than the Eiffel Tower and just slightly lower than the Empire State Building.
- Approximately 20 percent of the territory of France lies outside Europe in the overseas departments and territories and known as the "*domtom*." Some 2.5 million French citizens live in this area that covers four continents—Europe, North America, South America, and Antarctica—and has shores on the Atlantic, Pacific, and Indian oceans.

- The form of government in France has changed nine times since 1789, including five republics, two empires and two constitutional monarchies.
- France has the highest wealth tax in Europe.
- Some French inventions include the adding machine, hot air balloon, airship, parachute, submarine, ambulance service, photography, animation, and cinema.
- The first recipient and the most Nobel prizes winners for literature were from France. This includes Sully Prudhomme as the first in 1901, Maurice Maeterlinck, Romain Rolland, Anatole France, Henri Bergson, Roger Martin du Gard, Andre Gide, Francois Mauriac, Albert Camus, Saint-John Perse, Jean-Paul Sartre (who declined the prize in 1964), and Claude Simon.
- The French are the second biggest consumers of alcohol per capita, after Luxembourg, in the Western world.
- More than 67 million tourists visit France annually, which is more than any other country in the world.
- In 2004, the *Queen Mary II* was built in France. It is the largest and most advanced passenger cruise ship.
- The French TGV high-speed train had its inaugural run between Paris and Lyon in 1981. The network of the train is centered in Paris and has expanded across France and to adjacent countries. On 3 April 2007, it set the record for the fastest train in the world by reaching speeds of 357 mph (574,8 km/h).

BUSINESS ETIQUETTE

 ## Punctuality

- Arrive on time or early for meetings or dinners. Punctuality shows you are serious and motivated. However, expect to be kept waiting for a few minutes; this tendency indicates their desire to create an impression of being busy and successful.
- Telephone if you are running 10 minutes or more late for an appointment or dinner engagement.

 ## Meeting Manners

- Schedule appointments at least two weeks in advance. Avoid the heavy vacation months of July and August.
- Meetings generally will be arranged by the secretary via telephone or written communication. A lot depends on the hierarchy and the level of the people you are meeting.

- Decisions will not be reached in meetings. Meetings are used for discussion. Hierarchy is critical, and decisions will be made at the top.
- Courtesy and a degree of formality are part of the French business behavior.
- Respect and trust is required to complete any business.
- Creating a wide network of personal business acquaintances is critical.
- Since French is the official language, every attempt should be made to try to speak the language. A few key phrases will help create a long-term relationship.
- Education, social status, and the part of the country your counterparts were reared in will play an important role in your communication skills. There is a strong definition and competition between the classes.
- Over the past 20 years, women have been accepted into exclusive French schools and have achieved higher ranking positions, such as president in corporations or minister in the government.
- The direct approach is common. Good direct eye contact while you are speaking is necessary.
- The French do like their privacy, so always knock and wait before entering a room or office. Never just "drop in" without an appointment.
- Wait to be seated and allow your host to instruct you to sit and where.
- Do not rush. The business transitions are slow, patient, and according to protocol. Protocol is necessary to finalize the deal with formal contracts.
- Do not confront or use high-pressure tactics. Debating is welcomed.
- Careful analysis is always given to all details.
- Avoid a lot of chitchat. The French separate their business lives from their personal lives.

 ## Business Cards

- After the initial introduction, business cards are exchanged.
- There is no formal protocol for the exchange of cards.
- One side of your card should be translated into French. Though it is not mandatory, your attention to detail and respect will be noticed.
- Your advanced degrees should be included on your business card.
- The size of the French business card may be a little larger than the standard card exchanged in the United States.

Be On Your Best Cultural Behavior

Meals/Toasts

- Arrive on time if invited to either a home or a restaurant.
- Lunch is the recommended time for a business meal. You should wait until the dessert is served before discussing business.
- If attending a dinner party, send flowers the morning of the event. This will allow them to be displayed during the event.
- A dinner generally starts at 8:30 p.m. (2030) and can easily continue until 11 p.m. (2300). To politely excuse yourself, you should wait until the other guests have completed their coffee.
- Do not refuse wine during a meal, but sip it slowly.
- The French eat Continental style, with the fork held in the left hand and the knife in the right while eating. While you are not eating, rest your wrists on the edge of the table. Both hands should be visible during the meal, but avoid placing your elbows on the table.
- Wait to be seated. There could be a seating plan and you should follow your host/hostess.
- The honored position is at the head of the table, usually placed facing the door. The person of most importance is then seated to their left and then second ranking of importance to their right. If a couple is hosting an event, they will sit at opposite ends of the table.
- In France, they pass food to the left.
- Food portions may be small, but you will receive a lot more courses, so pace yourself.
- Wait until the host/hostess signals by saying, *"Bon appetit."*
- It is appropriate to finish everything on your plate, but do not ask for more.
- You may ask for more water but not more wine. Your host will serve you. If you are finished with your wine, then leave the wine glass almost full. If not, they will keep refilling. If you are the host, make sure your guests' glasses are filled.
- Fold your lettuce with your fork; do not cut it with a fork and knife.
- Peel and slice fruit before eating it.

 ## Entertainment

- If you invite others to a restaurant or bar, you are expected to pay.
- If you're invited to a French home, expect the meal to be elaborate and have numerous courses. Dinner parties could be late or even last to early in the morning.
- Gifts are expected as a thank-you for a social gathering. This could include flowers, chocolates, or liquor. Present your gift as your arrive and before any festivities.

- Just be careful with the flowers, remembering that they are presented in odd numbers and that chrysanthemums are for funerals, red roses for lovers, and carnations can be interpreted as a sign of bad will. Consult a local florist to be safe.
- Follow up the next day with a thank-you note to your host. This note should be handwritten and delivered by a messenger. You could also send flowers or a basket of fruit.

Forms of Address/Introductions/Greetings

- The handshake is a common exchange for greetings. They will welcome you with a handshake and offer another as you leave.
- The French do not shake hands as firmly as do people in the United States. Generally, it is quick and light with no pumping or heavy grip.
- If they have their hands full or may be dirty or wet, they will instead extend their elbow for you to touch or their finger for you to grip. Touch and let go.
- The French will stand close and touch your shoulder or pat your arm during conversation.
- Friends will meet and greet with two kisses. One light kiss on the left cheek and then one kiss on the right. (Often this is just cheek brushing and "air" kisses.) In some parts of the country, friends may exchange three kisses and maybe even four. If in doubt, just stand still and let them go back and forth. Then try to remember for future hugs and kisses how many they will exchange.
- Eye contact is important during the handshake. At times the French can be intimidating with their intense eye contact.
- Address colleagues by their last names. Wait to be invited to call a person by his first name.
- Men should stand when a higher ranking or superior person enters the room or at least make the effort to begin to stand.
- If you do not know the language, at least make attempts with a few greetings and phrases and apologize for not knowing their language.
- The French enjoy the exchange and the art of conversation. Frequent interruptions and arguments are part of their communication.
- Most French think that North Americans lecture instead of talking or conversing.
- Talk softly. North Americans come across as abrasive, with a loud, direct, and aggressive approach to conversation.

Appearance/Attire

- More formal and stylish is the norm for French business dress. The French are very conscientious about their appearance. Good quality accessories and well-tailored clothing are important for both men and women.
- Dark suits are still the standard for men during initial business encounters. As the meetings progress, your style will be determined by the standards of your French counterparts.
- Formality remains a constant in the office, with the men leaving their jackets and ties in place.
- Business suits and elegant dresses are worn by the women. Avoid bright or flashy colors.
- The professional business look means no tattoos for men or women and no earrings for men. Clean hair is important and men should be clean-shaven or have well-groomed beards. A little cologne is OK, but don't go overboard.
- If your invitation states "informal dress" do not be confused by wearing jeans and a t-shirt. Their informal dress is still very dressy and could include a jacket and tie for the men. If you have questions about the appropriate dress for a social or business occasion, check with your host/hostess in advance. It's always better to be overdressed in these situations than underdressed and apologizing for your appearance.

 Gift Giving

- Be careful if giving flowers. They should be presented in odd numbers but not 13, which is considered an unlucky number. White lilies and chrysanthemums are used for funerals, so should be avoided. Bad will is conveyed by red carnations. Another old tradition is not presenting white flowers because they are reserved for weddings.
- French love their wine, so if presenting a bottle of wine make sure it is of the highest quality.
- Other gift ideas are books, including a coffee table book from your home country, music, or other items from your home that you know will be appreciated by your host.
- Do not include your business card with your gift but instead a nice card.
- Gifts are generally opened when received.

% Tipping

- A service charge that is required by law is included in the bills in restaurants and bars. If you are satisfied with the service, it's customary to round up your bill or leave change in addition to this service fee.
- In upscale restaurants, an additional five percent of the bill is left on the table.
- Taxi drivers and hairdressers are tipped 10 percent of the bill.
- Theater ushers are given small tips from .40 to .75 euros (US$.62 to US$1.16).
- In some theaters and hotels, you may see a sign that states, "*Pourboire Interdit,*" which means tipping is forbidden for the coat room attendants. But if they may receive a tip, .64 euro (US$1) is appropriate.
- Washroom attendants could be given .32 euro (US$.50).
- Leave the housekeeper or chambermaid 1.4 to 1.6 euro (US$2.18 to US$2.50) per day.
- A bellman can be tipped .64 to 1.6 euro (US$1 to US$2.50) per bag, depending on the quality of the hotel.
- A concierge that performs a service above and beyond normal duties can receive 7 to 16 euro (US$10 to US$25), depending on the level of the service and the quality of the hotel.
- If you need your tires checked, then .64 to 1.6 euro (US$1 to US$2.50) is an appropriate tip.
- Museum guides can receive 1.6 to 2.8 euro (US$2.50 to $4.36) for their services.
- Bus drivers can receive 1.4 euro (US$2.18) for their duties after the excursion.

Gesture Awareness

- "*Mon oeil*" is displayed in a gesture of pulling down the skin under your eye with your index finger. You are telling that person that you do not believe what they are telling you—the U.S. version of "Yea, right!" or "Who are you kidding?"
- To show that a person is drunk, make a loose fist and hold it up in front of your nose. Make a motion with your fist like you are turning or going to rev up a motorcycle, as your tilt your head the other way.
- To show that you need money or that something is too expensive, hold your hand out with the palm up and rub your thumb across your fingers back and forth several times.
- To motion "let's leave" or "get out of here," hold both of your palms down and smack one hand down on the other.

Be On Your Best Cultural Behavior

- The French will start to count the number 1 with their thumb, two is with the thumb and index finger and so on. So if you hold up the usual two fingers as we do in the United States with your index finger and middle finger, then you will get three of whatever you are requesting. They count the thumb even if you do not display it.
- Snapping your fingers is considered offensive.
- Motion with your entire hand instead of using just the index finger to point.
- To summon for the check at the end of the meal, motion with a writing gesture in the air.
- The OK sign that is used in the United States by forming a circle with the thumb and forefinger means "zero" or "useless" in France. While the French OK sign is equivalent to the thumbs-up sign used in the United States.

 Faux Pas

- Be very careful about personal questions. They may just tell you, "It is none of your business."
- If you receive a card of congratulations or thanks for a gift or kind gesture, you need to return a card to them. So, yes, you are thanking them for thanking you. It's a bit confusing but better to err on the side of too many cards.
- Be careful about invitations and be very clear about exactly what you have been invited to attend. A wedding invitation could only be an announcement and you are truly not invited to anything. Or you may be requested only at the church and nothing else.
- *Bonjour* is the common greeting but it should also be followed with either a person's name or title, such as, *"Bonjour, Madame."*
- Chewing gum in public is considered disgusting.
- When in public, keep your hands out of your pockets.
- Avoid criticizing Napoleon or asking personal questions about someone's occupation, political stance, or how they voted.

USEFUL FACTS

President	Nicolas Sarkozy (2007)
Prime Minister	Francois Fillon (2007)
National Name	Republique Francaise
Size	210,668 square miles (545,630 square km)
Population	64,057,790 (2008)
Capital	Paris
Government	Fifth Republic
Currency	Euro (formerly French franc)
Religions	Roman Catholic 85%, Protestants 2%, Islam 8%, Jewish 1%, unaffiliated 4%
Language	French is the official and the first language of the country. There are a few minor languages, but this population also speaks French. Three percent of the population speaks German dialects; 0.2%, Flemish; 1.7%, Italian; and 0.1%, Basque.
Ethnicity	Celtic and Latin with Teutonic, Slavic, North African, Southeast Asian, and Basque minorities
Industry	Food and tourism play a major role in France. Other industries include machinery, chemicals, automobiles, metallurgy, aircraft, and electronics. France is invested in civil nuclear power and exports it. Numerous natural resources.
Time Zone	France is one hour ahead Greenwich Mean Time (GMT +1) or six hours ahead of Eastern Standard Time (EST +6). France does observe daylight saving time.

Telephone Code	Country Code: +33
	City Code: +1 (Paris)
Weather	Mostly cool winters and mild summers. Along the Mediterranean, you will find mild winters and hot summers. Occasional mistral, which is a strong, cold, dry, north-to-northwesterly wind.
Voltage/Frequency	220 V; 50 Hz

HOLIDAYS/FESTIVALS

1 January	New Year's Day
1 May	Labor Day
8 May	WWII Victory Day
14 July	Bastille Day
15 August	Assumption of the Blessed Virgin Mary
11 November	Armistice Day
25 December	Christmas Day (Noel)
26 December	2nd Day of Christmas (in Alsace and Lorraine only)

LANGUAGE TIPS

French	Phonetics	English
Bonjour	bohn-zhoor	Hello/Good Day
Bonsoir	bohn-swahr	Hello/Good Evening
Salut	sah-lew	Hello/Hi
Ca va?	Sah vah	How are you? (informal) and
Ca va		I'm fine
Tres bien/mal/pas mal	treh bee-ahn/mahl/ pah mahl	Very good/bad/ not bad
S'il vous plait	seel voo pleh	Please
Merci (beaucoup)	mair-see boh-koo	Thank you (very much)
Excusez-moi	ex-koo-zay mwah	Excuse me/sorry
A demain	ah duh-mahn	See you tomorrow.
Je (ne) sais (pas)	zhuhn say pah	I (don't) know

Chapter 10: GERMANY

LOCATION/GEOGRAPHY

Germany is located in central Europe and is bordered by Austria, Belgium, Czech Republic, Denmark, France, Luxembourg, The Netherlands, Poland, and Switzerland. To the north, Germany has ports on the Baltic and North Seas.

DID YOU KNOW?

- Five thousand varieties of beer are produced in Germany.
- In World War II, the German submarine U-120 was sunk by a malfunctioning toilet. (I promise this is true.)
- Adolf Hitler was one of the people responsible for the creation of the Volkswagen Beetle.
- The name Vaseline is a combination of the German word for water, *wasser,* and the Greek word for olive oil, *elaion.*
- The word snorkel comes from the German word *schnorchel,* which was a tube used by German submarine crews in WW II.
- The country of Prussia no longer exists. After WW II, it was divided among Poland, Germany, and the USSR.
- Germany was the first European country to create a health insurance system for its workers—in 1888.
- German Melitta Bentz created the coffee filter in 1908.
- Germany is approximately the size of Montana.
- In most areas there is no speed limit on the autobahn, a fact which makes driving extremely stressful or exciting, depending on your perspective. However, be very careful of the areas of the autobahn where speed limits are posted. They have video cameras and will catch you in the act. The fines can be very high. Tailgating is common and aggressive, especially with German motorcyclists on the left side of the autobahn.
- East Germany and West Germany, divided following WW II, were reunited in 1990.

BUSINESS ETIQUETTE

Punctuality

- Arrive on time because punctuality is taken very seriously.
- If you cannot arrive on time, telephone immediately and offer an explanation.
- Canceling a meeting at the last minute could jeopardize your business relationship and is considered extremely rude.
- Business meetings start when doors close.

Meeting Manners

- Appointments should be coordinated at least one or more weeks in advance.
- The best time for business appointments is between 10 a.m. and 1 p.m. (1000 to 1300). Avoid Friday afternoon appointments because some offices will close by 2 p.m. or 3 p.m. (1400 or 1500).
- Germans have a six-week paid vacation time, generally in July and August. December, Easter, and school breaks are other big vacation times.
- Titles are extremely important, so it's critical that you know the proper form of address, a person's full name, and correct title. This applies in both verbal and written communication. Address letters to the top person, using the proper name and title.
- Formality is the norm for most meetings.
- Germans are very forward thinking and are masters of planning. Extensive planning is important with business conducted at the specific time and day appointed. Agendas are critical, as are exact starting and ending times.
- Rules and regulations set the standards, so they know what is expected and they plan accordingly. If something works, then it is accepted and not changed.
- Initial meetings are generally used to establish trust and to get to know one another. Germans are direct and to the point. A personal relationship is not necessary to do business.
- While addressing your associates, direct eye contact is important.
- Hire an interpreter even if English will be the language of the meeting. This will help with any misunderstandings. All materials need to be in both German and English.
- Some Germans will signal the end of the meeting by rapping their knuckles on the top of the table.
- It is critical that you follow the protocol of the highest-ranking or eldest person entering the room first.
- Men will enter the room before women if their age and status are roughly the same.
- Do not sit until you are invited to and are told where to sit for the meeting.
- Germans are interested in credentials and like to get down to business after the initial relationships are set and with minimal small talk.
- Germans are detail-oriented, so do not rush or be frustrated with their delivery and follow-through with protocol. All details must be clear and completely understood before coming to a final agreement. Contracts are strictly adhered to and followed.

- Decisions come from the top, and hierarchy is still critical and enforced.
- Once the planning process is completed, the project will move along quickly and deadlines are expected to be honored.
- High-pressure tactics will prove to be counterproductive, so avoid unnecessary confrontations.
- Expect a lot of communications for back-up and maintaining a good record of the discussions and the decisions.
- Once a decision is made, it is generally final.
- Seating is critical, with the center seat at the table farthest from the door reserved for the most senior attendee. The counterpart should sit across from him or her, with the next most important to the right of the highest ranking and the next to the left of the highest ranking.
- "Open-door" policy is not followed, and most people work with their doors closed. Knock first and wait to be invited into the office.
- Germans are very structured, with a strict and clear divide between work and personal lives. Germans believe that at the end of the day, your work should be over. If you need to spend additional hours with work, then you did not plan your day well enough to complete it. Very true!

Business Cards

- Always have plenty on hand.
- Exchange business cards at your initial meeting.
- It's to your advantage to have your cards printed in German on the reverse side.
- Titles, including graduate degrees, are important.

Meals/Toasts

- Always remain standing until you are invited to sit down because they may have a particular seat for you.
- Germans follow the Continental style of eating, with the fork in left hand and the knife in the right while eating.
- Use utensils when eating. Even pizza is eaten with a fork and knife unless it is sold by the slice to go.
- Breakfast meetings are not part of German business culture. Lunch is the best time for business discussions and generally is served from noon to 1 p.m. (1200 to 1300). Evening business meals are less common because of the importance of their private time.
- Wait to begin eating until the hostess starts or someone gives the sign by saying, "*guten appetite*," which means good appetite.

- Do not cut your lettuce in your salad but fold it using your knife and fork.
- To show the cook that your food is tender and prepared correctly, cut as much as possible with your fork.
- Finish all the food on your plate. Leaving large portions of food on your plate might suggest that something is wrong with it.
- Meals can be heavy, since German cuisine is traditionally meats and sauces. Inform your host in advance if you have dietary, health, or religious reasons for not accepting certain foods. Do not wait until the meal is being served.
- To show that you are finished with your meal, place your knife and fork on the right side of the plate, with the fork over the knife.
- The person who invites pays. It is not expected that as a guest you should even offer to pay the bill. If you do want to pay, then this should be handled before you get to the restaurant.
- Dinner is served generally from 7 p.m. to 8:30 p.m. (1900 to 2030), which is the same time for parties to begin.
- An aperitif in the form of a cocktail or a liqueur can be served before dinner. If this same drink is served after dinner, it is called a *digesif.* Both are generally served cold.
- Allow the host to give the first toast. Later in the meal, the honored guest can and should return the toast.
- The most common toast with wine is *zum wohl*, which salutes good health. The most common toast with beer is *prost*, which also means good health.

 ## Entertainment

- Generally, only close friends and relatives are invited to homes. If you are invited to a German's home, arrive on time but not early. Do not arrive more than 15 minutes later than invited without telephoning to explain why you will be late.
- Always send your host a handwritten thank-you note the following day.
- Luncheon meetings will be conducted before and after the meal but not during.
- When a couple is hosting, many times they will be seated at the ends of the table opposite one another. The male guest will be seated to the right of hostess and female to the right of the host.
- It is not unusual to be in a restaurant and be approached by strangers who ask to share your table. You do not have to talk to them other than the initial greeting to confirm whether the chairs are available.

- Conversational topics to avoid are WW II, the Holocaust, and personal questions, including salary or costs of personal items.
- Good conversation topics include sports (especially their national sport of soccer), travel, recent holidays, current events, your work and profession. If you are comfortable talking politics, you can venture in that direction.

Forms of Address/Introductions/Greetings

- Greetings are formal. A quick, firm handshake is the traditional exchange. Shake hands at both the beginning and the conclusion of a meeting.
- When being introduced to a woman, you might wait a second to see if she extends her hand.
- A handshake may also have a slight bow. Reciprocate by returning the nod to show respect and make a good first impression.
- Good direct eye contact is critical.
- Titles are important and show respect. Use titles and surnames until invited to use first names. Say *herr* or *frau* or the person's title and surname.
- German men might still greet one another by saying *herr* and the last name, even after many years of friendship.
- Germans still prefer third-party introductions when possible.
- Hugs and kissing on both cheeks are common among good friends and family.
- Handshaking between parents and grown children and between adult siblings is a common practice.
- Wait for your hosts to introduce you to a group.
- When entering a room, shake hands with everyone individually, including the children.

Appearance/Attire

- Dress is conservative, understated, and formal for corporate business.
- Men wear dark, conservative business suits.
- Women also wear conservative business suits or dresses.
- Office staff and clerks dress more casually.
- Avoid excessive jewelry or accessories, especially in the former Democratic Republic of Germany (East Germany).
- "Informal" means not wearing a coat and tie, it does not mean jeans and a t-shirt.

Be On Your Best Cultural Behavior

- "Formal" attire indicates more formal eveningwear and much more dressy than American standards.
- Khaki and seersucker suits are not acceptable, at least for your first meeting.
- Teenagers and students will wear a more casual, sporty look.

Gift Giving

- If invited to a German's home, bring a gift of chocolates, wine, flowers, or a silk scarf for the hostess.
- Yellow roses or tea roses are a great gift, but do not give red roses because they express romantic intentions. Do not give carnations because they symbolize mourning. Do not give lilies or chrysanthemums because they are used at funerals.
- If you bring wine, it should be imported, preferably French or Italian. Giving German wines sends the message that you do not think the host will serve a good quality wine.
- Gifts are generally opened when received. Small gifts are considered polite, and substantial gifts are unusual.
- Quality pens or tasteful office items displaying your company logo make good gifts. Coffee table books from your country or something that reflects the interests of your hosts are also excellent.
- Send a handwritten note to your hosts to show your appreciation.

Tipping

- Tipping at restaurants is left up to you. Their laws include the tip in the bill, which is approximately 10 percent to 15 percent, but most people leave a bit more if service warrants it.
- Rounding up seems to be the standard. Tipping is not as liberal as in other countries.
- The procedure is the waiter will come to your table and tell you the amount of the bill. You tell them what you want to pay and they will give back the difference.
- Always give the tip to the server instead of leaving it on the table. If you allow the wait staff to return your change and then place your tip on the table, it is associated with dissatisfaction and unhappiness with the service.
- At German airports you will find only baggage carts and no skycaps.
- Housekeepers in hotels are left a tip in the room for their services.

- For doormen or bellmen who help with your luggage, two or three Euros are appropriate for service.
- The hairdresser may receive one or two euros, and the person who washes your hair may receive one Euro. In Germany, the salon owner does not get a tip.
- Ten percent of the amount shown on the meter is generally the tip for taxi drivers.

Gesture Awareness

- A group wave is not appreciated in a business situation. Save this for casual settings.
- Direct eye contact does not necessitate a greeting nor should it be threatening.
- The OK sign used in the United States is considered obscene in Germany.
- Pointing your index finger to your head is an insult to another person.
- To show luck, instead of crossing their fingers, German's will squeeze the thumb between the middle and index fingers. Only the thumb tip is between the fingers; to allow it to protrude is considered an offensive gesture.
- Public displays of affection are considered inappropriate in some areas.
- Germans will wear their wedding rings on their right hand, not the left as is customary in other countries.

Faux Pas

- It is considered rude to chew gum while talking to another person.
- Placing one hand on your lap and using only one hand to eat is not considered good table etiquette.
- Germans do not need or expect to be complimented. Their policy is that everything is satisfactory unless you are told otherwise.
- Humor is not expected or appreciated in business situations. They take business very seriously.
- Don't embarrass yourself by trying to keep up with Germans when they are drinking. Consuming two liters of beer may be an ordinary evening for them, but pace yourself and be sure to eat if you are unaccustomed to much alcohol.
- Germans value their private life, so avoid contacting an executive outside the office without prior arrangements or permission.

USEFUL FACTS

President	Horst Kohler (2004)
Chancellor	Angela Merkel (2005)
National Name	Bundesrepublik Deutschland
Size	135,236 square miles (350,261 square km)
Population	82,369,548 (2008)
Capital	Berlin
Government	Federal Republic
Currency	Euro (formerly Deutsche mark)
Religions	Protestant 34%, Roman Catholic 34%, and others include Islam, Buddhism, Judaism, and Hinduism.
Language	German 95%, with other minority languages including English, French, Italian, Russian, Polish, Dutch, Serbian, Romani, Turkish, and Kurdish.
Ethnicity	German 91.5%, Turkish 2.4%, Italian 0.7%, Greek 0.4%, Polish 0.4%, other 4.6%
Industry	One of the world's largest and most technologically advanced producers of iron, steel, coal, chemicals, cement, machinery, vehicles, machine tools, electronics, food and beverages, ships, and textiles
Time Zone	Germany is one hour ahead of Greenwich Mean Time (GMT +1) or six hours ahead of Eastern Standard Time (EST +6). Germany observes daylight saving time.
Telephone Code	International Code: +49 City Code: +30 (Berlin)

Weather	Germany's weather is varied throughout the country. Winters in the west of Germany will have freezing temperatures and well below freezing in the east. The temperature in the summer months is usually 20 C (68 F) to 30 C (86 F), with more rainfall during the summer months.
Voltage/Frequency	230 V, 50 Hz

 # HOLIDAYS/FESTIVALS

1 January	New Year's Day
6 January	Epiphany
March/April	Good Friday to Easter Monday
1 May	Day of the Worker/Labor Day (Very special day and the opening of the outdoor beer gardens.)
39 Days After Easter	Ascension Day
50 days after Easter Sunday	Whit Monday (also known as Pentecost Monday)
June	Corpus Christi (honor of the Holy Eucharist)
8 August	Peace Festival
15 August	Assumption Day (celebration in honor of the day Mother Mary's body and soul were united before she ascended to heaven)
3 October	Day of Unity (the day when East and West Germany were united in 1990)
31 October	Reformation Day
1 November	All Saints Day
Wednesday before Nov 23	Day of Repentance
25 December	Christmas "Holy Night"
26 December	St. Stephen's Day

LANGUAGE TIPS

German	Phonetics	English
Guten morgen	GOO-ten morgen	Good morning
Gute nacht	GOO-tuh nahdt	Good night
Ich heisse…	ich HYE-suh	My name is…
Ich bin…	ich bin…	I am…
Haben Sie…?	HAH-ben zee	Do you have…?
ein Mietwagen	eye-n MEET-vahgen	A rental car
der Bahnhof	dare BAHN-hof	The train station
der Flughafen	dare FLOOG-hafen	The airport
Bier/Wein/Saft	beer/vine/zahft	Beer/Wine/Juice
Wo ist die Toilette?	Vo ist dee toy-LETa	Where's the restroom/toilet?

Chapter 11: GREECE

LOCATION/GEOGRAPHY

Greece is located in southern Europe and borders on the Aegean, Mediterranean, and Ionian seas. It shares land borders with Albania, Bulgaria, Turkey, and the former Yugoslav Republic of Macedonia.

 DID YOU KNOW?

- Greece was the birthplace of democracy in the 5th century BC.
- Greece has almost 2,000 islands in its territory.
- At 2,917 meters (approximately 9,570 feet), Mount Olympus is the highest point in Greece.
- The Olympic Games originated in Greece around 776 BC. They were outlawed as pagan rites in the 4th century AD. The modern Olympic Games were revived in Athens in 1896.
- Easter is more important to most Greeks than Christmas.
- The Greek Orthodox Church plays a large role in political, civic, and governmental affairs.
- The younger generations are not so devout church-goers as their parents and grandparents.
- In Greece, it is believed that one family member bringing dishonor to himself brings dishonor to the entire family.
- When walking into a Greek Orthodox church, you should light a candle. You can put in any amount to light this candle but generally 50drs or 100drs (US$.25 or US$.50) is appropriate. After lighting a candle, Greeks will kiss the icon of their patron saint.
- The drinking age in Greece is 16.
- The Greek alphabet was the first true alphabet. It provided a symbol for each consonant and vowel and is the oldest alphabetic script that is still in use today.
- The government is now starting a new program requiring taxi drivers and police officers to attend seminars about the importance of treating people, especially tourists, more cordially.

BUSINESS ETIQUETTE

 Punctuality

- Arriving 30 minutes late to a Greek home is still considered on time.
- Arriving on time for meetings is expected, but your host may not be there.
- Promptness is not a priority in Greek culture. Don't take it personally.

 Meeting Manners

- Greeks prefer to do business with people that they know and trust.
- Family and friends are a key part in business transactions and are frequently called on because of their trustworthiness. Nepotism is common.
- Greeks prefer face-to-face meetings. The telephone and written communications are considered too impersonal.
- Allow enough time to establish a relationship. This can be done over lunch, dinners, and social events.
- Do not challenge the integrity or honor of a business associate. A person's integrity or their decisions should never be questioned publicly.
- Avoid being pretentious.
- Business may come across as very relaxed, but actually it is very serious. Treat all meetings and relationships with respect and formality.
- If your Greek counterparts become quiet or pull back, you might have done something to upset or offend them.
- Appointments are necessary. You will need to arrange these at least one to two weeks in advance. It is possible to arrange on shorter notice, but at least your initial meeting should have sufficient lead time.
- Confirm your meeting the day prior by telephone.
- Allow plenty of time for travel to your meetings because of the traffic in Greece. Parking is also a challenge, so taxi cabs or the subway system could be alternatives. Many Greek cabs do not have air conditioning, so be prepared to sit in a hot taxi.
- Lunch is generally taken from 1 p.m. to 3 p.m. (1300 to 1500), so it is not the best time to schedule a meeting.
- It may take up to three meetings before you actually get down to business. Allow this time for them to get to know you and establish the necessary trust and mutual respect. Do not lose your patience or show frustration in this process.
- Greeks enjoy negotiating. Hire a local lawyer to assist with the details of negotiation.
- Have all your printed information in both English and Greek.

- Be prepared for people to interrupt the meetings and for several people to talk at the same time.
- There will be deviations from the agenda. Agendas are important and are used as starting points for discussions, but then they will follow these discussions to the next level.
- Some of the business associates will speak English, but it's smart to hire an interpreter.
- Age and position are highly respected. The decisions are made at the top of the company.
- Deadlines or stressing a set time-frame could end negotiations. Be patient. Their pace is slower.
- Contracts are simple and secondary to the personal relationship.

Business Cards

- Greeks observe no formal ritual with the exchanging of business cards.
- One side of your business card should be translated into Greek.
- When you present your card, make sure the Greek side faces the recipient.

Meals/Toasts

- Remain standing until you are invited to be seated. You may even be shown to a particular place.
- The Greeks eat Continental style, with the fork in the left hand and the knife remaining in the right while they are eating.
- Generally the oldest person is served first.
- Allow the hostess to begin eating first.
- Your hands need to stay above the table while eating and your elbows off the table.
- Accepting a second helping compliments the host. You can also finish everything on your plate.
- Meals are great times for socializing, so expect a lot of discussion.
- You may be invited out for coffee. This coffee get-together may end up with a meal, but the invitation will be extended for coffee first.
- Small dishes, or *mezes*, are often served instead of a large plate. These *mezes* are generally shared with all the diners.
- This is one country where you can use a piece of bread to soak up gravy or sauce, so enjoy!
- It is common to share food from your plate.

- To show you are done with the meal, place your knife and fork parallel on your plate with the handles facing to the right and place your napkin next to your plate.
- The first toast will be given by the host. A toast can be given later in the meal by the honored guest.
- The most common toast is "to your health," which is *stinygiasou* in informal situations and *eis igian sas* at more formal events.

Entertainment

- If invited to a Greek home, you should dress well to show respect for the hosts.
- Offer to assist the hosts in their home with the setup and clearing of the meal. They may not accept your offer, but it will still be appreciated.
- It is considered punctual if you arrive 30 minutes late to a Greek home.
- You will be treated like a king or queen as a guest in a Greek home.
- Make sure to compliment the hosts on their home.
- If you are dining at a restaurant that provides live music, don't be surprised if everyone gets up and starts dancing. If you're invited, join them. You may not know their dances, but at least try. They will appreciate your effort.
- In a bar or tavern you may be offered a drink or a sweet. If so, thank the giver or say cheers (*yamas*). You are not obligated to drink or eat, but say thanks and take a sip or small bite to show appreciation.
- Smoking is common in Greece.

Forms of Address/Introductions/Greetings

- The first-time greeting is a firm handshake with a smile and direct eye contact.
- Good friends will embrace and could also kiss on both cheeks. This physical contact between men and women is very casual and common. These same signs of friendship are also shown by the same sex.
- Men that are friends will often slap each other on the arm at the shoulder.
- Greeks can be very expressive, with big arm and hand gestures while they are speaking.
- Since Greeks are so outgoing, their conversations could get loud. This does not indicate anger.
- Greeks are more formal with names. Even when they move to calling you by your first name, it still may have the title of Mr. or Mrs. followed by your first name as a sign of respect.

Greece

Appearance/Attire

- Men will wear dark, conservative business suits and ties.
- Women will wear either business suits or dresses also in dark, conservative colors.
- Just to leave the home, women will be a little dressier with make-up.
- Jeans and sneakers are worn but more around the home or for exercise.
- Casual gatherings are still dressy compared to U.S. casual dress.
- Because the summers are very hot, the styles will relax a little, with more informal and casual dress. But if you are at an official meeting, then even in the heat, dress more formally for business.

Gift Giving

- Greeks will exchange gifts with family and friends at Christmas and for their "name day" (the birth date of the saint that they were named after). Some will celebrate their birthdays, but name days are more popular for celebration.
- Gifts are reciprocated, so you need to be careful of the cost of the gift. The Greeks will feel obligated to give a gift to you of equal value and it could be a burden.
- Greeks can also be very generous, so be careful of too much complimenting because you just might end up with the object admired as your gift.
- Company logo gifts are appreciated and appropriate.
- If invited to a Greek home, bring a small gift of flowers or sweets. Flowers and floral arrangements could be sent in advance of an event.
- All gifts should be wrapped.
- Gifts generally are opened when they are presented.

Tipping

- A service charge is usually part of the bill in restaurants. You usually will need to ask for the bill because it probably will not be brought to you at the table.
- An additional tip of 10 percent to 20 percent of the total bill for waiters is appreciated and appropriate. This is usually left in the tray that is brought with your bill or given directly to them.
- If you would like to leave additional monies for the busboy, leave coins on the table that total about a Euro.
- Porters, doormen, and concierges are all tipped 2 to 3 euro or US$3 to US$4.60.
- Tip a small amount to the public toilet attendants.

- Taxi drivers do not expect tips but love receiving them. A small fee is charged by taxi drivers for handling each piece of your luggage. This is an official charge and should not be considered part of a tip.
- In remote areas, tipping is not expected or smaller tips are given.

 ## Gesture Awareness

- You should always avoid the OK sign of a circle with your fingers. It's considered obscene.
- The signal that is used is the United States to signify "stop," with the open hand facing outward is considered very offensive and should always be avoided.
- To indicate "no," Greeks do not shake their head from side to side but instead they tilt their head upward and backward and then back down to looking directly ahead. They only do the movement once. They may also click their tongue against their teeth. To add emphasis as in "no, of course not," they will tilt their head up and back in a very slow deliberate movement with even a partial or full closing of their eyes.
- To indicate yes, the head is tilted downward and slightly to one side. This is also done only once. To add emphasis, this movement is done slowly.

 ## Faux Pas

- Don't try to change their smoking habits. There are rules for non-smoking in stores, restaurants, cafes, banks, and other public places but it goes unnoticed. The best seats in restaurants are for smokers. Smoking is everywhere.
- When entering a Greek Orthodox Church, dress appropriately and cover your skin. Tourists should not walk from the beach in swimsuits and enter a church. Also cover up while shopping or dining in restaurants.
- Be careful with shopping. If you don't intend to buy something, don't pick it up, touch it, or try it on. Shopkeepers are known for "shadowing" their customers.

USEFUL FACTS

President	Karolos Papoulias (2005)
Prime Minister	Konstandinos (Kostas) Karamanlis (2004)
National Name	Elliniki Dimokratia
Size	50,502 square miles (130,800 square km)
Population	10,722,816 (2008)
Capital	Athens
Government	Parliamentary Republic; Monarchy rejected by Referendum 9 in December 1974
Currency	Euro (formerly drachma)
Religion	Greek Orthodox 98%, Muslim 1.3%, Other 0.7%
Language	Greek 98%, Macedonian 1.8%, others include English, French, Albanian and Turkish
Ethnicity	Greek 98%, other 2%
Industry	Tourism, food and tobacco processing, textiles, chemicals, metal products, mining, petroleum
Time Zone	Greece is two hours ahead of Greenwich Mean Time (GMT +2) or seven hours ahead of Eastern Standard Time (EST +7). Greece observes daylight saving time.
Telephone Code	International Code: +30 City Code: +21 (Athens)
Weather	Greece and the Greek Islands have mild winters and warm summers. Their summers have a lot of sunshine and little rainfall. The islands of the Aegean and the Ionian seas are a little milder.
Voltage/Frequency	230 V; 50 Hz

HOLIDAYS/FESTIVALS

1 January	Saint Basil's Day/New Year's Day
8 January	Midwife's Day/Women's Day
25 March	Independence Day
March/April	Good Friday, Holy Saturday, Easter, Easter Monday The week preceding Holy Week is called "Dumb Week" and the first Monday in Lent called "Clean Monday."
28 October	Oxi Day (The day that Greeks said no to the Italians when they wanted free passage to invade Greece in WWII)
25 December	Christmas

LANGUAGE TIPS

Greek Phonetics	English
Ya-sou	Hello or good-bye (greeting to one person or a friend)
Ya ssas	Hello or good-bye (greeting to more people or a more formal and polite way to greet an unknown person)
Kali-mera	Good morning
Kali-spera	Good evening
Kali-neek-ta	Good night
Ef-hari-sto	Thank you
Paraka lo	You're welcome
Mi la te Anglika	Do you speak English?
Then katala ve no	I don't understand
Me le ne	My name is …
Neh/O-hee	Yes/No

Chapter 12: INDIA

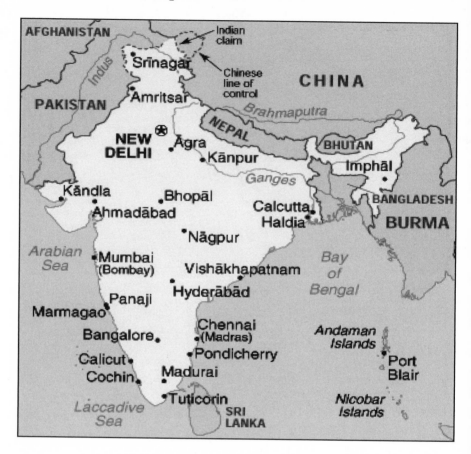

LOCATION/GEOGRAPHY

India is located in southern Asia, surrounded by the Arabian Sea, Indian Ocean, and the Bay of Bengal. It is bordered by Bangladesh, Bhutan, Myanmar (Burma), China, and Nepal to the east and northeast and Pakistan to the northwest. India is approximately one third the size of the United States.

DID YOU KNOW?

- In terms of size, India is the seventh largest country in the world. With a population of more than 1 billion, India is the second most populous country in the world (after China).
- The literacy rate is just over 50 percent, but India has one of the largest populations of technically qualified manpower. There are approximately 15 million doctors, engineers, and scientists.
- The Bombay Stock Exchange has approximately 6,500 companies; this is second only to the New York Stock Exchange.
- India is the largest producer of tea, second largest cement-producing country, fourth in the world in the pharmaceutical industry, second largest fruit and vegetable producer, the world's largest center for diamond cutting and polishing, and is emerging as a major center for technology.
- Bollywood produces more than 800 movies every year. Approximately 3 billion movie tickets are sold each year in India.
- The median age is 24, with 40 percent of the population between the ages of 22 and 44.
- Hindi is the official national language, but less than 40 percent of the people can speak or understand the language. India has 18 constitutionally recognized major languages and 1,600 other languages and dialects. English is the co-official language. It is spoken by the educated class and is the common language for business.
- Their parliament is bicameral, with the lower house Lok Sabha (house of the people) and the upper house Rajya Sabha (council of state).
- This is the only country that has a Bill of Rights for cows. The Hindu religion holds them sacred.
- Bananas were introduced to the West after Alexander the Great discovered them in India in 327 B.C.
- Arabic numerals are not actually Arabic. They were invented in India.
- Just recently Ken, the famous boyfriend of the Barbie doll, was banned for sale in India because he was considered in conflict with the standards of traditional arranged marriages.

Be On Your Best Cultural Behavior

BUSINESS ETIQUETTE

 ## Punctuality

- Punctuality ranges according to class, but it is advisable.
- Although the people of India appreciate punctuality and keeping their commitments, many are habitually late. They consider arriving for a social event on time to be bad manners.
- It is customary to arrive a few minutes late for a business meal.

 ## Meeting Manners

- A hierarchical system is observed, along with a strong work ethic. Many sons will automatically follow in their father's footsteps. They are trained and taught to carry on the trade of their family.
- The Indian culture is based on relationships and feelings. A deal could be closed or opened depending on their trust and belief in you and your company. It is important for your Indian associates to know the whole person they are dealing with, including social, personal, and historical background.
- Aim your first appointment for a person that is high in authority. Starting at the top will definitely be in your favor. This higher authority will probably direct you to a middle-level associate, but this is probably the person you need to be doing business with. Starting with superiors will help you as you progress through the chain of transactions.
- Stand and greet people when they enter a room, especially if they are higher ranking.
- Women executives in senior positions are still relatively new, so if you are a woman wanting to conduct business in India, you may need a few extra steps to get to the stage you want to be. The Indians will always be courteous and respectful to you, but you will likely encounter a slower process.
- Negotiations can be slower than in the United States and are much more relaxed.
- Be ready to negotiate and bargain for the final price or additional concessions. Build some buffers into your initial offer. Coming straightforward with your offer can come across as your final deal and they feel they have no negotiating room. Expecting a deal in your first meeting is unrealistic. This could be a long process because of the bureaucratic nature of their organizations.
- Also expect interruptions during your meeting. Indians tend to multi-task, but with that comes other conversations or interruptions while you are in the office or meeting with them. This does not show a lack of respect for your business or you. Just be patient.

India

- A detailed proposal sent in advance is advisable. A PowerPoint could be used to start your presentation in person. Indians will be cautious in accepting a new idea or proposal.
- Many Indian businesses are modern and Western in their operations, but it is important to understand the specific community culture, which can vary considerably. There are regional differences. In southern India, companies are more conservative compared to the north or the western part of the country. These three sectors, in turn, tend to be more individualistic and assertive than the eastern portion of India.
- Informality can be interpreted as disrespect. Be extremely respectful when addressing older people or people of higher rank.
- Many joint ventures and technical collaborations have been established for more than several decades, so Indians are comfortable and open to negotiation. An intermediary is not required to establish your credentials, but if your company is smaller or less well known, it would help to get some referrals from your other clients and partners in India.
- It is not absolutely necessary, but it helps to have an Indian contact for setting up your appointments. It is also advisable to hire an Indian lawyer or liaison to help you navigate the intricate Indian laws and regulations.
- Schedule appointments at least a couple of months in advance. Then reconfirm your meeting a few days before your scheduled appointment. Leave your contact information with the assistant or secretary, so you can be informed of any last-minute changes.
- The normal work day is from 10 a.m. to 5 p.m. (1000 to 1700), but there is a trend toward longer work days starting at 7:30 a.m. and lasting until 8 p.m. (0730 to 2000). Normally, lunch is between noon and 2 p.m. (1200 to 1400). The actual days of the work week vary depending on the company.
- Just recently, the practice of meeting over lunch or dinner or "power breakfasts" has gained popularity. Lunch is the preferred choice.
- In the evening, official dinners with large gatherings are meant for socializing and getting to know one another and connect.
- Meetings can start with a little small talk. They regard this period as a time of building trust and rapport. Your meeting will normally start with topics such as the weather or your travels to India. It may even go into personal questions about family or children. Indians are very open and friendly, and their questions may get personal.
- Indians like talking about politics, cricket, films, and Indian economic reforms. They also enjoy speaking about their history, traditions, and heritage. Prepare in advance so you know a little about and understand these topics. Cricket is their national pastime. They are very passionate about the game, and professional cricket players are national celebrities and are idolized.

Be On Your Best Cultural Behavior

- You will probably be offered tea, coffee, or snacks at the start of meetings. It is absolutely fine to accept the offer, but preferably after they ask two to three times.
- Indians will seldom show or express disagreement in a direct manner. After a trusting relationship has been established, then disagreements will be openly discussed. Avoid expressing direct disagreement.
- The roads can be very crowded. Plan in advance and allow plenty of time to reach your destination. You might want to hire a chauffeured car.
- Indians follow the western Christian calendar. Their dates are written as dd/mm/yy. January 2, 2009 would appear as 02/01/09.
- Their financial year is April to March. Try to avoid scheduling appointments that coincide with their year end in March.
- Vacations are planned during their summer season (April through June) and mid-December to mid-January. They also schedule vacations in October during the Dussehra/Pooja holidays.

 ## Business Cards

- Indians commonly include all educational degrees, current and previously held titles, and current position in the company on their business cards. Foreign businesspeople should include their university degrees.
- Always have plenty. Exchanging business cards is a necessary part of doing business in India. Business cards are also exchanged in non-business situations.
- English is a common language, so it is not necessary to have your card translated into any other Indian language.

 ## Meals/Toasts

- India has a variety of cuisines. The food can be very spicy. Remember to check with the wait staff before ordering if you prefer your food a little less seasoned.
- Because of their religious beliefs, some foods are forbidden. Hindus are forbidden to eat beef. If you are hosting a meal function, it is best to ask guests if they are vegetarians. It is also important to keep the vegetarian and meat dishes on separate tables during a meal function. Always mark the dishes so people will know what they are selecting and eating.
- Most Hindus fast once a week, eating only fruit. Make sure so you can accommodate dietary restrictions.
- Hindus do not eat beef. Muslims do not eat pork. Muslims will eat meat that is ritually slaughtered or *Halal*. Jains eat cereals and lentils, but avoid meat, honey, and even some vegetables.

India

- Chicken, lamb, and fish usually are safe options for meals.
- Cleanliness is very important to Indians. They wash their hands before and after a meal.
- Traditional Indian dishes are eaten with the hands. When using your hands, use only the right hand, never the left. The left hand is considered unclean.
- Offering another person food from your plate is considered culturally unacceptable. It is seen as unclean.
- Muslims, Hindus, and Buddhists do not drink because of their religious beliefs, but times are changing, and among some urban, educated populations, abstinence is not strictly observed.
- Toasting is not a common ritual. Over a business meal, you could offer a toast by raising your glass and saying, "Cheers!"
- A business woman in India can host a businessman. The male guest is expected to offer to pay for the meal. The woman can very nicely decline the offer.
- If you are invited to an Indian's home for dinner, you should arrive 15 to 30 minutes late. Remove your shoes when entering an Indian home.
- Women usually will remain in the kitchen during a meal in the home. They feel their responsibility is to provide a good meal and to make their guests feel at home. Show your appreciation by praising the food to the women of the house.
- Saying thank you at the end of the meal is considered inappropriate and very impersonal. You should offer to return the hospitality by inviting your hosts out to dinner.
- If you are hosting a social function, contact every person by phone. Indians usually do not RSVP. Send invitations early and then follow up with phone calls closer to the day of the function.
- Some of your Indian guests may bring guests of their own. This is considered to show that the Indians feel they are comfortable in the relationship. You, as a host, need to respond with an attitude of "the more the merrier."
- A buffet setting is advisable, since you cannot predict when your guests may arrive or how many will be coming.

Entertainment

- There is not a lot of nightlife outside the international hotels. Entertaining may take place in Indian homes.
- Traditionally, male and female coworkers will not socialize outside of work. India has a very strict social hierarchy, and mingling outside the workplace is uncommon.

Be On Your Best Cultural Behavior

- Invitations from your Indian host can be very casual or unclear, but it is truly an invitation. You might want to phone before showing up at someone's home. It is not uncommon for Indians to just drop in on you.
- If you need to refuse or decline an invitation, it is better to be vague with possibly "I'll try to be there" as opposed to a direct refusal. A direct response could seem impolite or even arrogant.
- Indians will offer beverages or snacks for refreshments. The custom is to refuse the first offer but to accept on the second or third offer. It is improper to reject their hospitality, even if you don't want the snack or drink. It is better to accept and take only a small sample.
- Business meals are generally held in five-star hotels or upscale restaurants. You may need to make your reservations in advance because of the popularity of these locations.
- Before selecting the restaurant or hotel for your meeting, make sure that the cuisine meets the taste of your guests. Check the preference of your guests for smoking or non-smoking sections.
- It is better to confirm what your guests will be drinking before ordering beer or wine. Even if your guests drink, they may not drink alcohol on certain religious festivals or if there is a respected, older person present. It is always safe to have non-alcoholic drinks and juices.
- Traditional Indian women do not smoke or drink regardless of their religion. An urban, elite Indian woman may smoke or may drink beer or wine.
- If you are with Indians who drink, serve imported, well-known brands of scotch or whiskey as opposed to Indian brands.

Forms of Address/Introductions/Greetings

- Men will shake hands with other men when arriving or departing. If introduced to a woman, a man should not shake her hand or extend his hand. Let her take the lead. Instead she could be met with a *namaste* (nah-mas-tay), which is done with palms together as in praying, about chest high and below your chin. Or *namaskar* (nah-mas-kar) adding a nod of the head or slight bow. The *namaste* can be useful if you are unsure about physical contact with another person. Traditional Muslim women are kept from the view of men outside their families, and even non-Muslim women seldom attend social gatherings, sit at the dinner table, or join in the conversation even in their own homes.
- Even though the *namaste or namaskar* are Hindu greetings, they are accepted by other communities. The Muslim traditional greeting is *Salaam-Wale-Kum*, and you respond by saying, "*Wale-kum-Salaam*."

Sikhs traditionally greet each other with *Sat-Siree-Akaal* (True is the Immortal Lord).

- The handshake is also acceptable to greet urban and Westernized Indians.
- With the younger urban Indians, saying hello and a wave of their hand is a more informal accepted greeting.
- Hugs and kisses should be expressed only in private and not as you meet a person on the street or at a social or business event.
- Use Mr., Mrs. or Miss plus the given name. Also address with professional titles, such as Doctor or Professor. Generally, people are addressed by their names only by close acquaintances, family members, or someone who is older or superior in authority.
- There are so many religious and regional customs that it can be very difficult to know how to address a person in India. Hindus in the south place an initial and their father's initial followed by given name. Hindus in the north use a family name that may be indicative of caste. "*Singh*" is used by all Sikh men, and is the equivalent of Mr., so use Mr. plus the given name.
- A Hindu man following more traditional practices will probably have two initials preceding his given name but no family name. The first initial stands for the name of his hometown, and the second is the initial of his father's given name. A Hindu woman will often follow her own given name with her husband's name.
- Christian Indians and Eurasian Indians often have given names followed by family names, such as Jane Smith. She could be addressed as "Miss Jane" or "Mrs. Smith."
- If in doubt, ask colleagues what they would like to be called. If you do not know the person, then always use Mr. or Mrs. to be safe.

Appearance/Attire

- Normal business dress for men is a suit and tie, but because of the warm weather, a long-sleeved shirt with a tie is acceptable. Men's business dress should be in neutral colors. Some companies have a more relaxed dress code, including t-shirts, jeans, and sneakers. But as a visitor, you should be more conservative.
- For women visitors, pant suits or long skirts are recommended. Be sure to cover the knees and wear blouses or dresses with higher necklines.
- Women can also wear a *salwar* for business. The *salwar kameez*, also spelled *shalwar kameez* and *shalwar qamiz,* is the traditional dress worn by both men and women. *Salwars* are the loose pajama-type trousers. The

legs can be wide at the top and then narrow at the bottom or more form-fitting from top to bottom. The *kameez* is the long tunic or shirt. The side seams, or *chaak*, are left open below the waistline for more freedom and movement. In northern India, it is worn mostly by women. There are many variations, with the modern versions being much less modest than the traditional dress. Some *kameez* may have more revealing necklines, sleeveless or cap-sleeve design, and the side seams slit much higher.

- Casual dress is acceptable at a social gathering, but be aware of the specific dress code for each event or function.
- Remember that the cow is sacred, so avoid leather clothing, including belts, boots, purses, or leather jewelry like a watchband or bracelet.
- Before entering a place of worship, be aware of the proper attire and abide by their beliefs and customs.
- Dress to cover your shoulders and as much skin as possible. Women should wear baggy clothes instead of form-fitting outfits. Consult an Indian counterpart before buying traditional clothing. It will show your respect for the culture if you select the correct and proper attire for an event or special occasion.
- Avoid pictures of pigs, cows, or dogs on t-shirts or ties, since it may be offensive and disrespectful to their beliefs.

 Gift Giving

- Gift giving is customary and is a sign of friendship, and it is not expected at the first meeting.
- Avoid expensive gifts. These are saved for family friends and close relatives.
- Indians try to reciprocate a gift, so if it is too expensive, it can cause embarrassment for the recipient.
- Use red, yellow, green, or blue for wrapping paper. White and black represent misfortune.
- Normally gifts are not opened in the presence of the giver, but your Indian host may insist that you open your gift and express appreciation for their choice.
- If invited to an Indian home, you may be met and presented with a garland of flowers. You should remove the flowers instantly to show humility.
- If invited to an Indian home for a meal, a box of chocolates or flowers is an appropriate gift to bring. Also bring a toy or book for children.
- Do not present gifts that are made of cowhide or resemble a cow.
- Muslims do not eat pork, and strict Muslims do not drink alcohol, so do not give anything that could convey a lack of respect and understanding of their beliefs.

- If visiting an Indian during a festival, carry of box of sweets.
- Indians appreciate a gift that represents your culture.
- A framed photograph of yourself with them would be considered a warm and friendly gift.
- Roses are safe flowers, but check with the local florist because other flowers have different connotations across India.
- Drinking alcohol is culturally unacceptable in many parts of India. But, if your hosts do have alcohol in their home, a bottle of wine, whiskey, or scotch would be appropriate.
- Jewelry is considered an intimate gift and viewed inappropriate if given by a man to an Indian woman. Gold jewelry is normally exchanged only among family.

 ## Tipping

- Excessive tipping is not encouraged, but a certain amount is common practice.
- A 10 to 15 percent tip in most restaurants is sufficient and may be added to the bill.
- In upscale restaurants in hotels, usually a 10 percent service fee is added to your bill.
- Porters at railway stations would be tipped Rs. 5-10 per bag (US$.12-US$ .25).
- If you are an overnight guest in a home, check with your host before giving tips to the domestic help.
- Tipping the three-wheeler and taxi is not common but is up to your discretion and the service received. Ten percent of the fare or leaving the change from your fare is sufficient.
- If you hire a car and driver for your stay, then the driver would be tipped Rs. 50-100 per day (US$1.25-US$2.50), depending on the distance traveled.

 ## Gesture Awareness

- Grasping one's ears is a sign of sincerity and apology.
- Tossing your head back or a chin toss means "yes."
- The traditional greeting is the *namaste*. The palms of the hands are together in a praying position and held about chest high and below chin along with a slight bow. This is also used when saying good-bye.
- To get someone's attention, just hold your hand straight out, palm downward, and make a scooping motion with your fingers. To call someone with a wagging finger, with the palm upward, is viewed as a condescending signal and is considered an insult.

- Do not point with your finger. Use your hand/palm or chin for pointing to someone.
- Standing erect with your hands on your hips is considered aggressive and dominating.
- Using your hand during conversations is normal, but folding your hands or placing your hands in your pockets is perceived as arrogant.
- Whistling and winking are rude and unacceptable and have sexual connotations.

Faux Pas

- Avoid irony and sarcasm. Watch jokes; Indians take things seriously.
- When walking, do not stare, especially at the impoverished. This is a grave humiliation. There is a large rich-poor divide. Indians openly discuss the country's poverty, but if a visitor does, it is interpreted as impolite criticism.
- Always ask first before taking a photograph of an Indian person.
- Ask permission to smoke cigarettes, pipes, or cigars.
- The head is considered a sacred part of the body. Do not touch or pat a child's head or touch an older person's head. Women should cover their heads when entering a sacred building.
- The feet and soles of your shoes are considered the dirtiest part of the body. Do not touch anyone or point at anyone with your shoes or their soles. If your feet or shoes touch another person, apologize.
- When you are offered food or drink, it is polite to refuse it at least once before accepting. But after that initial response, do not refuse again. It will be considered an insult.
- Try not to use the left hand. Pass food, gifts, and any other articles with your right hand. Always eat with your right hand and point using your right hand/arm. The left hand is used for bodily hygiene.
- Don't confuse or compare Indians with Pakistanis.
- Avoid public display of affection with the opposite sex, including hugging or kissing.
- Remove shoes before entering a temple or a mosque.
- Do not touch paintings or statues inside a mosque.
- Do not challenge or question people that are senior to you.

USEFUL FACTS

President	Pratibha Patil (2007)
Vice President	Hamid Ansari (2007)
Prime Minister	Manmohan Singh (2004)
National Name	Bharat
Size	1,147,949 square miles (2,973,190 square km)
Population	1,147,995,898 (2008)
Capital	New Delhi
Government	Federal Republic
Currency	Rupee
Religion	Hindu 82%, Muslims 12%, Christian 2%, Sikh 2% (Others Buddhists, Jains, Parsis, and 300 local tribes)
Language	English is the most important language for communication. Hindi is actually the national language, but less than 40 percent of the population can speak or understand Hindi. Fourteen other official languages: Bengali, Telugu, Marathi, Tamil, Urdu, Gujarati, Malayalam, Kannada, Oriya, Punjabi, Assamese, Kashmiri, Sindhi, and Sanskrit.
Ethnicity	Indo-Aryan 72%, Dravidian 25%, Mongolian and other 3%
Industry	Engineering, textiles, chemicals, food processing, steel, transportation equipment, electronics, cement, mining, petroleum, machinery, and software. These industries are the major source of economic growth, but two thirds of the workforce is in agriculture.

Time Zone	India is 5-1/2 hours ahead of Greenwich Mean Time (GMT +5.5) or 10-1/2 hours ahead of U.S. Eastern Standard Time (EST +10.5). India does not observe daylight saving time.
Telephone Code	International Code: +91 Area Code: +11 (New Delhi)
Weather	Varies from tropical monsoon in south to temperate in the north and from the snow in the Himalayas to the desert in the west. The best months to visit India are between October and March, which is their winter season. The temperature can go as low as 2-3C (35-37F) in the Northern mountains, but most of the country is comfortable 15-25C (59-77F). The summers can be very hot, with the temperatures reaching 50C (122F) in many locations. The summer season is April to June.
Voltage/Frequency	230 V; 50 Hz

 ## HOLIDAYS/FESTIVALS

26 January	Republic Day (Adoption of the Constitution, 1950)
15 August	Independence Day (Free from British rule, 1947)
2 October	Gandhi Jayanti
November	Diwali (Festival of Lights—a five-day new year's celebration)
25 December	Christmas

There are many other Hindu, Sikh, and Muslim festivals. Consult the local Indian Embassy/Consulate to confirm the exact dates each year for these celebrations. There are also many regional festivals.

LANGUAGE TIPS

<u>Hindi Phonetics</u>	<u>English</u>
dhanya-waad	Thank you
meharbani se	Please
jana parega	How do I get to…?
Kitne paise	How much?
Namaste	Hello
Phir milenge	Good-bye
Apka shubh nam	What is your name?
han/nahin	Yes/No
Kya baja hai	What is the time?
mujhe minu dikhao	Show me the menu
bill lao	The bill please

Chapter 13: IRELAND

LOCATION/GEOGRAPHY

Located in Western Europe, the island of Ireland is divided into the Irish Republic, which occupies five-sixths of the island, and Northern Ireland, which is part of Great Britain and lies across the North Channel from Scotland. The Atlantic Ocean is on the west; the Irish Sea separates Ireland from Great Britain on the east; and the Celtic Sea is to the south.

DID YOU KNOW?

- Two distinct jurisdictions can be found on the island of Ireland. Ireland is a sovereign state and maintains five-sixths of the island. Its capital is Dublin. The other sixth is Northern Ireland, which is part of the United Kingdom of Great Britain and Northern Ireland.
- The Irish scientist John Tyndall was the first person credited with explaining why the sky is blue.
- The shamrock, also known as "*seamroy,*" was used by St. Patrick to explain the Holy Trinity.
- An estimated 40 million people in the United States and 30 percent of Australians claim Irish descent.
- Ireland is the number 1 country for tea drinking. Britain is second.
- The Normans brought the English language to Ireland, but the Irish language evolved from Celtic immigrants in approximately 600 B.C.
- Ireland was the first country in Europe (in the late 1600s) to plant potatoes as their staple food crop.
- Nine cities in the United States are named Dublin.
- If you want to kiss the Blarney Stone, you have to do it upside down.
- There is a passage tomb in Newgrange, County Meath, Ireland, dating to 3200 B.C., which makes it older than Stonehenge and the Pyramids.
- The windmills in Ireland rotate in a clockwise direction, which is opposite to the rest of the world. Tradition and popular design pitches the blades to turn clockwise.
- The potato famine was responsible for the deaths of 1 million Irish from 1845 to 1850.
- The famous *Titanic* was built at Harland & Wolff Shipyard in Belfast, Northern Ireland.
- The Irish cyclist Stephen Roche won the *Tour de France* in 1987. Six years later a drug scandal cast aspersions on Roche. The statute of limitations won out, but the incident damaged his reputation.
- Grandstand Bar is the longest bar in the world. It is located at the Galway Racecourse in Ireland and measures 210 feet long (64.008 m).
- Twenty-one American Presidents have been of Irish descent.

BUSINESS ETIQUETTE

Punctuality

- You should always be punctual. By arriving late, you will be perceived as unreliable and unconcerned with your future business.
- If you are left waiting, be patient.

Meeting Manners

- It's easy to set up appointments. Do so two weeks in advance.
- A third-party representative helps move your business along much faster.
- In some cases you will need to work with the secretary to get to senior executives. Get to know these gatekeepers to move more quickly for meetings.
- Some companies may close for the lunch hour between 1 p.m. and 2 p.m. (1300 and 1400) and their phones will not be answered.
- A good place for an initial meeting is in a hotel for coffee. Another might be at a golf course.
- Chitchat is common in the beginning of meetings. It could cover anything from your trip to Ireland, the weather, or anything you have done since arriving in Ireland. Not to talk briefly in the beginning can be perceived as rude and unfriendly.
- It may be difficult to set up meetings during tourist season from June to August as well as during the Christmas and Easter holidays.
- Be careful about going overboard with your presentations or promises to a company or individual in Ireland. Stay concise, simple, and to the point. Generally meetings will be short, but they are looking for new ideas to be presented.
- Company policies are always followed, so be aware of their rules or laws.
- Family is very important, even during business negotiations, so discussions of your personal life and family may play a role. Family will mostly take precedence over skills and experience.
- Watch over-praising. You may come across as suspicious or misleading.
- Hierarchy is very important in the work environment, especially if it is a family-owned company.
- Once you get to the right person or the top person, the decision making will be fast.
- Even though you may not be told "no," if you get no response after a period of time, you can generally assume it means no.
- Irish women are still struggling to get equal pay and positions in business, but foreign women are accepted in business easily.
- Men will hold the door open for women; employees will hold the door

for bosses; and the youth will do this kind gesture for elders. So always make sure you turn to look behind you as you enter or leave a room or building.

Business Cards

- Business cards are used but are not necessarily presented at the very start of the meeting.
- Show respect in exchanging cards, but there are no formal procedures.

Meals/Toasts

- Their dinner manners are more relaxed, so just enjoy.
- The traditional meat and vegetables is still the norm for meals, but seafood is prevalent in the coastal regions.
- Pubs are generally for drinking and may not serve food.
- Chinese, Italian, Thai, and European foods are becoming popular and so are take-out eateries, but only in the main cities.
- You might find a small plate next to your dinner plate. This is used for peelings removed from boiled potatoes.
- Even after a brief acquaintance, you may be invited to an Irish home. Generally business and personal life are kept separate unless it is a family business.
- If invited to a home, you may eat everything on your plate without offending your host or sending an inappropriate signal.
- Refusing a drink could come across as an insult and don't forget to buy a round of drinks.
- "*Slainte!*" and "cheers" or "cheers to your good health" are the common exchanges for toasts.

Entertainment

- A pint of Guinness is enjoyed daily by many in Ireland. Drinking and even getting drunk is acceptable but not advisable as part of your business visits. The government is working to cut down on alcohol consumption because of missed work and the loss of productivity it causes. But drinking is truly a "social thing" in Ireland so be strong and pace yourself or plan to be sick!
- Refrain from bringing up business during a meal or a night in the pub unless your host does first.
- It is unmanly to have less than a pint of Guinness, but women can order a glass of Guinness, which is a half pint.

- Foreign women should invite an Irishman to lunch instead of dinner. A dinner invitation could be perceived improperly, but business dinner meetings are becoming more common.
- Be prepared to order from the bar for your drinks. It is unusual to have wait service in pubs. Be ready to pay for a round of drinks. It's considered impolite and will make a bad impression if you don't take your turn to pay.
- Most business people will not drink during a business lunch.
- Entertaining generally takes place in restaurants.
- Dinner gatherings are a great way to establish and develop relationships but are considered more social than business. Spouses or partners may or may not be included. Just check ahead with the host.
- Most Irish will automatically just pick up the bill when they invite you out to dinner. But be ready; they may not.

Forms of Address/Introductions/Greetings

- Direct eye contact is important. It's considered untrustworthy if you avoid making eye contact with other people.
- The handshake is the normal form of greeting at both the beginning and end of the meeting. This includes shaking hands with all present.
- Arm's length is the conversational distance. Personal space is important to the Irish people.
- Men should not be too physical with women. They also need to be careful making personal comments or winking at them.
- Touching, hugging, or patting other men in public socially is considered unacceptable. The exception is at a rugby game, when a slap on the back is expected to say "well done."
- Introductions are important and valued. Not following up is considered rude.
- Initially in written correspondence, use "Mr.," "Mrs.," or "Ms." with their last name.
- Moving to a first name basis is common and generally happens immediately. "Sir" and *madam* are rarely used. Titles are not important and are perceived as pretentious.

Appearance/Attire

- Your appearance should be modest and conservative.
- You will still see the traditional tweeds and wools.
- Come prepared with a raincoat year-round.
- Men should wear a suit or sport coat and a tie.
- Women should wear business suits or dresses.

Gift Giving

- Gift giving is usually not part of the business culture. Small gifts can be given at the end of negotiations.
- The gesture of giving the gift is more important than the cost of the gift.
- If you're invited to a home, flowers, chocolates, wine, cheeses, or a gift from your home country would be appropriate.
- Be careful with the flowers you select. Lilies are reserved for religious occasions and red or white flowers symbolize death. Ask the florist for advice.
- Coffee table books are appropriate as a gift.
- A food product is considered a good choice, but be careful about what can be brought through customs.
- Thank-you notes should always be sent in response to a gift or in appreciation for dinner.

Tipping

- Ten percent or more of the entire bill is customary for tipping in restaurants. It depends on the service and caliber of the venue.
- Hotel porters generally are tipped 1 euro per bag (US$1.57).
- It's customary to tip taxi drivers, hairdressers and most services. Just round up to the next euro. If you feel the service warrants it, then tip 1 to 2 euro more (US$1.75 to US$3.14). It is appreciated.

Gesture Awareness

- The reversed "V" for victory, with the palm facing the signer, is considered inappropriate.
- Irish do not like loud, aggressive, or arrogant behavior.
- Women generally are seated first and it's appropriate for them to cross their ankles or one knee over the over. Crossing their ankle over their knee is perceived as too informal.

Faux Pas

- Don't discuss religion or politics unless your Irish counterpart brings it up. Topics to avoid during conversations are the Catholic Church, the English, and immigrants. If your host should bring them up, get their view of the topics first before expressing your opinions.
- Don't brag. You'll come across as pompous.
- Don't criticize Irish policies or customs. Irish will criticize themselves but they don't want to hear it from others.

USEFUL FACTS

President	Mary McAleese (1997)
Prime Minister	Brian Cowen (2008)
National Name	Eire
Size	26,598 square miles (68,889 square km)
Population	4,156,119 (2008)
Capital	Dublin
Government	Republic
Currency	Euro (formerly Irish pound)
Religion	Roman Catholic 88%, Church of Ireland 3%, other Christian 2%, none 4%, other 3%
Language	Irish (Gaelic), English (both official languages) Even though Gaelic is taught in school, the younger generations are not showing as much interest in their traditional language.
Ethnicity	Celtic, English
Industry	Agriculture, steel, lead, zinc, silver, aluminum, brewing Clothing, pharmaceuticals, machinery
Time Zone	Ireland is the same as Greenwich Mean Time (GMT), or five hours ahead of U.S. Eastern Standard time (EST +5). Ireland does observe daylight saving time.
Telephone Code	International Code: +353 City Code: +1 (Dublin)

Weather	Ireland has a mild and temperate climate. Expect sun and rain. The weather ranges from an average of 65-75F (18-23C) to 35-45F (1-7C). Snow is rare but rain showers can occur year round.
Voltage/Frequency	220 V; 50 Hz

HOLIDAYS/FESTIVALS

1 January	New Year's Day
17 March	St. Patrick's Day
March/April	Easter Monday
First Monday in May	Labor Day/May Day
First Monday in June	June Holiday
First Monday in August	August Holiday
Last Monday in October	October Holiday or Halloween Holiday
25 December	Christmas
26 December	St. Stephen's Day

LANGUAGE TIPS

Irish	Phonetics	English
Dia duit	djiah gwich	Hello/Good Day
Conas ta tu?	co-nas tah tu	How are you?
Ta me go maith	tah may go mah	I'm well
Dia dui tar maidin	djiah gwich air mahdjeen	Good morning
Slan	shlahn	Good-bye
Ni raibh	nee roe	No
Bhi	vee	Yes
Mas e do thoil e	mushayduh-hulyah	Please
Go raibh maith agat	guramahhagut	Thank you
Oiche mhaith	ee-ha-why	Good night
Gabh mo leithsceal	gomolyesh-kale	Pardon

Additional Irish expressions with English translation:

Irish Expressions	Engish
Cheers	Thanks
Well Sir/well boy/well guy	Hi
How is it going?/	How are you?
How is it cutting?	(very country side expression)
No bother!	Don't worry about it/it's fine/no problem!

Chapter 14: ISRAEL

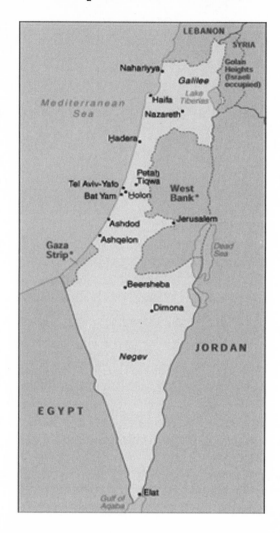

LOCATION/GEOGRAPHY

Located in the Middle East between Egypt on the south and Lebanon on the north. Bordering Syria and Jordan on the east and the Mediterranean Sea on the west.

- The highest percentage of home computers per capita is in Israel.
- Voice mail technology was developed in Israel.
- Motorola-Israel developed the cell phone.
- Israel has the highest per capita rates of patents filed and the highest per capita ratio of scientific publication in the world.
- More than 25 percent of Israel's work force is employed in technical professions. Their work force also leads the world in the number of scientists and technicians.
- Microsoft-Israel developed Windows NT software. Israel also developed voice mail technology. An Israeli software company designed AOL's instant message program. The only R&D facilities built outside the United States by Microsoft and Cisco are in Israel.
- Israel has the world's highest ratio of university degrees to the population.
- Tel Aviv is the primary air portal to Israel. Ground entrances are from Egypt and Jordan. If you carry an Israeli stamp, entrance will be denied into Syria and Lebanon and some other countries.
- Most cafes and restaurants are beginning to remain open over the Sabbath (Friday evening at sunset to Saturday evening) and during Jewish holidays.
- The Dead Sea is the lowest point on Earth's surface and the deepest hyper-saline lake in the world. It has more than 1,100 species of fish.

USINESS ETIQUETTE

 ## Punctuality

- Always arrive on time. Punctuality is respected.
- Meetings will generally start within 10 minutes of the scheduled start time.

Meeting Manners

- Most meetings are conducted informally.
- The protocol for seating arrangements is not critical, but still wait before taking a seat.
- Very little chitchat will be included at the start of meetings. Meetings progress quickly.
- English generally will be the language for meetings. Brochures, agendas, e-mails and other documentation should also be in English.
- Interpreters easily can be found if necessary.
- It isn't necessary to have a local contact for setting up your meetings, but it's highly recommended to have a local lawyer or a person who is familiar with Israel's bureaucracy to review all materials before finalizing any contacts. Local embassies or commercial attaches can give advice about local contacts.
- Israelis are aggressive negotiators, exhibiting hard-sell techniques.
- Scheduling a meeting usually takes only two or three days' advance notice. Allow more time when scheduling a meeting with high-ranking officials.
- Secretaries or gatekeepers are still very important, so get to know them.
- Meetings are usually conducted in offices, with possibly a preliminary meeting in a hotel lobby or business center.
- Provide an agenda with your objectives and the timetable for your meetings.
- Reconfirm your appointments, since Israelis tend to schedule as much as possible.
- Women are accepted in all levels of business, but still very few are in high-level positions.
- The foreign woman in Israel will have no challenges. The only exceptions are in synagogues or at certain religious sites, where there are separate areas for women.
- Marital status for a woman will not affect how she is treated in business or social settings. A woman can be unaccompanied in public without any criticism.
- Children may be present at meetings or even in business offices. If you do not want to lose the business instantly, then enjoy the children and proceed with your business.
- You are often judged by the selection of your hotel. There are many higher class hotels that can provide this good impression.
- Always carry your identification. You may be searched or asked if you are carrying arms when entering an office building.

Business Cards

- Business cards are exchanged during meetings and at informal get-togethers.
- English only is needed on the business cards, but to be impressive you could have them printed in Hebrew on the reverse side.
- Engraved cards make a good impression.
- When you accept a counterpart's card, take your time to read it.
- Protocol of the business card exchange is not highly important.
- Titles can differ from American standards. Presidents and CEOs in Israel can carry the title of General Manager. It's appropriate to ask about specific job functions.

Meals/Toasts

- Invitations could be extended to breakfast, lunch, or dinner, but no pork items will appear on the menu. Assume that your hosts observe *kashrut* (eating of *kosher* food).
- Eat what you like. There are no rules about leaving food on your plate or eating all of it. Be prepared to be given a lot more than you can eat.
- It's acceptable to decline alcohol. "*Lechaim*" (to life) is offered when alcohol is served. Beer, wine, and alcohol will be offered in most restaurants.
- Toasts are generally made only at formal occasions or to celebrate when a contract is signed.
- A toast is generally made with small glasses of cognac or wine, with the traditional "*Lechaim*" said by all present.
- You can just touch the glass to your lips if you do not want to take a drink.

Entertainment

- If you're invited to a meal in a restaurant, generally the business discussion will be minimal.
- If your host takes you to a restaurant, you should at least make the offer to pay. It will most likely be declined, but the offer will be appreciated.
- If you're invited to a home, a gift is appropriate.
- Men and women will eat together and expect to stay the entire evening.
- Generally the host will sit at the head of the table and his wife will sit across from him at the foot of the table.
- It's inappropriate to discuss business if you're invited to a home for a meal.
- Tell your host in advance if you have any dietary restrictions.

Be On Your Best Cultural Behavior

- It is acceptable to compliment the hosts on their home and possessions.
- Thursday and Friday evenings are the main entertaining evenings and normally start at 10 p.m. (2200) for dinner, a movie, or just to be with friends. An afternoon nap is also common leading up to the evening.
- Day trips to different parts of the country are fun ways your host might entertain you. It's a perfect way to strengthen your relationships, talk business, and enjoy the country.
- All cuisines can be found, from American hamburger to the traditional Mediterranean-Middle Eastern food of *kebab* and *hummus*.

 ## Forms of Address/Introductions/Greetings

- Both men and women will shake hands upon arrival and departure, but be careful with greeting, touching, or offering a handshake to both Jewish and Muslim devout women.
- In most situations, eye contact and a smile is also offered with a handshake.
- When a visitor enters the room, generally those seated will rise.
- When a woman enters a room, the men will often stand, but usually they will not when she leaves.
- Visitors will be introduced first to the highest-ranking person or to the host.
- Age generally does not play a role in the introduction.
- First names are used generally in the beginning of meetings, but wait until requested to move to their first name.
- Using Mr. and Mrs. is advised for the first meeting or more formal occasions. Once you move to a comfortable setting, then first names will be used.
- Personal space is not consistent in Israeli culture, so just follow the lead of your host. Touching or patting is also an individual matter. It's common after getting to know someone to exchange a slap on the back or a hug.

 ## Appearance/Attire

- Most parts of Israel are westernized, so special dress is not necessary. It's best to dress conservatively and follow your host's lead. Ask what you should wear to be safe and appropriate if a meeting is held away from the office or in a more formal business setting.
- In certain parts, particularly in Jerusalem, you do need to honor the traditions and religion. The dress code in traditional or religious areas

for women typically is more modest, covering the elbows and knees and even the ankles. Men will usually wear dark jackets, white open-collared, long-sleeved shirts with dark slacks and black shoes.

- Men will wear suits and ties during the winter months and just a shirt with slacks or lightweight suit with or without a tie for the summer.
- Women dress fashionably in dresses, skirts with reasonable length, or slacks.
- Casual clothes are appropriate for trips in the country or to the beach.
- Shorts should be worn only to the beach or for tourist trips.
- Sneakers are fine for informal occasions or workouts.

 ## Gift Giving

- Wine (*kosher*) or flowers are appropriate if you're invited to a home. Remember to bring a gift for children if you know they will be present.
- Do not bring food if invited to a home unless you are invited for tea or coffee; then a cake would be appropriate.
- A gift should not exceed 67 ILS (US$20). Modest but well chosen gifts are the best route. Expensive gifts will be questioned and are inappropriate.
- Acceptable gifts could be pens, books, desk items, or a gift with your company logo. Try to get to know the recipient's interests and tastes.
- In some companies, giving and accepting gifts is not allowed.
- If gifts are exchanged, wait until you feel that a good relationship has been created.
- It would be a nice gesture to send a gift during specific holidays.
- If presenting roses, offer them in odd-numbered bouquets.
- To say thank you, a phone call is appropriate and a card with a personal note is seen as a nice gesture.
- Make sure you present and accept gifts with your right hand or both hands, but not your left hand only.

 ## Tipping

- If a service charge is not included, then a 10 percent to 15 percent tip is customary in restaurants.
- Be generous with tips if the service is good. Most wait staff earn low salaries.
- A 12 percent to 15 percent is given to taxi drivers. You can also receive a receipt upon request.
- 3.38 ILS (US$1) is customary per bag for porters.

Gesture Awareness

- Left hands should not be used for gift-giving or to touch. The left hand and the soles of your feet are impure.
- An insult to an Israeli is to point down at the upturned palm of one hand with the forefinger of the other hand. This implies "grass will grow on my hand" before the words of the speaker can come true.

Faux Pas

- Avoid profanity.
- Israelis have a good sense of humor, but avoid racist or religious jokes or anything that could be perceived off-color or indecent.
- Do not be critical of ethnic groups or religious matters.
- Be careful not to invite your hosts to meet or socialize on the Sabbath or Jewish holidays without prior arrangements.
- Do not take photos of military installations or other government or sensitive areas.
- If you are dealing with orthodox individuals, do not call them or try to contact them on the Sabbath or on Jewish holidays.
- If you are not introduced to the host's wife, then do not pay attention to her. If you do, you will offend and anger your host.

USEFUL FACTS

President	Shimon Peres (2007)
Prime Minister	Ehud Olmert (2006)
National Name	Medinat Yisra'el
Size	7,849 square miles (20,329 square km)
Population	7,112,359 (2008)
Capital	Jerusalem
Government	Parliamentary Democracy
Currency	New Israeli shekel
Religion	Jewish 80%, Muslim 16% (mostly Sunni Muslim), Christian 2%, other 2%

Language	Hebrew (official), Arabic, English
Ethnicity	Jewish 80% (Europe/America-born 33%, Israel-born 20%, Africa-born 14%, Asia-born 13%), non-Jewish 20% (mostly Arab)
Industry	Technology, agriculture, tourism, diamond cutting and polishing
Time Zone	Israel is two hours ahead of Greenwich Mean Time (GMT +2) or seven hours ahead of U.S. Eastern Standard Time (EST +7). Israel does observe daylight saving time.
Telephone Code	International Code: +972 City Code: +2 (Jerusalem)
Weather	Climate is varied. The low coastal areas along the Mediterranean Sea are warm and humid in the summer, with cool winters. There is little or no rainfall and lots of sun between May and September throughout the country. Mountain regions in the North and in the Jerusalem area are much drier, with cold nighttime temperatures during the summer but near freezing in mid-winter. Mountains and higher elevations will have several snows in winter. The desert areas to the south are hot and dry during the day and cold at night.
Voltage/Frequency	230 V; 50 Hz

HOLIDAYS/FESTIVALS

Between 5 September and 5 October	New Year/Rosh Hashanah
Between 14 September and 14 October	Day of Atonement (Most Holy Day of the Year/Yom Kippur)
Between 19 September and 19 October	Feast of Tabernacles
Between 26 September and 26 October	Assembly of the Eighth Day/Simchat Torah/Shemini Atzeret
Between 27 November and 27 December	Feast of Rededication (Hanukkah)
Between 24 February and 26 March	Memorial Feast for the Triumph of Esther/Purim
Between 26 March and 25 April	Passover/Pesach
Between 1 April and1May	Seventh Day of Passover/ Shvi'i shel Pesach
Between 7 April and 7 May	Holocaust Remembrance Day/Yom HaZikaron LaShoah VeLaGevurah
Between 14 April and 14 May	Fallen Soldiers Remembrance Day/ Yom Hazikaron
Between 15 April and15 May	Independence Day/Yom ha-Atzmaut
Between 15 May and 14 June	Pentecost/Shavuot

All Jewish holidays will begin the evening before the date specified on most calendars. Jewish days begin and end at sunset as opposed to midnight. Work is not permitted on Rosh Hashanah, Yom Kippur, the first and second days of Sukkot, Shemini Atzeret, Simchat Torah, Shavu'ot, or the first, second, seventh, and eighth days of Passover. Many of these holidays will fall during the normal work week.

LANGUAGE TIPS

<u>Hebrew Phonetics</u>	<u>English</u>
Ken/Lo	Yes/No
Todah	Thank you
Shalom	Hello
Le hitra ot	Good-bye
Ma Ha'inyanim	How are you?
Kama ze ole	How much is it?
Eifo uxal limtzo	Where can I find it?
Be Vakasha	Please
Ani lo meveen (male)	I don't understand
Ani lo meveena	(female)I don't understand
Kor'im li	My name is . . .

Chapter 15: ITALY

LOCATION/GEOGRAPHY

Referred to as the "boot-shaped" peninsula, Italy is located in southern Europe and is surrounded by the Mediterranean, Tyrrhenian, Ionian, and Adriatic Seas and bordered by France, Switzerland, Austria, and Slovenia. Italy has two large islands, Sardinia and Sicily, and many smaller islands. The Vatican City (in Rome) and the Republic of San Marino are independent states within Italy's geographical borders.

DID YOU KNOW?

- Italy has more Catholic churches per capita than any other country.
- Actual church attendance is relatively low, but the influence of the church is still strong.
- Each day of the year has at least one patron saint associated with it. Children are named for a particular saint and celebrate their saint's day the same as they celebrate their own birthday.
- There are three active volcanoes: Stromboli, Vesuvius, and Etna.
- Vatican City, the home of the Pope and the Roman Catholic Church, is located in Rome but is considered a separate state. The Vatican has it own currency, flag, and stamps.
- The Gran Paradiso is the highest mountain in the Graian Alps in northwest Italy. The range reaches over 4000 meters (13,123 feet).
- *Life is Beautiful* (1998), an Oscar-winning movie, made $57 million in its initial run.
- Mickey Mouse is known as "Topolino" in Italy, and Santa Claus is called "Babbo Natale."
- In Ivrea, Italy, thousands of citizens celebrate the beginning of Lent by throwing oranges at each other.
- Canned herring became "sardines" because the caning process was first developed in Sardinia.
- Cantaloupes were believed to be first grown in the gardens of Cantaloupe.
- The Sovereign Military Order of Malta is the smallest sovereign entity in the world and is located in Rome. It is the size of two tennis courts.
- The first city to mint its own gold coins was Florence in 1252.
- If you are up for a "doggy disco," head to Italy where owners can actually dance with their dogs.

BUSINESS ETIQUETTE

Punctuality .

- You should be punctual, but your Italian counterpart probably will not be. Bring a book or extra work and plan to wait 15 to 45 minutes.

- Arrive 15 minutes late if invited to a dinner, 30 minutes late if invited to a party.
- Because you are arriving on time and possibly your Italian associate might not be, you might want to renegotiate the starting time so it works for everyone.
- Punctuality is more important in Northern Italy. They are likely to be on time.

Meeting Manners

- Third-party introductions will assist initially and provide longer-lasting relationships. Networking and connecting are critical in Italy to your personal contacts. Personal relationships are important prior to conducting business.
- It's to your advantage to go to Italy to create a stronger face-to-face relationship.
- Appointments are necessary and need to be made at least two or three weeks in advance in writing. Reconfirm your appointment by telephone, fax, or e-mail.
- The start and ending time will vary slightly from the North to the South, but generally there is a two or three hour break for lunch. Business can be discussed over these breaks and lunch.
- Suggested times to schedule meetings are between 10 a.m. and 11 a.m. (1000 and 1100) and after 3 p.m. (1500).
- August is the primary vacation month, so make sure you plan in advance to work with their schedules.
- English is spoken by many businesspeople, but still have all your materials printed in both English and Italian.
- Unless you are fluent in Italian, it is important to hire an interpreter.
- Don't be flustered or concerned if several conversations are going on at the same time or if you are interrupted during your presentations.
- Because of such conversations, some of the voices could get loud. This is not anger, just a case of being heard above the other voices.
- Written agendas are important but are not necessarily followed.
- Meetings are meant for creation of ideas and discussions. Debate and argument are expected as part of the discussion process.
- Northern Italians are more direct and want to get to the point with very little initial social conversation. Southern Italians are much more relaxed and want to get to know you. Follow the lead of your colleagues in making the transition from social to business.
- Italians prefer to work with high-ranking people. Hierarchy is the foundation of business and they respect the age and the power that comes with it.

- Avoid high-pressure approaches to doing business with Italians.
- Verbal commitments are respected, and not complying with such agreements will destroy your business relationship.
- Decisions can be based on how you are perceived more than on your astute business knowledge.
- Women have advanced to the highest levels of business and government in Italy, but most do not have equal recognition or authority in business settings.
- Office doors generally remain closed. Make sure you knock before entering. When you leave the room, make sure you pull the door shut behind you.

Business Cards

- Calling cards are used in many social situations. Calling cards are generally a little larger than the traditional business card and will include their name, address, title or academic honors, and phone number. If your visit is extended while in Italy, you should have calling cards made.
- Do not give your business card instead of a calling card in a social situation.
- Business cards are presented in a business setting after formal introductions.
- Once you receive the card take the time to review the card and read the material on it before slipping it into your card holder.
- Have your business card translated into Italian on one side.
- Make sure you include any graduate degrees on your business card. Include your title and status in your company. Italians like to know how you fit into your organization.
- More senior Italian businesspeople generally will have less information on their business cards.
- Italian business cards are often basically plain white with black print.

Meals/Toasts

- Food and drink is very important and a focal point.
- Plan on at least two to three hours for a business lunch. It's a great opportunity to discuss business and to get to know one another.
- Breakfast meetings are not common but may be held in the major cities.
- Remain standing until you are invited to sit down. You possibly could be shown to a specific seat.
- Follow your hostess because she will sit at the table first. She will also start to eat first and is the first to get up at the end of the meal.

- No bread plates are provided and generally no butter.
- Family-style serving is common. Pass dishes to your left. Take smaller amounts because you will be invited to have seconds. The portions will seem smaller than in the United States, but you will receive more courses.
- Italians eat Continental style with the fork in the left hand and the knife held in the right.
- It's rude for hands not to be seen above the table. Do not rest your elbows on the table.
- To get the attention of a server or clerk, use the phrase "*senta,*" which means "come here."
- At the completion of your meal, place the knife and fork parallel to one another across the right side of the plate. If you put both utensils down on the plate for an extended period of time, it is a sign that you are finished and your plate will be removed.
- Lunch is the main meal of the day and generally is served after 12:30 p.m. (1230). It can be an elaborate meal with many courses. It could include a light start or antipasti of grilled vegetables, salami, cheeses, and olives, followed by soup, pasta or rice, then meat or fish with vegetables, or a side salad. Then it will end with dessert or cheese with fruit, and espresso.
- When you enter a café, you will probably seat yourself.
- When you ask for the bill, it will be presented and be prepared to pay. The waiter will typically wait for your payment.
- Olive oil could be used instead of butter.
- A small amount of food can be left on your plate.
- Use a knife to pick up your cheese instead of using your fingers.
- Wine is common at both lunch and dinner. Leave your wine glass nearly full if you do not want more or it will be refilled. Sip your wine slowly and drink moderately.
- Dinner is generally served starting at 8 p.m. or 9 p.m. (2000 or 2100) in the north; 9 p.m. (2100) in Rome, and 10 p.m. (2200) in Naples.
- Dinner in major cities can last far beyond midnight, especially if it serves as the main meal of the day instead of lunch.
- The host will give the first toast. An honored guest should return a toast later in the meal. A woman can offer a toast. The most common toast is "*salute*" (to your health), or more informal is "*cin-ci*n" (pronounced "chin-chin") and meaning "cheers."

 Entertainment

- If invited to an Italian home, come prepared with gift-wrapped chocolates, sweets, or flowers.
- If you are invited to a home, do not wander from room to room unless the host invites you to or guides you.

- Being invited to a private dinner party is an honor. Never refuse. Refusing an invitation will be perceived as an insult. Dinner parties could go well into the early hours of the morning.
- If you are the host of a business dinner, make sure you check with your Italian contact regarding the invitation list.
- Business luncheons can last for two to three hours but are a great avenue to discuss your business.
- Generally business decisions are not made over a business meal. Allow your Italian associate to initiate the business segment of your meeting.
- If you are hosting a meal in a restaurant, make all payment arrangements in advance. This is particularly important if you are a woman, as the male guests will want to pay.
- The most honored position is at the middle of each side of the table. The individual with the greatest importance is seated to the immediate right of the host. If a couple is hosting, then one will be at one end of the table and the other at the opposite end.
- Couples could be separated at a dinner party to encourage meeting new acquaintances and to stimulate new conversation.

Forms of Address/Introductions/Greetings

- Greetings are formal but very enthusiastic.
- Between strangers a handshake with direct eye contact and a smile is a good starting point. Direct eye contact is important. Looking away may be perceived as a sign of rudeness or boredom. But don't let your eye contact linger because it could be confused as having a romantic interest.
- The Italian personal space is much smaller than that of United States, Canada, and even of northern Europeans. Italians will stand so close some people become uncomfortable. Don't back away from them.
- The handshake is common for both men and women and may also include grasping the arm with the other hand. When you are introduced and again when you are leaving, everyone will shake hands individually in a group.
- Once your relationship develops, air-kissing on both cheeks is the norm. Men may also add a pat on the back with other men.
- Remember first impressions. You will be judged instantly on your respect when greeting other people, especially on the first encounter.
- The American "group wave" is not appropriate for a small group.
- You will be introduced to older people and women first. It's good policy to follow this format when introducing yourself or other people.
- Use "*Signore*" (Mr.) and "*Signora*" (Mrs.), plus the family name, when you're introduced to strangers.

- Titles should be included, and a university degree (doctor, professor) ranks higher than "*Signore*" or "*Signora*."
- Wait until you are invited before moving to a first-name basis.
- It's common for people of both sexes to walk arm in arm or holding hands in public.

 ## Appearance/Attire

- Appearance and attire are very important and indicate your social status, your family background, and your educational level. Your first impression is lasting. "*Bella figura,*" or good image, is very important and goes beyond just dressing well. It includes your confidence, style, and demeanor. The first seconds are critical, as you are judged before any words are exchanged.
- Men wear fashionable, high quality suits with accessories, including a quality shirt, designer tie, and shoes. They will also wear cuff links, tie clips, and stylish watches.
- Women dress in business suits, dresses, fashionable shoes, and accessories, including elegant jewelry and beautiful scarves. Avoid wearing stockings in the summer.
- Avoid wearing scuffed, unfashionable or shoes that are not shined.
- Men and women both use perfumes and colognes.
- Their "informal" dress could still include a jacket and tie for men. Formal dress is evening wear. This attire is considered very dressy by United States standards.
- Shorts are not acceptable in public and generally are worn only by tourists. You will be refused entrance into churches if you are wearing shorts, a sundress, or even a sleeveless top. Come prepared to throw a cover-up over your shoulders.
- Jeans and sneakers can be worn but are seen mostly on younger people or in gyms.

 ## Gift Giving

- Do not give a business gift until you receive one first.
- If invited to a dinner in a home, you should present gift-wrapped chocolates or flowers. Be careful with the types of flowers and the amount given. Give an odd number of flowers.
- Chrysanthemums are used at funerals so do not give as a gift. Red flowers convey secrecy and should not be given as a gift. Do not give yellow flowers because they indicate jealousy.
- Do not give anything in the quantity of 17, because 17 is considered bad luck or a doomed number.

- Wine should be of good quality. If invited to a home, bring one or two bottles and, if possible, select something from your home country.
- If staying with a family, then a coffee table book from your home country is always appropriate. Make sure your gift reflects your host's interests.
- Do not wrap gifts in black and gold because those are their mourning colors. Wrapping gifts in purple is a symbol of bad luck.
- Gifts are usually opened when they are presented.
- Gifts should be in good taste but not obviously expensive.
- Alcohol or crafts from your own country are welcomed and appreciated. Know the history of the gift in case they ask an explanation for why you would present it to them.
- To show appreciation to someone who has helped you in the office, a good gift selection could include fine pens, framed prints or pictures, or something electronic. Just make sure it is a reputable brand name.
- Remember secretaries or assistants and show your appreciation with a gift of flowers or chocolates.
- Sending a holiday card is appropriate and appreciated. Just make sure it reaches them in time for Christmas. Exchanging Christmas cards is not common in Italy.
- Avoid items on which your logo is too large. Avoid brooches and handkerchiefs because they are associated with funerals. Knives or any type of sharp item can be symbolic of severing your friendship.

Tipping

- Restaurants usually include a 15 percent gratuity as part of the bill.
- Even if the tip is part of the bill, it is still appropriate to leave an additional 5 percent to 10 percent if the services were above your expectations.
- If you are in doubt whether the tip has been included, just ask.
- Ten percent is appropriate for taxis.
- Hotel attendants should be given tips. This should include bellmen, doormen, housekeeping, washroom attendants, and coatroom clerks.

Gesture Awareness

- Eye contact is very important. Looking away is perceived as a sign of boredom or just plain rudeness. On the other hand, romantic attraction is generally implied when two stranger's eyes connect and linger.
- Putting your hand on the stomach conveys dislike for the other person.
- Rubbing your chin with your fingertips, and then moving them forward quickly, shows contempt.

- Making the devil's horns with your fingers pointed outward is an obscene gesture. Pointing the fingers inward is a sign to ward off the devil. So be careful with the directions you place your fingers.
- Pointing at someone with your index and little finger means you're wishing them bad luck.
- Slapping your raised arm above your elbow and thumbing your nose are both considered rude and offensive.
- Gum chewing, leaning, and slouching in public are unacceptable.
- To alert your server in a restaurant, motion with your fingers pointing down or simply make eye contact. Avoid raising your hands or fingers.

 ## Faux Pas

- Conversations to avoid include religion (the Vatican), politics, World War II, the Mafia, taxes, criticizing Italian culture, family concerns, their profession or income, and off-color jokes.
- It's insulting to ask a person you just met at a social gathering about their profession.
- Young people should give up their seats on public transportation to older people.
- Drink moderately and avoid ever being inebriated. It could reflect poorly on your business relationship.
- Do not take pictures where you see an X posted. They take this very seriously.
- It's considered bad form to leave the table to go to the washroom or for any other reason.
- Do not season your food before you taste it. It sends bad messages to your host that the food is bland or inadequate.
- If you are eating pasta, do not use a spoon for assistance. Discreetly use a fork and the sides of the bowl or plate to twirl the pasta. Slurping the strands of pasta is very poor manners.
- You can use your bread to soak up some of your sauce or gravy. But don't go as far as mopping the bread around the plate to get the last drop.

 ## USEFUL FACTS

President	Giorgio Napolitano (2006)
Prime Minister	Silvio Berlusconi (2008) (President of the Council Of Ministries)
National Name	Repubblica Italiana

Size	113,521 square miles (294,019 square km)
Population	58,145,321 (2008)
Capital	Rome
Government	Republic
Currency	Euro (Previously lira)
Religion	Roman Catholic 90%, with Protestant, Jewish and Islamic
Language	Italian is the official language. Approximately 50% of the population have a regional dialect. Other languages include Ladin, Slovene, German, French, Albanian, Croatian, Sardinian, and Greek.
Ethnicity	Italian with also German-, French-, and Slovene-Italians in the north and Albanian-Italians and Greek-Italians in the south.
Industry	Tourism, machinery, iron and steel, chemicals, food processing, textiles, motor vehicles, clothing, footwear, and ceramics.
Time Zone	Italy is one hour ahead of Greenwich Mean Time (GMT +1) or 6 hours ahead of U.S. Eastern Standard Time (EST +6). Italy does observe daylight saving time.
Telephone Code	International Code: +39 City Code: +06 (Rome)
Weather	Winters can be damp and cool in the south and very cold in the north. Summers can be very hot and humid. There is little snow except in the mountainous regions.
Voltage/Frequency	230 V, 50 Hz

HOLIDAYS/FESTIVALS

1 January	New Year's Day
6 January	Epiphany
8 March	Women's Pride Day
March/April	Easter Sunday and Monday
25 April	Liberation Day
1 May	Labor Day
2 June	Anniversary of the Founding of the Republic
15 August	Feast of the Assumption
1 November	All Saints Day
8 December	Feast of the Immaculate Conception
25 December	Christmas Day
26 December	Boxing Day/St. Stephen's Day

LANGUAGE TIPS

Italian	Phonetic	English
Salve/Ciao	Sal-veh/Chow	Hello/Hi
Arrivederci	Ah reeve ah dare chee	Good-bye
Buon giorno	Born jorn no	Good morning
Buonasera	Bwoe nah sa rah	Good evening
Come stai	Co may stah	How are you?
Si/No	See/Noh	Yes/No
Quanto ?	Kwanto	How much?
Per favore	Per fa-voray	Please
Grazie	Grat-ze-a	Thank you
Scusi	Skoo-zee	Excuse me

Chapter 16: JAPAN

LOCATION/GEOGRAPHY

Located in eastern Asia, Japan is an island chain lying between the North Pacific Ocean and the Sea of Japan, east of the Korean Peninsula. Japan is just slightly smaller than California.

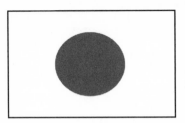

 DID YOU KNOW?

- Many over-the-counter cold medicines, such as Vicks Inhalers, Sudafed, and Actifed are illegal in Japan because they contain small amounts of amphetamines.
- The best items to shop for in Japan are pearls, silks, pottery, *cloisonné*, lanterns, furniture, lacquer ware, red coral, cameras, dolls, karate gear, carp kites, *Imari* porcelain, green tea, good-luck charms from Shrines, and packaged seaweed.
- Approximately 200 volcanoes can be found in Japan, and Japan is home to 10 percent of the active volcanoes in the world.
- To conserve space, some Japanese farmers grow watermelons in a square shape.
- Sumo wrestling is the national sport of Japan.
- The literacy rate in Japan is close to 100 percent, and 95 percent of the Japanese population has a high school education.
- The national anthem of Japan (as well as those of Jordan and San Marino) has only four lines.
- Japanese chopsticks are pointed and Chinese chopsticks are blunt.
- What do Ringo Starr and apples have in common? In Japanese, Ringo means apple.
- Kublai Khan's fleet was destroyed by a hurricane while trying to invade Japan in 1281.

USINESS ETIQUETTE

 ## Punctuality

- Be punctual at all times. It's considered rude to be late.
- If you're taking a taxi, allow plenty of time due to the hectic and busy traffic. The most efficient way to travel is by train. Allow time to find the office once you depart the train. Tokyo streets do not follow a grid, and even with a map, navigating the city can be challenging.

Meeting Manners

- The senior person of the team generally will enter the room first, followed by his subordinates in order of rank. The least senior person of the team will sit closest to the door.

- As a guest, you will most likely be seated on the farther side of the room. The senior members will sit in the middle and the lower management on the ends. Stand at your seat and wait for the top person to tell you to be seated. When the meeting has concluded, allow the highest ranking person to stand first before you stand.

- Many people from a company may attend initially, so come prepared with enough handouts and business cards.

- You will need a translator or agent. All arrangements will need planning. The best advice is to keep your presentation visual, short, clear, and to the point. Watch any slang or English jargon that could be misunderstood.

- Intermediaries are important in securing Japanese contacts and connections. Use these intermediaries for consultation regarding negotiations, endorsements, and assistance in closing the deals. The higher ranking connection the better.

- If possible, direct your first remarks to the most senior person. Following remarks you can proceed to the appropriate individuals.

- Remember that "silence is golden." It is not always important to talk or to break the silence. Silence in Japan is just as important as your speaking. Silence provides Japanese the time to think and evaluate before they respond. By breaking the silence, you may appear to be rushing them and not sincere in your proposal or presentation.

- The "poker face" is very common in dealings with Japanese. It's considered rude to convey emotions in public and the uncommitted face will cover any negative emotions. The smile can also be used to cover any embarrassing situations.

- Japanese might feel challenged or rebel under constant direct eye contact. Americans have been taught to have good and sincere eye contact with a smile, but many Japanese will look away or down to show their respect and sincerity. It is becoming more common for Japanese to have direct eye contact as in Western countries.

- Small talk is fine before the negotiations. Your Japanese counterpart might ask questions regarding your education, family, and social life. Japanese may be very direct in their conversations and may ask how much money you make, the type and size of your home, and other personal questions.

- During three weeks of the year, many Japanese visit the graves of their ancestors. You should avoid scheduling appointments or business trips during New Year's holidays from 28 December to 3 January; Golden Week, 29 April to 5 May; and *Obon*, mid-August.

- Agreements can be made by a nod or a slight bow rather than our usual shaking hands. But also know that they will renegotiate their contracts.
- Do not be confused by "yes" or "no" answers. They may just be "thinking about it" but will answer with a "yes." "I'll consider it" is more likely to mean "no."
- Avoid all confrontations or showing negative emotions during business negotiations. Express your opinions but avoid direct refusals.
- Avoid giving praise to an individual. It's much better to address the entire group because they consider the group more important than the individual.
- Watch using broad hand gestures, facial expressions, or big movements.
- It is critical for women to stress their role, abilities, and title. It is becoming much better and easier for a woman to deal in Japan, but it is important not to be aggressive and to maintain a professional and dignified working relationship during both business situations and social events.
- Everything is considered during negotiations, including the history of your company, the financial status, your expressions and remarks, and your acceptance from the group. The decision-making process can be extremely slow, even as long as two to three years.
- Remember that age equals rank in Japan. Respect for the elderly is extremely important.

 ## Business Cards

- The business card exchange ("*meishi*" pronounced may-shee) is critical and a key part in the business relationship. Never be without your business cards because your Japanese associates will exchange them frequently.
- Generally the higher ranking will exchange cards first and the others will follow in order of seniority.
- Present your card after the bow or handshake. Business usually will not begin until the "*meishi*" exchange has taken place.
- Have one side of the card in English or your native language and the reverse side in Japanese. Present your card with the Japanese side facing up and toward the recipient.
- The process is to present your card with two hands, let one hand go to receive their card and then immediately place both hands on the card you receive.

- Read a business card carefully. Memorize it if you have to so you can make remarks regarding their title, education, or any other information that might appear on their card. Avoid going back to the card constantly to remember their name or important information.
- Be careful not to drop their business cards. It is a sign of disrespect.
- Avoid placing the card in your pocket and most definitely avoid placing it in your wallet and then in your back pocket. That is considered extremely disrespectful.
- On the same note, do not pull your card out of your back pocket to preset. They may even refuse to accept. Carry your cards in a professional business card case.
- Do not write on a person's business card. Carry a notepad or another form to take notes.
- Do not place your business cards in a stack on the table and allow people to take a card from the stack.

Meals/Toasts

- Generally the highest-ranking person hosting a meal will sit at the center of the table, farthest from the door and facing it. To the host's immediate right, the most important guest will be seated. The least important guest will be seated near the entrance or the door.
- The host will generally lead by starting to eat first. Then the guests may proceed.
- In a traditional Japanese restaurant, the host will generally order for you. If you are familiar with Japanese dishes, then it is fine to let the host know your preferred selections.
- Thanking your host for the meal is critical.
- A standard meal in Japan will consist of grilled fish, bowl of rice, cup of soup, and a small dish of pickles.
- Japanese delicacies include *sakura-nabe* (horse meat), *inoshishi* (wild boar), *uzura* (quail), *suzume* (sparrow), and *shika-no-shashimi* (raw deer meat). These are very expensive and rarely served.
- Even if the food is not appealing, you should try everything that is presented or be ready with a good health reason if you do not sample. Avoid saying you do not like something. If you are asked, you can respond, "I prefer this to that," so not to offend your host.
- Your chopsticks should not be used to point at a person or something. If you are not eating with or using your chopsticks, then place them on the chopstick rest or lay them down in front of you with the tip to the left.
- Do not give food from chopstick to chopstick. This is done only with the bones of a cremated body at a funeral. Do not stick your chopsticks into

your food, especially rice. The chopsticks are placed in rice at funerals and placed on the altar.

- Pouring soy sauce on rice is not a Japanese custom. The soy sauce can be placed in a small bowl for dipping. Be careful not to pour an excessive amount that will be wasted and unused.
- This is one place that it is fine to slurp your noodles and tea.
- Both hands should be used to hold a bowl or cup that you want refilled.
- Any bones should be placed on the side of your plate.
- If you are a guest, wait for another person to replenish your beverage. If you do not want any more to drink, leave the glass or cup partially full. When served *sake* in a little cup called an *ochoko*, turn the cup upside down to indicate no more. Otherwise, your drinks will be refilled. If you are the host, it is expected that you will refill beverages for at least a second round.
- A small portion of your meal should be left on your plate to show that the meal was appealing and satisfying.
- To return a favor for a meal, select a restaurant of your own culture if that is possible. This will give you a chance to establish a little better rapport and a closer personal relationship. Your hosts may initially decline because they feel it is a burden to you, so continue to insist.
- The most senior person generally offers the first toast. If you propose the toast, it will be repeated by the companions and they will clink glasses before taking a sip. The host traditionally will take the first sip. *Kampai* (kahm-pie) is the equivalent of "cheers."
- If a toast is given to you, it is important that you return one.

Entertainment

- Remember that if you are invited, the host will possibly order the meal and will always pay. This is not negotiable.
- Business can be discussed over these meals, but allow your host to initiate these discussions.
- Most entertaining will take place in restaurants. Pour your companion's drink and wait for them to pour yours. It's impolite to pour your own drink.
- *Karaoke* bars are very popular, so be ready to start singing even if you can't carry a tune. Think of it as just part of doing business.
- If a Japanese counterpart invites you out after work, it is impolite to refuse to socialize. However, they separate their work from nightlife, and although they may loosen up during socializing, they may not mention it during subsequent business sessions.
- If you are invited to a social event, this is one time you can show up "fashionably" late.

Be On Your Best Cultural Behavior

- It is rare to be invited to a Japanese home, so if you are, show sincere appreciation. In Japanese homes, it is customary and expected for you to remove your shoes and wear the slippers that are provided. (And don't forget that there will be another pair of slippers to change into if you go into the bathroom.) You may be expected to sit cross-legged or with your legs to the side around a low table with the family. A backrest may be offered.
- In temples, homes, and in some traditional Japanese restaurants, you are expected to take off your shoes. Slip-on shoes make it so much easier. Just make sure you wear clean socks with no holes.
- Women are not welcomed at geisha houses, hostess bars, or Sumo wrestling rings.

Forms of Address/Introductions/Greetings

- A bow, or *ojigi* (oh-jee-ghee), is their most common form of greeting to express thanks, to say "I'm sorry," or to ask for a favor.
- The Japanese have adopted the Western tradition of shaking hands to show a kind gesture in business. Visitors should show their appreciation by returning a slight bow of the head, still looking forward while shaking hands.
- The Japanese handshake might be weaker than the Western grip. Don't be fooled by their weaker handshake. They are still very strong business people.
- The recipient's rank and status will determine the depth of the bow. If a person is of higher rank than you, then your bow should be a little lower to display respect. Play it safe and bow a little lower if you are not sure of the status of the person you are facing. If it is a person of the same rank or status, a bow at the same height is appropriate.
- Initially stay away from touching. A pat on the back or an embrace would be extremely inappropriate in an initial meeting.
- First names are generally saved for family and close friends. Wait to be invited before using their first names. Avoid suggesting being called by your first name during the first several meetings.
- Even after you have established first-name relationships, call people by their last names in the presence of their colleagues to avoid any embarrassment.
- Include titles or Mr., Ms., or the suffix *san* used with their last name as in *Aoki-san*. When introducing yourself, do not add *san* to your own name. It would be "Hello, *Aoki-san*, my name is Steven Smith."
- There could be many people in the meeting or room with the same last name, so it is up to you to keep them all straight.

- Ask if you do not know how to pronounce a name.
- Taxi drivers rarely speak English. Before entering the taxi, have the concierge or doorman at the hotel assist with either giving the directions or writing the destination in Japanese and presenting them to the driver. Make sure you have directions and the name of the hotel in Japanese with you to return to the hotel. If necessary, have someone assist with the payment.

Appearance/Attire

- Never dress casually for a business meeting or function. A good image in appearance and clothing is important in Japan.
- Conservative suites of blue or gray with a white shirt and dark tie are the traditional dress for Japanese men. Styles are changing and becoming more colorful and fashionable, but dress conservatively until you get to know the customs, dress codes, and people of a particular company.
- You will find many men without a tie and just short sleeve shirts in the summer. Pastel shirts are becoming more common and popular in the business place.
- Slip-on shoes are recommended, since shoes are removed frequently.
- Business women should dress conservatively and minimize the use of jewelry, perfume, and make-up.
- Japanese women are now starting to wear slacks and high heels to work and taking on a more Western look. There are still some older companies that continue to dictate a conservative style. Just remember that you want to present a professional look, so avoid wearing slacks and higher heels so you do not offend your Japanese counterparts or tower over them.
- Summers can be extremely hot and humid, so have lightweight clothing. The Japanese are very concerned with neatness, so it's advisable to have several changes of clothes.
- *Kimonos* are the national costume of Japan. They are worn now mostly by women and for special occasions. They are wrapped around the body with the left side over right. For funerals, corpses wear a *kimono* wrapped right over left.
- The *geta* (thonged wood-platform footwear) are worn with the *kimono* with the split-toe socks called *tabi*.

Gift Giving

- Gift giving is very important, and gifts are exchanged mid-year *"chugen"* and at the end of the year *"seibo."*
- Bring various gifts to exchange. The emphasis of gift giving is on the exchange of the gift instead of the actual gift. The style and ceremony is what matters.
- It's best to present your gift at the end of the visit. Make it known that you will present a gift and avoid surprising your host.
- If a gift is for an individual, then it's best to present it in private. If gifts are to be given to groups, then have all the people together to make your presentations. Do not make the mistake of giving the same gift to two or more Japanese of unequal rank.
- Gifts are generally opened in private. A lot has to do with "loss of face." The gift could be a poor choice for the recipient's rank or status.
- Present and accept gifts with both hands, similar to the presentation of business cards.
- Before accepting a gift, it is polite to refuse the gift at least once or twice before finally accepting.
- Ask the hotel or store to wrap your gifts. Selecting the wrong paper could ruin your presentation before gifts are even opened. Black and white paper are unacceptable; the best choice is rice paper. Pastel colors are good, but avoid bright colors and bows.
- If invited to a home in Japan, bring an uneven number of flowers, cakes, or candy.
- Never show up *"tebura,"* or empty-handed.
- Good gift ideas are foreign, well known name-brand items; imported scotch, cognac, bourbon, brandy, or top quality wines; electronic toys for children if appropriate; fruit, pen and pencil sets; top choice beef; a special photograph during an important gathering; or something that you know the recipient will enjoy. Saks and Neiman Marcus gifts are always appreciated.
- Even giving watermelon is considered a good gift in Japan and China.
- Gifts to avoid are flowers associated with funerals, which include lilies, lotus blossoms, and camellias. White flowers of any kind should not be presented. Potted plants are believed to signify taking root where you are, so you would never want to send a potted plant to someone in the hospital, for example.
- Presenting four or nine of anything is considered unlucky. Also gifts in odd numbers are considered bad luck. Four is pronounced *"shi,"* which is the same as death and nine is pronounced *"ku,"* which is the same pronunciation as torture or agony.

- Watch admiring anything that belongs to your host. Japanese love to please, so they may give you that item to take home.
- Funeral notices are generally printed in red, so stay away from red ink, even on greeting cards.
- If you receive a gift, be sure to reciprocate.
- Just in case you are ever invited to a wedding in Japan, remember all the procedures with colors and wrapping paper. A superstition still prevails that if the bow on the present opens too easily, then the couple are destined for a quick divorce, so tie it very tightly.

Tipping

- Tipping is not a common practice and not expected in Japan.
- An automatic service charge is placed on the bill in some restaurants, so tipping is usually not necessary.
- At a country inn ("*ryokan*"), you may provide the housekeeper with a five percent tip.

Gesture Awareness

- To touch or point to your nose is to indicate "me."
- Do not be confused that nodding your head up and down means "yes" as in the United States. It means that you are listening and not necessarily agreeing with the comments of the person.
- To motion for a person to "come here" just wave your hand in a back and forth motion with the fingers pointed down.
- To motion that you are "eating" is to pretend you are holding a bowl in your left hand and shovel rice into your mouth with chopsticks in your right hand.
- "Drinking" can be expressed as if you were taking a drink from a *sake* cup by moving your wrist back and forth.
- A woman will cover her mouth with her hand if embarrassed or to show modesty.
- To show negative reaction, they will fan their hand back and forth in front of their face, similar to fanning a fly away.
- Showing a devil with horns by pointing your index finger up from the temples expresses anger.
- Crisscrossing the index fingers or tapping them together signifies "fighting."
- The western sign that is used to signify "OK" by forming a circle with the thumb and index fingers together is similar to the Japanese meaning "money."

- To wave your hand with the palm outward in front of your face conveys that you do not understand or that you do not deserve it.
- Unusual facial expressions and motioning in dramatic ways can be misinterpreted.
- Scratching their head is a gesture for confusion and embarrassment.
- Pointing is considered rude, so wave your hand with the palm facing up.
- If in deep thought, Japanese may fold their arms. Do not take this as a gesture of hostility or of not having any interest in you or the conversation.

 Faux Pas

- Not bowing lower when greeting or thanking a person that is older or of a higher social status is extremely disrespectful.
- It is polite to initially refuse an offer of help.
- It's not acceptable to spit, snort, or sniff in public. It is considered even more impolite to blow your nose in public. If you absolutely need to use a tissue, make sure you throw it away instantly after use. Keeping a used tissue is considered disgusting by Japanese. Turn your head and cover your face when sneezing or coughing.
- Don't crowd people or stand too close. Japanese value their space. However, pushing and shoving in crowded train or subway stations is common. A form of "excuse me" is to slightly bow and hold your hand open in front of you and a slight wave as if to gesture please go ahead or that you are clearing the way for them.
- Be careful of facial expressions. A smile can express either joy or displeasure.
- Never pour a drink for yourself. Have someone else do it for you.
- Do not display money openly. If you must give it from person to person, then place it in an envelope.
- When speaking with a person, do not put your hands in your pockets.
- Avoid discussing post-war issues and politics.
- Avoid standing with your legs crossed. Do not lean against a door or a wall. Do not sit with your ankle over your knee. You can cross your legs at the ankles or knees, but it's better to sit up straight so you look involved and interested.
- It's impolite to have your leg above a table or desk. It denotes relaxation and shows disrespect. Sit on the edge of a chair or sofa to show respect. Sitting back the whole way shows familiarity. Do not put your legs out in front of one another on *tatami* (mats and traditional Japanese flooring) or in a chair. Do not sit so that you show the soles of your shoes.

- Be careful with the usual filler "uh" in your conversations. Japanese consider this a rough sound and it could jeopardize the flow of the conversation.
- Remember: The traditional concepts of "saving face" and *wa* (peace) of fitting in and remaining modest still exist. The Japanese will avoid embarrassment and avoid hurting another person or themselves.
- Although public display of affection is becoming more common with young adults, it still not accepted by some of the elders.

 ## USEFUL FACTS

Emperor	Akihito (1989)
Prime Minister	Yasuo Fukuda (2007)
National Name	Nippon
Size	152,411 square miles (394,744 square km)
Population	127,288,419 (2008)
Capital	Tokyo
Government	Constitutional Monarchy with a Parliamentary Government
Currency	Yen
Religion	Shintoist and Buddhist 84%, 16% other religions including 0.7% Christians
Language	Japanese
Ethnicity	Japanese 99%; Korean, Chinese, Brazilian, Filipino, other 1%
Industry	Leading technology producer of electronic equipment, motor vehicles, ships, chemicals, processed foods, machine tools, steel, and metals. Also agriculture and natural resources

Time Zone	Japan is nine hours ahead of Greenwich Mean Time (GMT +9) or 14 hours ahead of Eastern Standard Time (EST +14). Japan does not observe daylight saving time.
Telephone Code	International Code: +81 City Code: +3 (Tokyo)
Weather	Varies from tropical climates in the south to cooler temperatures in the north. June and the beginning of July are the rainy season, called *Tsuyu*. July and August are usually very hot and humid. August to October is the typhoon season. Winter in Japan can be cold, but the temperatures rarely drops below freezing. January and February are good times for skiing.
Voltage/Frequency	100 V; 50 Hz in Eastern Japan and 60 Hz in Western Japan This frequency difference affects only sensitive equipment.

HOLIDAYS/FESTIVALS

1 January	New Year's Day (*Gantan*) (The most important holiday, celebrated 28 December to 3 January)
2nd Monday in Janurary	Coming of Age Day (*Seijin-no-hi*) (People who are 20 years old celebrate becoming adults)
3 February	Setsubun (The Bean-Throwing Festival) (A tradition of chasing away evil spirits)
11 February	National Foundation Day
14 February	Valentine's Day (Typical for Japanese women to give chocolates to men on this day)
3 March	Japanese Girl's Day
14 March	White Day (Japanese men give candies to women)
20 or 21 March	Spring Equinox Day
March	Cherry Blossom season
29 April	Green Day (*Midori-no-hi*) (Former Emperor Showa's birthday)
29 April – 5 May	Golden Week (Group of national holidays in Japan)
3 May	Constitution Memorial Day
4 May	Citizen's Holiday or "Between Day"

5 May	Children's Day (*Kodomono-hi*) Japanese Boy's Festival
7 July	Star Festival
3rd Monday July	Ocean Day
13 to 16 August	*Obon* (Time of praying for the repose of the souls of their ancestors. They also believe that these spirits come back to their homes to be reunited with family during *Obon*.)
3 September	Autumn Equinox Day
3rd Monday September	Respect for the Aged Day
2nd Monday October	Sports Day
3 November	Culture Day
15 November	*Shichi-go-san* (Around this day people wish for the healthy growth of 7 (*shichi*) year-old girls, 5 (*go*) year-old boys, and 3 (*san*) year-old girls at shrines)
23 November	Labor Thanksgiving Day
23 December	The Emperor's Birthday
25 December	Christmas

LANGUAGE TIPS

<u>Japanese</u>	<u>Phonetics</u>	<u>English</u>
Arigato gozaimasu	Ah-ree-GAH-toh go-ZIGH-moss	Thank you
Onegaishimasu	Oh-neh-gigh shee-moss	Please
Doitashi mashite	Doh EE-tah-shee mosh teh	You're welcome
Ohayo gozaimasu	Oh-hah-YOH go-zigh-moss	Good morning
Konnichiwa	Kon-nee-chee-WAH	Good afternoon (hello)
Konbanwa	Kohm-bahn-wah	Good evening (good night)
Sayonara (long-term)	Sa-YOH-nah-rah	Good-bye
Hajimemashite	Hah-jee-meh-MASH-	Nice to meet you (first time)
Ogenke desu ka?	Oh-GEN-kee-dess-KAH	How are you?
Sumimasen	Soo-mee-mah-sen	Excuse me

Chapter 17: MEXICO

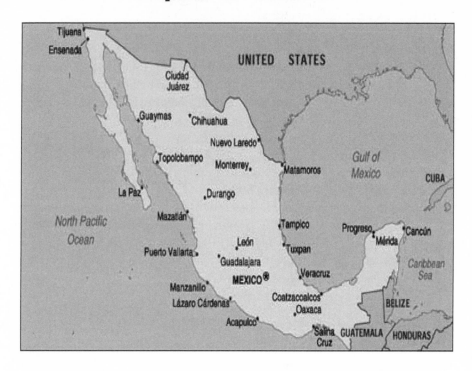

LOCATION/GEOGRAPHY

Mexico borders the Caribbean Sea and the Gulf of Mexico between Belize and the United States. It borders the North Pacific Ocean between Guatemala and the United States.

 DID YOU KNOW?

- Plaza de Toros, located in Mexico City, is the world's largest bullfighting ring.
- The poinsettia is named after a 19th century U.S. ambassador to Mexico, J.R. Poinsett, who brought the poinsettia plant to the United States.
- The Aztec Indians of Mexico believed that turquoise would protect them, so they used turquoise to decorate their battle shields.
- The Caesar salad is named after Caesar Cardini, who prepared the salad in his Caesar's Palace Restaurant in Tijuana, Mexico.
- Mexico is the third largest exporter to the United States.
- The family is the center of all social structure in Mexico.
- The drinking age in Mexico is 18. Drinking and driving is a serious crime in Mexico.
- Taxi cabs in Mexico are relatively inexpensive and are metered and charged by zones.
- Spain ruled Mexico for 300 years from 1521 to 1821.
- Mexico lost Texas in 1836. After the 1846-1848 war with the United States, Mexico lost the area that is now California, Utah, Nevada, most of Arizona and New Mexico, and parts of Wyoming and Colorado.
- Mexico joined Canada and the United States in January 1996 in the North American Free Trade Agreement.
- In 2002, the PRI (Partido Revolucionario Institucional, or Institutional Revolutionary Party) lost the presidency, ending 71 years of one-party rule.

USINESS ETIQUETTE

 Punctuality

- You are expected to be on time, but time is very flexible in Mexico. It is not uncommon for people to be 15 to 30 minutes late, but they do try to make every effort to arrive on time to show their appreciation for your punctuality.

- It's common for social events to begin as much as an hour later than planned. But plenty of drinks or alcohol will be provided while you wait.
- Usually meetings will not start until everyone is in attendance.
- *Manana* means morning, tomorrow, or later. So if you are told *manana*, it could mean actually sometime in the near future or not at all.

Meeting Manners

- Hierarchical relations are very important and are emphasized. Do not break the chain of hierarchy.
- Authority is respected; look to people in higher positions for guidance and decision making. Rank is important and treated with respect.
- The dignity of a person is regarded with great value. Do not criticize publicly or do anything that would embarrass or humiliate someone.
- Personal relationships are the key to doing business and to your success in Mexico. Intermediaries are used to make your connections. Your "business family" connection is critical and can make the introductions needed to do business in Mexico.
- Appointments can be made via e-mail or phone and should be done at least two weeks in advance. Be sure to confirm all visits again at least one week in advance. Once you arrive in Mexico, contact the office of the person you will be meeting to provide a local contact and once again to confirm the meeting and that you have arrived in Mexico. Communications can be handled through e-mails or phone calls. Just be very clear in all instructions and avoid possible miscommunication due to the language.
- Face-to-face meetings are much better than trying to conduct business by phone, letters, or e-mail. Since family is so important in Mexico, most Mexicans generally do not work on Saturday or Sunday.
- Arrive on time for meetings even though your counterpart could be 30 minutes late or more. Your meeting could be cancelled or postponed with little or no notice. You need to determine the importance of your meeting and not act irritated or frustrated by the lack of punctuality or the delays and slower negotiations.
- Check in advance with your intermediaries or their office to determine whether you need your material prepared in both English and Spanish and if an interrupter is necessary. If so, make all necessary arrangements so the meeting can be handled in Spanish. Allow extra time in the meeting for translation.
- Make sure presentations are of good quality.
- Agendas are not generally provided, and if they are, they are not necessarily followed. Materials and documents should be placed on

Mexico

the table and never tossed across the table. This is regarding as highly offensive.

- "No" is avoided. "We will see" or "maybe" is expressed and may sound positive but could actually mean no. Make sure all your agreements are in writing to avoid confusion.
- Trust and achieving strong personal relationships are important during negotiations.
- Do not back down or show weakness during negotiations. Be prepared to conduct several meetings to come to an agreement.
- Do not provide your best and final offer first. Be ready to negotiate. These negotiations could take a long time, so be patient.
- If attending a program with several speakers and the agenda is behind schedule, do not worry. They will get to you and you will be given the exact amount of time that was promised. It may be several hours later. Just be prepared and be patient. No one in the audience seems to be offended or worried that the meeting is several hours behind schedule. They still participate and show respect to all speakers and the program.
- Even though all are encouraged to participate in a meeting and provide their input, generally the final decision comes from the highest in authority or the owner of the company.
- Always follow up with a written agreement once a decision has been made.
- Good topics of discussion can include your family, your job, and things that interest you. Mexican history, art, museums, and culture are always excellent topics. Soccer (*futbol*), baseball, basketball, and bullfighting are good topics to discuss.
- Topics to avoid include any historical issues that are sensitive to the Mexicans. Definitely stay away from discussing Mexicans who are working illegally in other countries, the Mexican-American war, their poverty, religion, politics, earthquakes, or comparisons to the United States.

Business Cards

- Cards are exchanged in meetings during the introductions.
- Have one side of your card in Spanish and present with that side facing the recipient.
- Business cards should contain both your professional and educational degrees and qualifications.

Meals/Toasts

- Meetings can be scheduled for breakfast, lunch, or dinner. Agree on the time and location, but lunch is preferred over dinner for meetings and generally begins at 2 p.m. or 3 p.m. (1400 or 1500) but can last three to four hours. Allow plenty of time for personal conversation as well as business discussion.
- Breakfast meetings are common and usually start at 8 a.m. or 8:30 a.m. (0800 or 0830) and generally do not last more than two hours.
- Make sure to check with associates about the proper arrival time. Generally, arriving 30 minutes late is the standard. Actually arriving on time or early at a Mexican's home can be inappropriate.
- Do not plan to eat dinner before 8:30 p.m. or 9 p.m. (2030 or 2100). This generally is the lightest meal of the day.
- Women still need to be careful about inviting a man to a business meal without inviting the spouse, colleague, or coworker.
- Women should also make prior arrangements for paying the bill for business meals. This can be handled in the restaurant of her hotel or by just arriving early at the restaurant to make all arrangements. This will avoid any resistance or embarrassment when the male associate tries to pay for the meal.
- One person will usually pay the bill in a group setting. Usually that is the oldest person in the group. But to show your manners, you should offer to pay several times. To show your thanks, reciprocate the invitation and insist that you will be picking up the tab.
- Introduce yourself at a larger event or function. Initially it may be difficult to work your way into a conversation, but be persistent and you will find a group that will welcome you.
- The host will generally introduce you at smaller gatherings.
- Remain standing until you are invited to sit. You will also be instructed where to sit. Wait for the hostess to begin eating before you begin to eat or pick up your utensils.
- During a meal function, always keep both your hands visible. Your wrists can rest on the edge of the table. After the meal, place your fork and knife across your plate with the prongs /tines facing down and the handles facing to the right.
- It is considered polite to leave some food on your plate.
- *Quinceanera* is a party in celebration of a girl's 15th birthday, and it's an honor to be invited. You should definitely accept this invitation.
- Make sure you know how to drink their national drink, *tequila*. Place a pinch of salt in the depression of your left hand between thumb and forefinger. Lick the salt, and quickly take a drink of *tequila*. Follow this by sucking on a lime wedge.

- Generally men will give the toast. If you are a female and want to reciprocate a toast or show your appreciation for the meal and the business transactions, then check with an associate or your intermediary about how you should handle it.
- *Salud* is the traditional toast in Mexico.

Entertainment

- Business is not discussed if you are the guest in a Mexican home. It is a time to meet the family and socialize. It is an honor to be invited to a home and a great step toward the success of your business.
- If business is to be discussed, allow your host to bring it up first.
- Friendship is important for a successful business relationship. Consider an invitation to someone's home a major step toward a trusting and long-lasting association.

Forms of Address/Introductions/Greetings

- Men will shake hands initially. Be prepared to move into an embrace, or *abrazo,* after a few meetings. This is a warm hug along with some hearty backslapping and then a handshake. This is a part of their business culture and generally is just exchanged between men, but not always. A woman can be hugged after getting to know associates a little better.
- Women will pat each other on the right forearm or shoulder rather than shake hands in social situations. They will also kiss and hug if they are close.
- In business situations, both men and women will offer their hand. A man might wait for the woman to initiate the handshake.
- Do not immediately call a person by the first name. Continue to use *Senor, Senora,* or *Senorita,* or Mr., Mrs., or Ms., with the family name until told differently. If you don't know their last name initially, then just say *Senor, Senora,* or *Senorita.*
- Titles such as Doctor or Professor are important. When addressing a person, use only their title without including their last name.
- During a less formal setting or at a party, it is common to see a person giving a slight bow when he enters the room. Make it a point to greet and shakes hands with the guests upon your arrival. It is important that you shake hands with each guest again as you depart the party.
- Two kisses are exchanged (air kisses), first on the left side and then the right.

- A *senorita* may receive three kisses, two as a greeting and the third is a wish for marriage.
- Intermediaries can help with the proper introductions and which name to use. In formal speech and written correspondence, the mother's last name is added after the father's family name. But in face-to-face introductions, the man may be addressed by both names or by only the father's name. Never use just the mother's surname. Also in writing, a Mexican may reduce his or her second surname to just an initial.
- Married women will add their husband's father's name at the end of their name, shown as *de* (name) if written, but will be formally addressed as *Senora de* (name). If less formal, then simply address as *Senora* (name).

 ## Appearance/Attire

- Dress is very similar to European attire. Men wear dark, conservative suits with classic lines and the tailored look. Women wear stylish business suits, high heels, and hosiery.
- Dress for meetings and professional events is business-style. For more formal occasions, men will wear a white shirt, tie, and suit.
- Women wear slacks or skirts and men wear pants and shirt for more casual dress.
- The *guayabera*, or the traditional lightweight shirt, can be worn for the warmer weather and at resorts. Just make sure you do wear it outside and not tucked into your pants. This garment is not worn in public in Mexico City other than by waiters and other servants.
- Avoid tight or low-cut clothing. More revealing styles should be worn only at resorts.
- Be careful with showy or expensive jewelry. Leave more valuable items at home.
- It is rainy from May to November. Mexican men generally do not wear raincoats but do carry umbrellas.
- Jeans are appropriate and acceptable for more casual situations, but they need to be in good condition. Only children wear shorts.
- To attend meetings, come in business dress with shirts well-pressed and shoes polished to a very high shine.
- No matter the financial status, Mexicans will dress impeccably in the best they can afford.

Gift Giving

- If you give a gift, it will be opened immediately.
- If you receive a gift, open it and then show appreciation and enthusiasm.
- If you are invited to a Mexican home, bring a gift such as flowers (or send ahead of time), something sweet, or an item from your home country.
- If there are children, then toys from your home country, a sports team cap or shirt from your home team, and computer games or software are appropriate.
- Do not bring marigolds or yellow flowers because they symbolize death. Red flowers have a negative connotation or send a bad spell. White flowers as gifts provide a good feeling and will lift the spells cast on someone.
- Avoid giving silver items. Don't give anything resembling the trinkets that tourists buy in the markets. Mexico has some of the best silver in the world, so this is a gift you want to avoid giving unless it's top-notch.
- Knives should not be given in Latin America because they represent the severing of a friendship.
- Small gifts can be given in your initial meeting but are not required. A nice gift with your company logo is appropriate. Pens or quality office items are appreciated.
- Electronic gadgets, such as iPods or MP3 players with music already loaded, make great gifts. Just make sure you know the type of music the recipient enjoys.
- Don't forget secretaries or assistants. They like gifts for all the help they have provided in setting up meetings and dealing with their bosses.
- Not until a friendship is established and secure would a more expensive gift be appropriate.

 ## Tipping

- Tipping is customary and expected when good service is provided.
- People working in the tourism or service sectors in Mexico rely on tips to supplement their pay.
- In restaurants, tips are generally 10 percent to 15 percent and depend on the level of service provided. The national value added tax (IVA in Spanish) of 15 percent is part of restaurant bills. It is important to know that this is not the tip but a tax. An easy way to determine your tip is to leave an amount equal to the IVA, provided the service merits it.
- A 10 percent to 15 percent tip should be provided for fast food deliveries.
- For hotels, the standards are 10 pesos (US$1) per bag; concierge, 10 to 50 pesos (US$1 to US$5) or more depending on the service they provide.

- In hotels, housekeepers might be left 5 to 10 pesos (US$.50 to US$1) per day, depending on the establishment. Because staffers' schedules change, you should leave the tip each day.
- Other tips vary from 5 percent to 15 percent, depending on the service and the location.
- Gas station attendants are even given tips ranging from 2 to 5 pecos (US$.25 to US$.50).
- If you are shown to your seat in a stadium, the person that directs you could be given a small tip.
- Minimal tips are provided for men (generally they are men) that keep watch or patrol in the car park. They help drivers find a free space, watch their cars, or even help drivers back out of their spaces.
- In medium to large retail stores, a uniformed helper (generally children or elderly) that bags your products will also be tipped because of the low income they receive from this job. They are called *cerillos* and will receive 2 to 5 pesos or up to 15 pesos if they assist you at your car (US$1.50).
- If strolling musicians play at your table, they expect to receive a small tip.
- Taxi drivers or bus drivers do not expect to receive tips unless it is a tour, but it is always appreciated.

 Gesture Awareness

- Don't back away from a person. Mexicans stand much closer, and hugs and kisses are common.
- Putting hands on your hips indicates a challenge, and putting your hands in your pockets is considered rude.
- Mexicans will look away and not make constant eye contact. This gesture is a sign of their respect and not an insult or lack of interest in your conversation.
- Using the "hang loose" gesture that is seen in Hawaii (made with the index and pinkie finger) to say "stay cool" or "relax" has a little variation in Mexico. The same gesture done vertically in front of the body (knuckles pointing outward) means, "Would you like a drink?" The hand and fingers represent a handle to a mug.
- Be careful when knocking on a door. If the door to the bathroom is closed avoid tapping on the door to the tune of "dum-de-de-dum-dum... dum-dum" or the tune of "Shave and a haircut, two bits." This catchy little tune sends a crude message in Mexico.
- In restaurants, there are several ways to get the attention of the waiter. One is a "psst-psst" sound. The second is making a kissing sound. The

third and the most polite is to just lift your arm and signal with your hand.

- To call to others, extend your arm, palm down, with the fingers making a scratching motion inward.
- Remember to keep both hands on the table while eating, and not on your lap.
- If passing an object to a person, then hand it to him or her and do not throw or toss it. If you are handing change, place it in the hand and not on the table or counter.
- When paying the bill at a restaurant or purchasing an item in a store, hand the person your money or credit card. Do not place the money or credit card on the table or counter.
- A very rude gesture is to make a V with the index and middle fingers with your palm facing you and then placing the V over your nose.
- The OK sign with the thumb and index finger touching is considered vulgar.

Faux Pas

- Elderly are respected, so honor should always be shown to them, especially in public places.
- Do not visit a church or a religious site while dressed improperly, such as in short shorts, tank tops, or cutoff shorts or shirts.
- Avoid using the Lord's name in vain. It's considered very offensive to many Mexicans.
- Do not bargain in the large stores. Bargaining can be done in smaller stores and outdoor markets. With street vendors, it is very natural and expected.
- Ask permission before you take pictures of the local people.
- Remember to show patience. Delays and interruptions are common, so do not show anger or disappointment.
- Never use red ink if writing a person's name.
- Making jokes about "Montezuma's revenge" is inappropriate.

USEFUL FACTS

President	Felipe Calderon (2006) The President is both the Chief of State and Head of Government
National Name	Estados Unidos Mexicanos
Size	742,485 square miles (1,923,039 square km)
Population	109,955,400 (2008)
Capital	Mexico City
Government	Federal Republic
Currency	Mexican peso
Religion	Roman Catholic 89%, Protestant 6%, Others 5%
Language	Spanish is the official language. More than 100 Native American languages are spoken in Mexico, including Nahuatl, Mayan, and other regional indigenous languages.
Ethnicity	Mestizo (Amerindian-Spanish) 60%, Amerindian or predominantly Amerindian 30%, white 9%, other 1%
Industry	Food and beverages, tobacco, chemicals, iron and steel, petroleum, mining, and tourism
Time Zone	Mexico's Standard Time Zone is six hours behind Greenwich Mean Time (GMT -6) or one hour behind Eastern Standard Time (EST -l). Mexico observes daylight saving time and is in the same time zone as U.S. Central Standard Time zone (CST).
Telephone Code	International Code +52 City Code: +55 (Mexico City)
Weather	Varies from tropical to desert. Hurricane season is typically from late April to October.

Mexico

| Voltage/Frequency | 110 V; 60 Hz |
| | (same as in the United States and Canada) |

HOLIDAYS/FESTIVALS

1 January	New Year's Day
February, first Monday	Anniversary of Constitution of 1917
March, third Monday	Anniversary of the Birth of Benito Juarez
1 May	Labor Day/May Day
5 May	Anniversary of the Battle of Puebla
16 September	Independence Day/National Day
12 October	Discovery of America
November, third Monday	Anniversary of the Mexican Revolution
12 December	Guadalupe Day
25 December	Christmas

LANGUAGE TIPS

Spanish	Phonetics	English
Habla ingles?	Ah-blah een-glehs	Do you speak English?
(No) Hablo...	noh ah-bloh	I (don't) speak...
(No) Entiendo	noh ehn-tyen-doh	I (don't) understand
Puede ayudarme?	Pweh-deh ah-yoo-dar-meh	Can you help me?
Como se dice ___	koh-moh seh dee-seh ___	How do you say ___
en espanol?	ehn eh-spahn-yol	in Spanish?
Que es esto?	Keh ehs ehs-toh	What is this?
Buenos dias	bway-nohs dee-ahs	Hello/Good morning
Buenas tardes	bway-nahs tard-ays	Good afternoon
Adios	ah-dee-ohs	Good-bye
Hasta pronto	ah-stah prohn-toh	See you soon.

See other chapters of Spanish-speaking countries for additional words and phrases.

Chapter 18: THE NETHERLANDS

LOCATION/GEOGRAPHY

The Netherlands is located in Western Europe between Belgium and Germany and borders the North Sea.

DID YOU KNOW?

- Holland is one of 12 provinces that make up the country. The country is officially called The Netherlands. Even though Amsterdam is the capital, the royal home is located in The Hague.
- Amsterdam and Venice each have approximately 400 bridges. Venice's bridges cross approximately 150 canals, while the bridges in Amsterdam cross only 40 canals.
- Two-thirds of Holland was once covered by water. After water was pumped out, the drained areas called, *polders*, became some of the richest farmlands in The Netherlands. Almost half of The Netherlands lies beneath sea level, with the lowest point in Nieuwerkerk aan den Yssel at minus 6.76 meters (22 feet).
- The Dutch fought Spain 80 years to gain their independence.
- The Caribbean islands of Antilles and Aruba are part of The Netherlands.
- The city of Rotterdam has the largest seaport in the world.
- The largest museum in Amsterdam, the Rijksmuseum, is home to the famous paintings of Rembrandt.
- Prostitution is legal in The Netherlands. Recognizing that brothels in the "Red Light District" are a given fact, the government collects taxes, maintains health inspections, and controls minors there.
- Same-sex marriages were legalized in 2000 and euthanasia was legalized in 2002.
- Natural gas was discovered in the Netherlands in 1959 and provided a needed boost to the Dutch economy.

BUSINESS ETIQUETTE

Punctuality

- For both business and pleasure, being on time is essential and expected. Efficient use of time is of tremendous importance to the Dutch.
- Showing up late creates a perception of being untrustworthy, and it is perceived that you will not be able to meet deadlines. A phone call is necessary if you anticipate that you will be a little late.

- Being impatient and rushing is an indication that you have not planned properly.
- The abbreviation asap, or their *z.s.m.*, generally means at your earliest convenience.

Meeting Manners

- Plan and schedule appointments carefully and avoid changing at the last minute. Spontaneity is not appreciated in the business culture. Canceling could jeopardize any future meetings.
- Allow one to two weeks to schedule an appointment by phone or fax. If scheduling through the mail, allow at least one month. July and August and late December are considered their main holiday periods, so don't try to schedule meetings at these times.
- Making contacts is a major portion of doing good business in The Netherlands. More established companies may want a third-party introduction.
- Very little chitchat or pleasantries are exchanged before a meeting. But after some time, a more personal approach will be accepted if they feel the business will last over a longer period of time. Generally, meetings are more formal and will follow the agenda. Always state a starting and ending time.
- Printed material should be translated into Dutch, but if it is not, then make sure it is clear and concise. Only use high quality brochures and material.
- If using PowerPoint for presentations, keep the slides to a minimal number. The Dutch want solid, statistical facts describing your products or idea.
- Acknowledge by mail when you receive a contract or important business letters. Use international courier services such as FedEx, UPS, or DHL to track delivery and guarantee a quicker and more efficient delivery. Other correspondence can be done by e-mail.
- Keep a formal appearance and tone in all correspondence. Your letter may be shared with other departments. Even if you have moved to a first name basis with the person to whom you are corresponding, use the professional title and surname.
- Avoid stating you are "number one" or "the best" in what you do. Build trust by proving yourself, delivering what you promise, and being honest and straightforward in all aspects of business.
- If you mean no, say no. The Dutch appreciate a candid reply instead of tentative or indecisive answers.

- Women business travelers are treated with considerable respect. However, women in the Dutch labor arena have not made as much progress as they would hope. Fewer women work outside the home, and women in higher ranking positions are not common.
- Reaching a final decision may be a slow process. Generally, all employees that might be affected by a business decision will be consulted.
- Since the family and personal time is so valued, be careful not to ask to meet over the weekend or stay late to work.
- Avoid giving individualized compliments, since so much of the work is done in groups. Even the problems will be credited to the system and not the individual. Compliments or criticism are given in private. Rarely will workers be publicly recognized.
- Privacy is respected and most doors are kept closed both at home and in the workplace. Always knock first and wait to be invited to enter.

Business Cards

- Business cards may not be exchanged initially but at the end of the meeting.
- If your native language is something other than Dutch or English, have your home language on one side of the business card and Dutch on the other. Most Dutch businesspeople are fluent in English. You should translate promotional material into Dutch when dealing with complicated terminology.
- Higher education is very important, so degrees above a B.A. are listed on their cards, but it is improper to bring it up in conversation.

Meals/Toasts

- Do not be offended if you are not invited to a business lunch. Generally their lunch period is shorter and not considered enough time for a business discussion. Most companies will even have an eating area for employees.
- Remain standing until you are invited to sit down as there might be a particular seat for you.
- Women generally will take their seats before the men are seated.
- Allow the hostess to start eating before you begin.
- The utensils are held throughout the meal, not put down.
- Always use utensils when eating, even finger foods other than small snacks, French fries, and rolls. Fruit, cheese, bread, sandwiches, and pizza should all be eaten with a fork and knife. Avoid cutting the lettuce; instead fold it onto your fork.

- If appropriate, take small amounts of food so you can accept second helpings. Finish everything on your plate because it is considered offensive to waste food.
- When you have finished your meal, place the knife and fork parallel across the right side of your plate.
- Women may pay for drinks or meal after a longer relationship.
- Wine is common at meals and the host will propose the first toast and use the term *proost* (cheers). Generally *proost* is for beer and soft drinks. The French *sante* or just glances will be used for a toast of wine. It's important to always raise your glass in the direction of the toast.
- The honored guest should return the toast later in the meal.

 ## Entertainment

- Good topics of conversation include your home country or city, your flight and accommodations, politics (if you are well versed in them), and sports.
- Avoid conversations bragging about your possessions and income, criticizing the Dutch Royal Family (you can ask about them), religion, sex, or legalized prostitution.
- The Dutch drink a lot of stronger blend coffees.
- Dinner for business entertaining generally will take place in a restaurant rather than in a private home.
- If invited to a home, consider it a great honor. The Dutch protect their privacy.
- The Dutch will eat dinner fairly early. If you are extended an invitation for 6:30 p.m. (1830), then you are their dinner guest. If you're invited to come at 8 p.m. (2000), then don't necessarily expect dinner to be included.
- The host and hostess generally will sit facing one another at opposite ends of the table. The male guest of honor will be to the right of the host and the female guest of honor is seated to the right of the hostess. This position is considered an honor. Wait to be shown to your seat instead of just coming in and sitting.
- Keep you hands resting on the table, not in your lap, during the meal.

 ## Forms of Address/Introductions/Greetings

- A firm and quick handshake will begin and end a conversation for both men and women. Men and women will shake hands, but allow the woman to extend her hand first. Shake hands with everyone individually. If walking into a larger office, a polite nod to anyone you are not introduced to is acceptable. The "group wave" to say hello is saved for more casual and private gatherings.

- Never sit as you are being introduced.
- An arm's length is the comfortable distance for contact.
- Eye contact is a sign of sincerity. Constantly looking away is perceived as sneaky, dishonest, or a lack of social skills.
- Academic titles are reserved for correspondence and for work. They are not used in speech or in private contacts.
- A professional title followed by the last name should be used until you are invited to transition to a less formal greeting.
- Mr. is spelled *Meneer* and abbreviated in writing as *Dhr.* Mrs. and Ms. is abbreviated in writing as *Mevr.* and *Mw.*
- Formality is evident in first meetings. Allow the Dutch contact to introduce you to others that are present. If this does not happen, then you can introduce yourself, including your name and your company.
- If you do get to the point of exchanging a kiss, be ready for three of them (left, right, left) and do this as a welcome and farewell.
- At informal gatherings and when partners are involved, the woman may kiss all the guests good-bye, which would be two or three air kisses on the cheek. The men might do the same with the ladies.
- No bear hugs. This is not common in the Netherlands nor is it welcomed.

Appearance/Attire

- Dress is fairly conservative and depends on the level of position and profession. Appearance is very important to the Dutch.
- In banks, you will still find dark suits and ties and women in dark suits and white blouses, while most Dutch will dress more informally.
- In some industries, you will find the higher ranking in more casual dress of jeans, while the sales team will be in suits.
- If the Dutch remove their jackets as you start your meeting, by all means follow their lead.
- If in doubt about what to wear, call ahead to find out the appropriate attire.
- Formal wear is reserved for formal dinners, an opening night, or the theater.
- Shorts are for only jogging or hiking.

Gift Giving

- The Dutch are uncomfortable in giving or receiving large gifts, favors, or preferential treatment. A small gift is more appropriate and much less of an obligation. Large gifts are also perceived as bribes or unfair treatment to others.
- Presents are generally not given until a relationship has been established.
- Even though not expensive, the gift should be of good quality.
- A bouquet of flowers or a potted plant is recommended for the hostess if you're invited to a Dutch home. Flowers could also be sent the next day if more appropriate. Give flowers in odd numbers, avoiding 13, which is unlucky. White lilies and chrysanthemums are not recommended, since they are associated with funerals.
- Wine can also be given, but wine collecting is very popular, so your selection needs to match the host. The wine presented may not be opened because it may not be appropriate for the food being served.
- Belgian chocolate or other candy is also a good gift to bring to a home, especially if there are children. If you know in advance that children will be in the home, then bring gifts of small toys or candy for them.
- Other gift ideas include a book from your country or city, imported liquor, desk accessories, a good pen, and designer quality electronic devices.
- Avoid all pointed items, including knives or scissors, because they are considered unlucky.
- Make sure all gifts are wrapped nicely. Generally gifts are opened when received.

 Tipping

- Tipping in a restaurant is generally 5 percent to 10 percent. Gratuities, according to the law, are included in the bill. If you were pleased, then tip accordingly.
- Rounding to the closest euro is sufficient for taxi drivers.
- A chambermaid should be left one to two euros (US$1.50 to US$3) per day.
- A washroom attendant should be tipped 50 eurocents (US$.40).

 Gesture Awareness

- Body language and speaking should be quiet, relaxed, and never extravagant.
- To summon a waiter, just make eye contact and nod to get attention. If neither works, then raise your hand but not in a commanding gesture.

- Since the Dutch are more serious, smiling is not required or expected in business or for customer service. Constant smiling is felt to be a sign of insincerity.
- If in a smaller space like a theater or in an elevator, it is rude to press past a person with your back facing them. At least apologize, but it's much better to turn around and face them as you pass.
- Tapping the center of your forehead with your index finger is a sign for "crazy" and is considered an impolite gesture.

Faux Pas

- It is bad manners to just say "*hoi*" or "hi" to people that are definitely older than you or higher ranking.
- Avoid yawning, chewing gum, and using toothpicks in public.
- Do not have your hands in your pockets while you are talking. It's considered rude.
- Do not break promises. The Dutch are serious about what they say or they won't make a promise.
- Avoid displaying your wealth or accomplishments; boasting is against their customs.
- Don't ask personal questions of the Dutch. Their personal life is kept very separate from their work.

USEFUL FACTS

Sovereign:	Queen Beatrix (1980)
Prime Minister	Jan Peter Balkenende (2002)
National Name	Kingdom of the Netherlands
Size	13,104 square miles (33,939 square km)
Population	16,645,313 (2008)
Capital	Amsterdam
Government	Constitutional Monarchy
Currency	Euro (formerly guilder)

Religion	Roman Catholic 31%, Protestant 21%, Muslim 4%, other 3%, unaffiliated 40%
Language	Dutch and Frisian (both official language)
Ethnicity	Dutch 83%, other 17% (9% of non-Western origin, mainly Turk, Moroccan, Surinamese, Antillean, and Indonesian)
Industry	Agriculture, metal and engineering products, electrical machinery and equipment, natural gas, chemicals, petroleum, microelectronics, fishing
Time Zone	The Netherlands is one hour ahead Greenwich Mean Time (GMT +1) or six hours ahead of U.S. Eastern Standard Time (EST +6). The Netherlands observes daylight saving time.
Telephone Code	International Code: +31 City Code: +20 (Amsterdam)
Weather	Summers in The Netherlands are mostly warm, with some variation, but rarely excessively hot. The winters are fairly cold with some snow. Rainfall is common year-round.
Voltage/Frequency	230 V: 50 Hz

HOLIDAYS/FESTIVALS

1 January	New Year's Day
March/April	Good Friday
March/April	Easter
30 April	Queen's Day (Celebrated on the birthday of the late Queen- Mother, Juliana.)
4 May	Remembrance of the Dead
5 May	Liberation Day (Celebration of the 1945 capitulation of German forces in World War II. Celebrated yearly until 2000, then an official holiday once every five years.)
5 December	Saint Nicholas' Eve

| 25, 26 December | Christmas (The Dutch celebrate two days of Christmas. *Eerste Kerstday* (the first day of Christmas) and *Tweede Kerstdag* (the second day of Christmas.) |

LANGUAGE TIPS

Dutch	Phonetics	English
Hallo	Hah-low	Hello
Goedemorgen	Goo-duh-More-gun	Good morning
Hoe gaat het?	Hoo gaht hut	How are you?
Goed, dank u.	Goot, dahnk uu	Fine, thank you
Alstublieft	Ahl-stuu-bleeft	Please
Dank u	Dahnk uu	Thank you
Graag gedaan	Grahg guh-dahn	You're welcome
Ja/Nee	Yah/Nay	Yes/No
Waar is het toilet?	Wahr is hut twah-LET	Where is the toilet?
Tot ziens	Tot seens	Good-bye
Waar is het museum?	Wahr is hat muu-zay-uhm	Where is the museum?

Chapter 19: NEW ZEALAND

LOCATION/GEOGRAPHY

Even though many people automatically presume that New Zealand and Australia are geographically close, they are actually 1,250 miles (2,012 km) miles apart. They are neighbors, but a lot of water separates them. New Zealand consists of many small outlying islands and two main islands. The North Island is 44,281 square miles (115,777 square km) and 515 miles (829 km) long. This island has many hot springs, beautiful geysers and volcanic in its south-central area. The South Island is 58,093 square miles (151,215 square km). The Southern Alps are along the west coast with Mount Cook as the highest point

DID YOU KNOW?

- The literacy rate is 100%
- New Zealand was the world's first country to give women the right to vote in 1893.
- Even though the head of state is Queen Elizabeth II, the government is actually conducted by a Prime Minister and Cabinet selected from an elected Parliament.
- New Zealand was the first country in the world to have all of its highest offices occupied by women (from March 2005 to August 2006). This included the Queen, Governor-General, Prime Minister, Speaker of the New Zealand House of Representatives and the Chief Justice.
- New Zealand has always been advanced with all social welfare legislation; including adopting old-age pensions in 1898; a national child welfare program in 1907; social security for widows, orphans and the elderly along with family benefit payments; minimum wages; 40-hour workweek and unemployment and health insurance in 1938; and socialized medicine in 1941.
- The Maori language is only used in New Zealand.
- Maoris are well known and highly regarded for the art of tattooing.
- The Maori, a Polynesian people, were the first to inhabit New Zealand.
- Your passport must be valid for at least three months past the date you intend to leave New Zealand.
- Tap water is safe to drink.
- The kiwi (a flightless bird) is the national emblem and New Zealanders often refer to themselves as Kiwis.
- In June 2003, parliament legalized prostitution.
- In December of 204, New Zealand recognized same-sex unions.
- No one is more than 75 miles (120 km) from the ocean.

BUSINESS ETIQUETTE

Punctuality

- Arrive on time and plan your appointments in advance.
- Your tardiness shows a careless attitude and is not acceptable.

Meeting Manners

- Appointments are necessary and should be made at least one week in advance. These meetings can be set up by telephone, fax, or e-mail.
- If planned well in advance, it will be easy to set up a meeting with a senior level executive.
- Always arrive a few minutes early for all your meetings. Arriving late, even if for a few minutes, indicates that your time is more important than the person you are meeting.
- New Zealanders agree with Australians in regard to an egalitarian society. They show respect for all, regardless of wealth and social status. The same applies regarding the hype and production in business. Be direct and honest in your negotiations.
- The meetings will take on a more relaxed atmosphere but do not be confused because they are still taken very seriously.
- Their negotiating process does take time, so do not rush or attempt high-pressure sales approaches.
- The meeting will begin with minimal small talk and then you will proceed with the business portion.
- They operate a lot slower than the United States but a little faster than in Australia.
- Stay focused and stick to the point during your discussions. Avoid any emotions or feelings. They want your bottom line with facts and figures. Do not offer unrealistic promises that you cannot keep. New Zealanders are direct and expect the same in return.
- Honesty and directness are appreciated in your business dealings.
- Make sure your proposals and contracts clearly state all conditions and points in detail.
- The initial meetings will normally happen in an office. Later meetings may move to a lunch in a restaurant or hotel.
- Lunch is appropriate for business, but dinner is reserved for a more social event. Leave the business for the next day. It is also appropriate to include your partner for an evening get-together.
- December and January are their prime times for summer vacation so it's hard to schedule or set up meetings then.

Business Cards

- Keep your business cards in good condition by using a business card holder.
- Generally the visiting person will hand their business card first.
- Present with two hands with your name facing the recipient.

- Read the card when presented and may place the cards so they are visible during a meeting to refer properly to the people in attendance.
- Avoid ever placing the card in your back pocket.
- Avoid ever writing on the person's card.

Meals/Toasts

- Arrive on time for all appointments and meals.
- Wait to be seated. They will tell you where to sit.
- Meals may be served family-style.
- While eating, keep your elbows off the table and both hands above the table.
- Eating is Continental style with the fork in your left hand and the knife in the right hand while eating.
- When it is time to eat, they mostly eat. Talking generally will take place before and after the meal.
- To show that you have completed the meal, place the knife and fork parallel on your plate with the handles facing to the right.
- Even though dinners are more for social gatherings and minimal business discussion, it is appropriate to discuss business over lunch.

Entertainment

- Entertaining in a home is something they love to do and is very common.
- Make sure you understand the difference between "tea" and "afternoon tea." Afternoon tea is served between 3 p.m. and 4 p.m. (1500 to 1600). Tea is an evening meal served from 6 p.m. to 8 p.m. (1800 to 2000). Tea will provide enough food, so do not plan to go out to eat after that. Supper is a late night snack.
- Stay in control while you are drinking. Learn to pace yourself.
- If invited to a home, bring gifts of flowers, chocolate, or whiskey.
- The more formal the occasion, the more formal the protocol.
- You are always safe with topics regarding politics and sports. New Zealanders love the outdoors and sports. Their sports include golf, netball, soccer, rugby and cricket. They enjoy competitive sports as well as hiking, fishing, and sailing.
- Stay current and informed on their cultural topics.
- Avoid any racial topics and the treatment of the Maori people.

Forms of Address/Introductions/Greetings

- It is customary to shake hands at the beginning and end of meetings or gatherings.
- Good eye contact is essential during the handshake. This shows genuine interest in the other person.
- Allow a few feet for personal space.
- Women do shake other women's hands and will often exchange a greeting with a kiss on the check with a friend.
- Men may wait for a woman to extend her hand first for a handshake.
- Remember that hearing "*G'day*" over and over gets to be a little old. "How do you do?" or "hello" is a much more common exchange.
- Titles do not impress.
- Even though New Zealanders are more reserved, they are kind, polite, and warm.
- Always address people using their titles, or Mr., Mrs., or Miss plus the full name.
- "Mate" is used more often than sir. It is used to refer to one's own sex. Women also refer to another woman as "mate." "My mates," refers to one's friends.
- Many have been christened with two names—an original Maori name and an adopted English one. In some cases, these names are used interchangeably.
- You might see two people pressing their noses. This is the traditional Maoris greeting.

 Appearance/Attire

- Generally their dress is a little more informal than Europe or Asia.
- Fashions follow the North American trends but are a little more formal than the United States.
- Since the weather is temperate, lightweight clothes with a jacket or sweater work most of the time. Keep the rain gear handy in some areas.
- Business dress is more conservative, with dark suits and ties for men. Jackets are usually discarded in the summer months.
- Women's dress for business can be a suit, dress, slacks, or skirt.
- To convey the casual but classy look for social events, stay with neutral colors of navy, gray, camel, ivory, and white. Your casual shoes still need to be in proper shape.

Gift Giving

- When invited to a home, bring a modest gift, but it is not expected.
- Flowers, chocolates, wine or whiskey, or gifts from your home country would be appropriate gifts for a home invitation.
- Gifts will be opened when they are received.
- Try to know the interests of the person receiving the gift.
- Gifts are not generally given or exchanged in a business situation but are appreciated. Come prepared.
- A coffee table book from your home country is a great gift and appreciated.

Tipping

- Tipping is rare.
- A tip could even be refused if offered.
- More common is rounding up taxi fares to the nearest couple of dollars.
- Some restaurants, bars, and hotels do have an extra service charge on public holidays that amounts to a 10 percent to 20 percent increase.

Gesture Awareness

- The "V" sign for victory is obscene, especially when your palm is facing inward.
- Chewing gum and using a toothpick in public are both considered rude.
- New Zealanders have a very soft speech and loud voices are annoying to them.
- Nothing is overdone. They watch their actions and gestures and maintain the traditional British reserve.

Faux Pas

- Politics can be very opinionated. Be ready for a debate but without any insulting or personal attacks. Take a stand; you are respected for having knowledge and defending your beliefs.
- Don't confuse New Zealand with Australia. They are different countries with their own identity; they just happen to be in the same area of the world.
- If you yawn in public, make sure you cover your mouth.
- Ask permission before you take a photo of a person, especially the Maori.
- New Zealanders are extremely concerned about their environment and a major issue is the importing of predators. They are extremely tight on

border controls and will give huge fines for importing food or any other natural products (wood, cane, etc.).

- There is a strong belief that if you damage the environment you damage their "life force," or *mauri*. If the *mauri* loses its energy or vitality, then the lives of the people are affected as well and their ecosystems.

 ## USEFUL FACTS

Sovereign	Queen Elizabeth II (1952)
Governor-General	Anand Satyanard (2006)
Prime Minister	Helen Clark (1999)
National Name	New Zealand
Size	103,737 square miles (268,680 square km)
Population	4,266,537 (2008)
Capital	Wellington
Government	Parliamentary Democracy
Currency	New Zealand dollar
Religion	Anglican 15%, Presbyterian 11%, Roman Catholic 12%, Methodist 3%, Baptist 1%, Pentecostal 2%, Other Christians 9%, none 26%
Language	English and Maori both are the official language of New Zealand. In 2006, New Zealand became the first country to announce sign language as their third official language.
Ethnicity	European 73%, Maori 7%, mixed 7%, Pacific Islander 4%, Asian 7%, others 2%.

New Zealand

Industry	Food processing, wood and paper products, textiles, machinery, transportation, equipment, banking, insurance, tourism, agriculture, and mining
Time Zone	New Zealand is 12 hours ahead of Greenwich Mean Time GMT (GMT +12) or 17 hours ahead of U.S. Eastern Standard Time (EST +17). New Zealand observes daylight saving time.
Telephone Code	International code: +64 City code: +4 (Wellington)
Weather	Coldest months are July and August, with average lows of 44-47 F (6.6-8.3C) with 5.2 rainfall per month. Warmest months are January, February, and March, with highs of 71-79 F (21.6-26.1 C). The rainfall is only 2.8 to 3.4 in Auckland.
Voltage/Frequency	230/240 V; 50 Hz

HOLIDAYS/FESTIVALS

1-2 January	New Year's Holiday
6 February	Waitangi Day (Signed in 1840 as the Treaty of Waitangi and considered New Zealand's founding document)
March/April	Good Friday
March/April	Easter
March/April	Easter Monday
25 April	ANZAC Day (War Remembrance Day)
3 June	Queen's Birthday
28 October	Labor Day
25 December	Christmas Day
26 December	Boxing Day

LANGUAGE TIPS

Even though New Zealand is an English-speaking country, they have their own dialect.

Mate	Friend
Digger	Australian
Amber	Beer
Neck oil	Beer
Roo	Kangaroo
Heart starter	First drink of the day
Cargo	Garbage person
Barby	Barbecue
Full bottle	Knowledgeable
Whinger	Complainer

Chapter 20: PORTUGAL

LOCATION/GEOGRAPHY

Portugal is located in southwestern Europe. It is bordered by Spain on the east and north and by the North Atlantic Ocean on the west and south.

DID YOU KNOW?
- Statistically, the Portuguese are the worst drivers in Europe.
- Portugal was founded by Alfonso Henriques in 1152.
- Rio de Janeiro, Brazil, was the capital of Portugal from 1807 to 1821, while Portugal was fighting France in the Napoleonic Wars.
- Dinosaur tracks can still be seen clearly in the Parque Natural das Serras de Aire e Candeeiros and Parque Natural da Arrabida. There are also rock carvings in the Coa Valley that date from 22,000 BC to 10,000 BC.
- Ferdinand Magellan and Vasco da Gama studied at a school for mapmakers, astronomers, and navigators in Portugal. Vasco da Gama discovered the sea route to India at the end of the 1490s and Ferdinand Magellan was the first to complete a circumnavigation of the world in 1522.
- The Portuguese explorer, Bartholomew Diaz was the first to sail the southern tip of Africa, which he named the Cape of Good Hope.
- Since the eighteenth century, it has been illegal to kill bulls in Portuguese bullfighting.
- An earthquake in Lisbon in 1755 destroyed most of the city and killed over 30,000 people.
- The slave trade was outlawed in Portugal in 1850.
- The Virgin Mary was said to have appeared to children in the town of Fatima in 1917. This city today is a major pilgrimage site.
- Mario Soares was elected the first civilian President of Portugal in 1986.

USINESS ETIQUETTE

Punctuality
- Since business is generally more formal, it is important that you arrive on time.
- A business deal could be at risk by arriving late, since punctuality displays respect for that person.
- Even if you are kept waiting for your meeting, do not display irritation.
- You will find that people from the north will be more punctual than those from the southern sector.

- If you are attending a large social event, arriving 30 minutes to one hour after the stipulated start time is acceptable.

Meeting Manners

- Loyalty to the family takes precedence over any business, and the Portuguese extended family is very close.
- It's a good idea to have a mutual contact to provide initial introductions.
- The Portuguese prefer to do business with people they trust and with whom they have established a comfort level. The Portuguese build their relationships with an individual as opposed to a company. If the contact person or representative from a company changes during the negotiations, chances are that relationship and business process will start all over again.
- It's advisable to set up appointments at least one or two weeks in advance. Reconfirm your meeting a few days in advance.
- Avoid the month of August for meetings, since most Portuguese citizens take this time for holiday. Also try to avoid the week between Christmas and New Year.
- Initially, your correspondence should be written in Portuguese.
- You should have your printed material in both Portuguese and English.
- Much time is spent developing a good relationship. So allow ample "getting-to-know-you" time before you begin your business conversations.
- Try to schedule more face-to-face meetings. These meetings are still preferred over what is perceived as impersonal e-mails, letters, or phone conversations.
- Respect throughout the business process is important, and the embarrassment of a fellow colleague destroys trust and respect.
- Strict rules of protocol are followed and the meetings are formal.
- Agendas are important, but you can deviate from the schedule.
- Presentations need to be thorough, with statistical charts and figures.
- Generally the Portuguese have a more relaxed attitude toward time and deadlines.
- Interruptions or questions generally will wait until the end of a presentation.
- If you have questions, ask. The Portuguese are honest, but if it to their advantage, they may remain silent rather than offer information.
- Contracts will be respected.
- Women are in positions of authority.
- You will find nepotism very common in business, since they feel employing people they know and trust builds a stronger foundation.

- Portuguese are conservative and extremely polite, while always tending toward formality.
- The Portuguese culture still maintains and respects hierarchy, so their businesses are stratified and structured vertically. These structures are based on the Catholic church and family structure.
- Decisions are more often determined by one person than a group of individuals.
- Generally, decisions are not made at meetings.

Business Cards

- There is no formal etiquette for exchanging business cards other than just normal politeness.
- Generally, business cards are exchanged at the first meeting immediately after shaking hands.

Meals/Toasts

- Remain standing when you arrive. Wait to be invited to sit down because you most likely will be escorted to a particular seat.
- Table manners are formal. Their table manners are continental, with the fork in the left hand and the knife in the right.
- Wait for your hostess to signal the start of the meal with *"bom appetito"* before you start to eat.
- Make sure your hands are visible at all times during the meal but do not place your elbows on the table.
- Most of your food will be eaten with utensils. This even includes fruit and cheese.
- Your napkin should stay to the left of your plate while eating or it may be placed on your lap. When your meal is completed, move your napkin to the right of your plate.
- To rest or signify you are not finished eating, cross your knife and fork on your plate with the fork over the knife.
- Leave a little food on your plate when you have finished with your meal.
- To indicate you are finished with your meal, place your fork and knife parallel on your plate, tines facing up with the handles facing to the right.

Entertainment

- Avoid discussing business in a social gathering.
- If invited to a home, arrive no later than 15 minutes from the designated start time.
- It's common to invite an associate out for lunch or dinner. The dinner is the more social event, but it's good to ask your Portuguese associate to select the restaurant. To create a solid relationship, it is important that you have the correct setting.
- Be clear and up front that you will be paying if you are the inviter. You can handle this with the wait staff by specifically asking for the check. Your Portuguese colleagues will generally try to pay, as hospitality is part of their culture..
- If just enjoying a casual meal with colleagues, then it's common for everyone to pay for themselves.
- To signal the wait staff that you want the check, get their attention by writing in the air.
- If you want something during the meal, it's perfectly fine to signal by just raising your hand for the waiter.
- If you are invited to a Fado restaurant, where the traditional *Fado* music is performed, then plan to enjoy. It is extremely rude to talk during the music, so these settings are not good for discussing business.

Forms of Address/Introductions/Greetings

- Initial greetings are polite but reserved.
- The handshake with good eye contact is the standard form of greeting.
- Don't be too weak, but also do not give a power handshake with a firm grip.
- Once a more personal relationship is developed, men may greet one another with a handshake and hug. Women may kiss both men and women two times on the cheeks, starting with the right cheek. But rather than start by kissing, offer your hand first and allow them to progress. It may go to a hug and then the kisses after you build a good, solid relationship.
- It's very common to grip the arm or place a hand on your shoulder.
- You may see people walking down the street with their hand on another's upper arm. This is a gesture of warmth and trust.
- People in Portugal will stand closer than in North America and Northern Europe. They will also maintain more intense eye contact. Do not back away from them or divert your eyes.
- Titles are observed with "*senhor*" and "*senhora*" and the surnames.
- People with university degrees are addressed with their honorific titles plus "*doutour*" or "*doutoura*" (doctor), with or without their surname.

- Do not use first names until invited to do so. Stay more formal until your Portuguese associate suggests the change.

Appearance/Attire

- Dress is conservative and there is a slight difference between business and social dress.
- Keep your jacket on during meetings unless your Portuguese associates remove theirs first. If it gets hot and you don't see them removing their jacket, you may ask if you could remove yours. Just avoid rolling up your sleeves unless they do first.
- Senior level businessmen will wear sports jacket, pants, and tie. Some will remain more businesslike with a suit.
- Men will wear long-sleeved shirts. You will find foreign men wearing short sleeved shirts with a tie.
- If men are invited to a meal, then they will show up in a tie. Social events like the theater (play or opera) will be more formal. It's rare to see a black tie or more formal dress for women.
- Women will wear pants (trousers) as part of a suit or a more in-style outfit.
- Most companies are still in business dress but some are making the exception with "dress down" Fridays.
- The Portuguese are dress conscious, so clothes need to be coordinated and always clean.
- Come prepared with a jacket or sweater even in the summer because the evenings can get a little cold.
- You will still find the national dress in the northern Minho province for weddings and other festivals or in Madeira for the local markets and flower stalls.
- The traditional garments like the red and green stocking cap of the Alentejo cattleman and the *samara* (a short jacket with a collar of fox fur) can still be found.
- Wearing black for mourning is still very common in the villages.

Gift Giving

- If invited to a Portuguese home, bring flowers, good quality chocolates, or candy for the hostess.
- If you do not arrive with a gift, then send flowers the next day.
- It is considered unlucky to give 13 flowers.
- Lilies and chrysanthemums are used for funerals so it is not wise to present them to your host.

- Red is the symbol of the revolution so do not present red flowers.
- It's better not to bring wine unless you know what your host enjoys and prefers.
- Gifts are generally opened when presented or exchanged.

Tipping

- A 10 percent tip is generous. Service charges are not included in checks.
- If you need a receipt for expenses, you may need to ask for a copy.
- If you plan to pay by credit card, check in advance. Not all establishments will take credit cards or they may accept just certain ones. Visa is the most widely accepted card.

Gesture Awareness

- Be careful with hand gestures while you are speaking, since this can be perceived as overly demonstrative.
- To get a person's attention, they will extend their arm upward with the palm out and wiggle their fingers up and down. It looks like they are patting a person on the head.
- The thumbs-up sign is used to signal OK and sometimes will be done with both hands.
- Kissing the side of your index finger and then pinching your earlobe between the kissed finger and the thumb is a gesture used in Portugal to show that you enjoyed the dinner and want to extend a compliment to the hostess.
- To signal "I don't know" is displayed by the chin flick gesture of brushing your fingers (palm inward) off the bottom of your chin and away from your face. Doing the same gesture but with the thumb would indicate that something no longer exists or has died.

Faux Pas

- The Portuguese are very respectful of age and position, so be careful when addressing or dealing with people in hierarchical positions.
- Even if you feel comments are justified, the Portuguese do not appreciate direct criticism.
- Avoid aggressive tactics during a business deal.
- Do not use the American style of eating, placing your knife on the plate and switching to the fork. It's considered poor manners.
- Do not stretch in public.
- It's rare to find Portuguese people eating with their fingers. Avoid licking your fingers no matter how yummy or sticky the food may be.

- Don't turn your back to a person in a group; it is disrespectful. If you are sitting next to a person at dinner and want to turn to the person on the other side, excuse yourself first.
- Don't write anything in red ink. It's considered an insult. The only ones allowed to use red ink are teachers correcting their student's work.
- Although smoking is common, don't light up before asking those around you.
- You can cross your legs in both formal and relaxed situations, but avoid putting your feet on furniture or taking a more relaxed position. Maintain good posture.

USEFUL FACTS

President	Anibal Cavaco Silva (2006)
Prime Minister	Jose Socrates Carvalho Pinto de Sousa (2005)
National Name	Republica Portuguesa
Size	35,382 square miles (91,639 square km)
Population	10,676,910 (2008)
Capital	Libson
Government	Parliamentary Democracy
Currency	Euro (formerly escudo)
Religion	Roman Catholic 84%, other Christian 2%, other 0.3%, Unknown 9%, none 4%
Language	Portuguese (official) and Mirandese (unofficial, but locally used)
Ethnicity	Homogeneous Mediterranean stock with less than 100,000 citizens of black African descent who immigrated to the mainland during decolonization. East Europeans have entered Portugal since 1990.

Industry	Agriculture, textiles, footwear, pulp, paper, metals, oil refining, machinery, chemicals, fishing, and tourism
Time Zone	Portugal is the same as Greenwich Mean Time (GMT) or five hours ahead of U.S. Eastern Standard Time (EST +5). Portugal does observe daylight saving time.
Telephone Code	International Code: +351 City Code: +21 (Lisbon)
Weather	The weather varies considerably from region to region but Portugal has a temperate climate. In most parts of Portugal, the best time to visit is between April and October. The summers are mostly dry and clear, spring and fall sunny and warm and winters mild. The rainy season runs from November to March.

 ## HOLIDAYS/FESTIVALS

1 January	New Year's Day
February	Mardi Gras – Shrove Tuesday
March/April	Good Friday and Easter
25 April	Liberty Day (Anniversary of the peaceful military revolution in 1974 that overthrew the fascist regime)
1 May	Labor Day
10 June	Camoes Memorial Day (In memory of the death of Portugese poet Luiz Vaz de Camoes [1524—1580] who is best known for the epic poem, The Lusiad)
June	Corpus Christi (Christian feast celebrating the Eucharist)
15 August	Assumption of Mary
5 October	Republic Day (Commemorates the establishment of a Republican form of government in 1910, when the monarchy that had been in power since the 11th century was overthrown in a bloodless revolution)
1 November	All Saint's Day (Day for visiting deceased relatives)
1 December	Restoration of the Independence (Event of 1640)
December 8	Immaculate Conception
25 December	Christmas

LANGUAGE TIPS

Portuguese	Phonetics	English
Bom dia	Bomm dee-a	Hello/Hi
Sim/Nao	Seem/Now	Yes/No
Adeus	A-day-osh	Good-bye
Me descuipe-me	May des-cul-pee	Excuse me
Obrigado (m)	Oh-bree-gad-o	Thank you
Obrigada (f)		
De nada	Da nota	You're welcome
Quanto que e este?	Quantoo ki eh esstee	How much is this?
Nao falo Portugues	Now fa-lo poor-too-gase	I don't speak Portuguese
Eu nao entendo	Eh no en-tendo	I don't understand
Voce aceita cartao de credito?	Vo-say ass-ayta car-tao de credeet-o	Do you accept credit cards?

Chapter 21: RUSSIA

LOCATION/GEOGRAPHY

Russia is the largest country in the world and is located in Northern Asia
bordering the Arctic Ocean between Europe and the North Pacific Ocean.
Russia borders Azerbaijan, Belarus, China, Estonia, Finland, Georgia,
Kazakhstan, Latvia, Lithuania, Mongolia, North Korea, Norway, Poland,
and Ukraine.

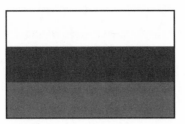

- Communist rule ended in 1991, when the United Soviet Socialist Republic (USSR) separated into independent states. Boundaries are still changing and new independent states are emerging.
- In August 1914, when WWI broke out, it was decided by their leaders that the name of the Russian capital, St. Petersburg, sounded too German so the name was changed to Petrograd. After the death of the Bolshevik leader Vladimir Lenin (1924), the Soviet Union changed the name again but this time to Leningrad. Sixty-seven years later, when the Soviet Union collapsed in 1991, the name returned to St. Petersburg once again.
- At the age of three, Ivan the Terrible (1530-1584) took the throne and was the first ruler of Russia to take the title of czar.
- The USSR was an atheist nation but now religion is increasing.
- The Russian literacy rate is 100 percent.
- English is taught in schools beginning in third grade.
- Families depend on one another and live together in small apartments, with several generations sharing the home.
- Many times parents have only one child, and women work outside their homes in addition to caring for the household and their children.
- Since so many people have the same names, a person's birth date is used to differentiate between identically named individuals.
- Siberia has more than 25 percent of the world's forests.
- There is a term in Russia called "*nyekulturny*," which is a way to tell you that you just created a faux pax did something that is considered socially unacceptable or that you are showing bad manners.
- The oldest mountains in the world are the Ural Mountains.
- The culture in St. Petersburg is amazing, with 221 museums, 80 theaters, 100 concert organizations, 45 galleries, 62 cinemas, 80 club establishments of culture, and 2,000 libraries. If this isn't enough, then every year you can attend at least 100 cultural and art festivals.
- Russia is the only state that has 12 seas in its territory, with 100 reserves and 35 national parks.
- During the time of Peter the Great, if a Russian man wanted to wear a beard, he was required to pay a special tax.

- Russia has twice as many chess Grandmasters than Germany, which is its closest competitor.
- The Soviet-born gymnast Olga Korbut won four gold Olympic medals in the 1972 and 1976 games for the USSR team. She helped popularize gymnastics around the world.

BUSINESS ETIQUETTE

 ## Punctuality

- You are expected to be on time for all business appointments, but your Russian associate will probably be late. Do not expect an apology. This lateness could even extend one to two hours. Do not lose your patience or say anything to the person. This could be a test of your patience. Patience is a great virtue to Russians, but punctuality is not.
- It is acceptable to be 15 to 20 minutes late for social events.
- If invited to a Russian home, arrive on time or no more than 15 minutes late.

 ## Meeting Manners

- Be prepared for a possible late start in your meeting. Schedules are constantly changing, and meetings may exceed the expected length. Even at the last moment or on short notice, a meeting can be cancelled. A reason for this is the style in which Russians often do business. Westerners generally will have formulated several possible solutions before bringing up a problem; whereas, Russians will discuss their problems or challenges openly with no set solutions or plans, in hopes that discussion will lead to a solution. The resulting debate and discussion can completely alter the agenda and far exceed the allotted time for a meeting.
- Russians can be very patient and tolerant so can "out sit" you in negotiations. But at the same time, the negotiations can become very flared, with your Russian associates walking out of the meeting.
- It is hard to do business without a local contact. Connections or influences will help tremendously. *Svyasi* means connections in high places, and these friendships will move you through the usual stumbling blocks.
- Appointments are necessary. Allow ample advanced time (up to six weeks) for a meeting with a government official.

- Confirm your meeting once you arrive in Russia and then again a day or two before the meeting.
- The first week in May is not a good time to try to schedule a meeting because of holidays. The end of July and the month of August are popular times for vacations.
- Some Russians view compromise as a weakness and bad business.
- The "final offers" may not be the final offer. A little more negotiation may be necessary.
- Long-term relationships do not need to be established for a good business deal, but a network of people that you know and trust is recommended. Expect long socializing periods and personal conversation before you get down to business.
- The first meeting could be a trial run to determine if you and your company are credible and if the Russians want to continue working with you or your company or to schedule the next meeting.
- Formality is important during your initial meetings and making contacts.
- You might even want to include a technical expert during your negotiations.
- Russian executives like to meet with people of the same rank. Hierarchy is still much respected.
- Women business travelers will be accepted in conducting business in Russia. It's important to dress and act professionally at all times and to be completely prepared with correct contacts and materials. Eighty-nine percent of the small businesses in Russia are now women-owned. This makes them the highest in the world for women-owned businesses. The men still have the lion's share of higher positions and pay, with 80 percent of the top management positions in the country. But it is slowly beginning to change in both public and government positions and they anticipate within the next few years that the top management positions will become more even between men and women. The younger generation is helping this ratio move along more quickly.
- To be asked a favor is a good sign of acceptance.
- If you are the host and conducting the meeting, be sure to have an ample supply of drinks, snacks, Danishes, and cookies.
- Be prepared for various conversations going on during your meeting.
- At the end of meetings, both sides usually sign a *protocol*, which is a summary of what was just discussed.

Business Cards

- Have plenty of cards available to exchange. There is no formal ritual for exchange of cards.
- Telephone books are not provided in certain areas, so cards can be essential.
- Have one side of the card printed in your native language and the other in Russian using Cyrillic text.
- Present the side translated in Russian to your counterpart.
- Include any advanced university degrees on your business card.

 **Meals/Toasts**

- Breakfast meetings are not a part of Russian cultural, but dinner meetings are now much more popular and are often used to close the deal. Dinners generally will start at 6 p.m. (1800).
- Continental is the style of eating, with the fork held in the left hand and the knife in the right. Keep your hands visible above the table. Your wrists will rest on the table.
- The elder or the most honored guest is served first.
- The most senior official will be placed in the center of the table, and the guest of honor should be placed across from this person.
- Allow the host to invite you to eat before starting your meal.
- Second helpings will be offered and it's fine to accept, but leave a small amount of food on your plate to show the hosts that they provided great hospitality.
- Russia is one place where you can actually use bread to soak up gravy or sauce.
- To get the attention of the wait staff, just use eye contact. If that can't get their attention, discreetly raise your hand with your index finger pointed up. Avoid waving or calling for a waiter.
- Allow men to pour drinks for women who are seated next to them.
- Remain at the table until the guest of honor gets up to leave or until you are invited to leave the table.
- If you invite, you pay. If you are the guest, you can offer to pay. As a host, make arrangements in advance and handle the payment, especially if you are a woman. Men are insulted if women even try to pay but this is slowly changing.
- Drinking is a very important part of Russian culture. You should not refuse a drink or a toast except for a health or religious reason.
- If you drain your glass, they are fast to refill. Pace yourself.

- A toast will be said before you begin your meal. Toasting is a critical part of the meal and at times can be long and even humorous.
- The first toast will be given by the host and the guests reply.
- Wait until the first toast has been given before you start to drink.
- Expect to clink your glasses together after the toast is offered. But do not participate in this process if you are drinking a non-alcoholic drink.

 ## Entertainment

- If invited to a Russian home, arrive on time or no more than 15 minutes.
- Remove your shoes when entering a Russian home. You may be offered a pair of slippers to put on in place of your shoes.
- Clothes that you wear to the office would show respect if you would wear to a home.
- Remember to bring flowers for the woman of the home. Pay attention to their customs and traditions about flowers. Choose pink, cream-colored, orange, or blue flowers and you should be pretty safe.
- Offer your assistance to help the hostess set up the meal and clean up after the meal. You may initially be turned down, but offer again and perhaps your offer will be accepted.
- Be careful not to be overly excited about anything in a Russian home; they may insist that you take it.
- Showing pictures of your own children or grandchildren is a sure way to establish good relations. Russians generally love children.
- Smoking is common during meals in both homes and restaurants.
- Be ready to stay late if invited to a home.
- It is not uncommon to be joined by a stranger in a restaurant. The Russians have an affinity for family and friends and would rather sit with a total stranger than eat by themselves in a restaurant.
- Don't ask for ice cubes in your drinks. They possibly may be made from water that was not purified.

 ## Forms of Address/Introductions/Greetings

- Greetings between men are an extremely firm handshake, direct eye contact, and the appropriate greeting for the time of day.
- Handshakes between men and women are less firm.
- Women will meet friends with three kisses on the cheek, starting on the left side.
- Male friends will meet with pats on the back and hugs.
- To be touched by a Russian during conversation shows they have confidence in that person.

- In formal situations, all three names are used. The first name is the person's given name. The middle name is a patronymic or a version of the father's first name and adding *vich* or *ovich* for the male and *avna* or *ovna* for the female. The son of Ivan would have a patronymic of Ivanovich and the daughter would be Ivanovna. The last name is the family or surname.
- It's appropriate to use "*gaspodin*" (similar to "Mr.") (gos-PODE-in) or "*gaspazhah*" (similar to "Mrs." or "Miss") (gos-PO-zhah) plus his or her surname. When you use full names and patronymics, then the honorific is unnecessary.
- Married women will take their husband's name but to show their gender will change the last letter when it is a vowel (and generally it is) into an "a."
- Friends will call each other by their first names and patronymics. Close friends and family will call each other by their first name only.
- Titles are important to this culture. Be prepared in advance so you make sure you are aware of all titles and distinctions.

Appearance/Attire

- Dress demonstrates the individual's image as a businessperson and a professional.
- Russians will spend more of their family budget on clothing than people do in other countries.
- They will select top designers and will avoid the imitations.
- Men usually wear well-tailored suits, ties, and good dress shoes.
- Jackets will generally remain on during negotiations.
- Women generally will dress conservatively.
- Women must cover their heads, arms, and knees when entering a Russian Orthodox Church.
- Skirts are a better choice than slacks. And the skirts should cover the knees.
- Make sure that your shoes have a nice shine.
- Jeans and sneakers can be worn as casual wear.
- If visiting during their winter, come prepared with warm coats, gloves, and well-insulated boots. It's smart to dress in layers for the fall and spring, and no matter what time of the year, have a sweater. It can be chilly in the evening in the summer.
- Come prepared with an umbrella if you are visiting rainy St. Petersburg.

 **Gift Giving**

- If invited to a Russian's home, it is appropriate to bring a gift. It could be a bottle of wine, dessert, or a bouquet of flowers. If there are children, a toy or candy would be a nice gesture.
- Avoid inexpensive gifts like pens, pencils, lighters, cheap wine, vodka, and notebooks. The same items, but of a higher quality, will be appreciated.
- Gifs are exchanged between family and friends on birthdays, New Year, and Orthodox Christmas.
- Male guests are expected to bring flowers as a gift for the hostess. If you bring flowers, make sure it is an odd number. You bring even numbers for funerals.
- Russians may refuse to accept a gift when it is first offered. Offer it again and they will most likely accept it.
- Russians do like to give and receive gifts, so bring plenty.
- Generally children's gifts are opened later in private, while adults will open gifts when received.
- To give a baby gift before the baby is born is considered bad luck.
- Just a card or thank-you note is not considered enough for a social event. A gift should be given for dinners or an overnight stay in a person's home.
- Even though gifts are basically expected for social gatherings, the thank-you note is not. They just do not consider thank-you notes appropriate or necessary, so don't expect to receive one from your Russian host or guest. But as a guest in Russia and your tradition or culture is to send a note of thanks to your host or guest, then I would err on the civility side and send the note.

 Tipping

- Tipping was actually illegal in Soviet times but now a 9 percent to 10 percent tip is included in most restaurant bills.
- Additional tipping is appreciated for extra service. You might tip from 10 percent to 15 percent, depending on your service.
- Tips or "*chaeviye*" do not have a set amount so people will vary their tips with restaurants, venues, or services provided.
- Intense studying of the bill is rude and makes the wait staff feel uncomfortable. Just review the final bill and submit payment, even if they overcharged.
- The wait staff will also very openly show their dissatisfaction if they feel you did not leave enough for the tip. They also prefer their tips in hard currency.

- Credit cards are not widespread throughout Russia nor is it even easy to draw cash other than in the main cities of Moscow and St. Petersburg. You might want to check first before assuming your credit is good. Also, if you pay your bill with a credit card, then leave your tip in cash.
- Make sure when you are exchanging your currency from another country that you only use the designated official locations. Using other venues, locations, or people is illegal and unofficial sites may be a scam. Enter the country with some money that was exchanged at the airport or have traveler's checks.
- Toilet attendants and housekeepers will be provided small change, while the bellmen and coat check will be provided 23 ruble (US$1) in better hotels.
- Hairdressers and barbers will receive 10 percent of the total bill.
- Tour guides will be tipped 236 to 478 ruble (US$10 to US$20) for more individualized and special tours. A guide is provided 23 to 188 ruble (US$1-US$2).
- Tip taxi drivers and other service providers from 10 percent to 30 percent, depending on the service. Your taxi fee should be discussed with the driver prior to the trip.

 ## Gesture Awareness
- Thumbs up is acceptable and means that you give or have been given approval.
- Avoid calling out names or making loud sounds to get the attention of a waiter. Either make eye contact or raise your hand with index finger pointed.
- Avoid using your index finger to motion for a person to come to you. Instead place your hand with the palm facing down and motion inward with all four fingers at once.
- Rude gestures include the OK sign or shaking your fist.

 ## Faux Pas
- Speaking loudly in public is considered rude. Russians remain very reserved in public.
- Whistling is considered bad manners and there is even an old superstition that it will cause financial loss.
- Avoid sitting with legs apart or one ankle resting on your knee.
- Standing with your hands in your pockets is considered rude.
- Remove your gloves when shaking hands with another person.
- Also remove your shoes as your enter an apartment or home. You may not be asked, so just show respect and remove them. You will most likely be offered a pair of slippers.

- Showing the soles of your shoes is impolite. They are considered dirty and never should come in contact with any part of the seat, like on a bus or subway.
- Steer clear of discussions about the Holocaust, the Czar and the monarchy, ethnic minorities, personal questions, and religion.
- The term *tovarisch* or comrade is now out of date and should not be used.
- Avoid comparing Moscow to Saint Petersburg and Russia to other developing countries.

 ## USEFUL FACTS

President	Dmitry Medvedev (2008)
Prime Minister	Vladimir Putin (2008)
National Name	Rossiyskaya Federatsiya
Size	6,592,812 square miles (17,075,400 square km)
Population	142,008,838 (2008)
Capital	Moscow
Government	Constitutional Federation
Currency	Russian ruble
Religion	Russian Orthodox 15% to 20%; other Christian 2%; Islam 10% to 15%; no religious preference, about 60%
Language	Russian, 81% as their official language and is written with Cyrillic alphabet instead of Latin. There are 48 other languages spoken by 120+ nationalities. Some of the languages include Tatar, Ukrainian, Chuvash, Bashir, Mordvin, and Chechen.
Ethnicity	Russian 80%, Tatar 4%, Ukrainian 2%, Bashkir 1%, Chuvash 1%, other or unspecified 12%

Industry	Mining and extractive industries producing coal, oil, gas, chemicals, and metals; machine building, high-performance aircraft and space vehicles; defense industries including radar, missile production, advanced electronic components, and shipbuilding; communications equipment; medical and scientific instruments; consumer durables, textiles, foodstuffs, handicrafts.
Time Zone	Russia covers 11 time zones, including Greenwich Mean Time +2 to +12 Hours (GMT +2 to +12) or 7 to 17 hours ahead of EST (EST +7 to +17). Russia observes daylight saving time.
Telephone Code	International Code: +7 City Code: +495 (Moscow)
Weather	Ranges considerably with every type of climate throughout this vast area from pleasantly warm in the summer in Moscow and St. Petersburg, to winters cool along the Artic Coast, to frigid in Siberia.
Voltage/Frequency	230 V; 50 Hz

 HOLIDAYS/FESTIVALS

31 December – 1 January	New Year's Day (Main holiday in Russia. Father Frost (not Father Christmas) comes on New Year's Eve and delivers presents)
7 and 8 January	Orthodox Christmas
23 February	Defender of the Fatherland Day
25 February	Defender of the Fatherland Day Observed
8 March	International Women's Day
12 April	Cosmonauts' Day
1 May	Labor Day
9 May	Victory Day (World War II)
12 June	State Sovereignty Day/Russia Day
4 November	Unity Day
7 November	Socialist Revolution Day
12 December	Constitution Day

LANGUAGE TIPS

Russia	Phonetics	English
Privet	Pre ve it	Hello/Hi
Do svidanya	Dos-vee-DAHN-ya	Good-bye
Kak dela?	Kahk DEE-lah	How are you?
Dobroye utro	DOE-broy-eh OO-troe	Good morning
Dobroy nochi	DOE-broy no-chay	Good night
Spasiba	Spa-SEE-ba	Thank you
Pozhaluysta	Puh-ZHAL-yoosta	Please
Ne za shto	NAY za shto	You're welcome
Da/Nyet	Dah/nyet	Yes/No
Izvinite	Iz-vin-EET-eh	Excuse me

Chapter 22: SINGAPORE

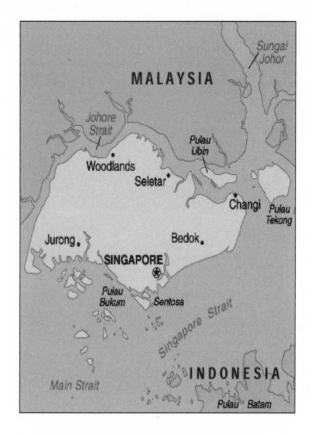

LOCATION/GEOGRAPHY

The main island and 57 other islands of Singapore are located at the southern end of the Malay Peninsula. The country is mainly flat and low-lying but there are a few small hills on the main island. Singapore is densely populated but smaller than New York City. It is very close to the Equator, so it has tropical climate year-round.

 DID YOU KNOW?

- Saving face is very important in all phases of their lives. This cannot be taken away, given, earned or lost.
- Singaporeans have a strong cultural value and believe that the concepts of group and harmony are more important than that of the individual.
- In 1996 a law was passed that children were responsible financially for their elderly parents if it became necessary.
- Body language and nonverbal communication is very important. They determine the feelings of people by their posture, facial expressions, and tone of voice. So be very careful about what your body language is saying.
- There are four major groups —Chinese, Malay, Indian, and European.
- Chinese are the greatest majority (78 percent), but each group has its own culture. It's critical that you understand these differences.
- Leadership and management rely on Confucian principles.
- The crime rate is extremely low in Singapore and you can be given fines or even imprisoned for spitting, littering, chewing gum, jaywalking, smoking in prohibited areas, and even neglecting to flush a toilet. There will be signs regarding the smoking or jaywalking and their laws also involve their visitors. This is why this country always looks clean and beautiful.
- In 1994, Singapore introduced a Goods and Service Tax (GST) to strengthen their economy.
- The maximum height for skyscrapers in Singapore is 280 meters (918 feet).
- Singapore is the smallest country in Southeast Asia and one of the few remaining city-states in the world.
- On 9 August 1965 Singapore received its independence from the Malaysian Federation and on 21 September 1965 became a permanent member to the United Nations.
- Singapore's name is derived from Sanskrit for "The Lion City." Even though it is believed that there were never lions in Singapore, when the Sumatran prince first landed there, he believed he saw lions. They actually were the Malayan tigers, but he thought it was a good omen and built the city.

Be On Your Best Cultural Behavior

- Only one Olympic medal has been won by Singapore since they have been sending athletics to the games. This was at the 1964 Rome Olympics, when Tan Howe Liang won the silver medal for weightlifting.
- The name "Raffles" is very well known in Singapore and you can walk down the streets and visit shopping centers or the beautiful hotel that all carry the name. But one thing you might remember is "The Long Bar" in the Raffles Hotel, which is the home of the "Singapore Sling." It is also said that a frequent visitor to The Long Bar was Rudyard Kipling. Maybe that was his creative spot.
- Orchard Road is four km (2.48 miles) of shops and malls.

BUSINESS ETIQUETTE

 ## Punctuality

- Punctuality is very important and should be respected for all business gatherings.
- Arrival at social events should be on time or just a little late.
- Old traditions say if you arrive right on time or a little early for a meal, then you are greedy. So arrive just slightly late when food is going to be served.
- For social events with good friends, then punctuality is important and you can arrive early.
- If a meeting is scheduled and a taxi is needed, allow enough time, especially if it is raining. Hailing a taxi could take hours. Plan in advance and call for a taxi. Arrange at your hotel if possible.
- If you are running late for whatever reason, then call personally to ask if you can arrive late or rearrange.

 ## Meeting Manners

- Appointments should be made one to two weeks in advance.
- Proper introductions are critical and being a part of the proper network is important in developing lasting business relationships.
- Groups, rather than individuals, play a major role in their business situations. The more elder person and the more competent person will take over the leadership role.
- Numerous meetings will be needed before final decisions are made.
- Building personal relationships is critical and in the long run even more important than the company you represent. So if you are replaced in your company, then the new person will need to start over in building the personal relationship.

- There is a very strong work ethic and intense competition.
- Courtesy, humility, calm manner, good listening, and preparedness are all key factors.
- Be patient. The overall process takes a much longer time than in the United States.
- Age and seniority are very much respected. Make sure that the most senior person's name is introduced first.
- Never criticize or disagree with anyone senior to you in rank. It could destroy your business relationship and may cause both of you to lose face.
- Protocol is important, including sending names and titles of all that will be in attendance in meetings.
- Formally a meeting should be arranged in writing, but more and more are now made by telephone, fax, or by e-mail.
- Avoid scheduling meetings over the Chinese New Year (late January/early February). Many businesses will be closed for the whole week.
- There will be a little chitchat prior to the meeting.
- Come prepared with material and information for the meeting.
- Rank and seniority are critical and applies to the seating arrangements, so wait to be told where to sit.
- Be careful when you are told "yes." It does not necessarily mean yes and could actually be a disagreement.
- Do not be discouraged by delay in conversation. A respectful pause of 15 seconds is very common. Do not get nervous or impatient and disturb their concentration. Slow down in your communication so it gives the impression you are thinking of their question.
- Have concessions in your back pocket that will not jeopardize your overall bottom line.
- Singaporeans know how to negotiate, so be ready. Their decisions are consensus driven.
- If working with Ethnic Chinese, the actual date you sign the contract may need to be determined by an astrologer or a geomancer (*feng shui* man).

 ## Business Cards

- English is the language that is generally used for all business, so cards need to be in English, except if meeting with ethnic Chinese. Then you would want to print one side of the card in Mandarin with their characters printed in gold. Make sure you present the card so the Mandarin side faces the recipient.

- Cards are exchanged in the beginning of the conversations or business meetings.
- Bring lots of cards and expect to exchange with everyone. Make sure they are in perfect condition.
- There is a formality for exchange. Present with both hands with the card facing the recipient. Always stand and give with a slight nod.
- Accept the card with both hands, and then take the time to read the material on the card. Then place the card in your business card holder, your pocket (not back pocket), or on the table to reference the name later in the meeting.
- Do not write on another person's card. It's considered rude.
- Reference the person by the name as stated on their card.
- How you handle the business card is an indication of how you will treat the relationship.

Meals/Toasts

- Chinese would much rather have seated dinners. They feel uncomfortable at stand-up receptions.
- The hosts will serve their guests.
- This is one place that you can pick up the food and eat it if it falls on the floor.
- Use your chopsticks, to remove any unwanted food that is in your mouth, (instead of your fingers).
- Chinese have various habits, including making noise with their lips, touching their dish or plate with lips, smoking at the table, and even spitting on the floor. Some might be extreme but don't be surprised.
- Food can be placed on your plate by another person using their cutlery. You should refrain from returning this gesture.
- In Indian tradition, the serving spoon should not touch the plate when placing food on your plate.
- It is common for Indians and Malays to eat with hands.
- If serving yourself, take only the food nearest you. Do not stir your food like you are looking for certain food.
- If you don't like the food, be prepared to tell your host why. It's safe to say it is for health reasons.
- Always compliment your host for the excellent choice in food, even if you didn't like it.
- As a senior guest, thank your hosts over soup, near the end of the meal. As a host, thank everyone for coming at the end. The host will bring the event to an end, not the guests.

- You can toast with any drink.
- At a more formal Chinese dinner, it is customary for the host to raise his glass and say "please" or "*ch'ing.*"

Entertainment

- Entertaining and social events are an important part of doing business.
- Respond to all invitations with either your attendance or a representative from your company.
- Spouses will most likely be invited to dinners but not to luncheons. If spouses are included, business will not be discussed.
- Government officials cannot participate in social events.
- Food is the focal point in social events.
- Religion is very critical in the selection of foods. Be very careful if you are planning the event and make sure you seek assistance in selecting the food and drink.
- If you arrive at a Chinese home right before everyone is ready to go to the table, you should decline.
- Coffee is important and many meetings could be held over a cup of coffee.
- Night life is prevalent, so be ready to be entertained in a nightclub or even *karaoke*. Nights can be very long.
- Golf clubs are in abundance. You could even be invited to a golf outing on one of the islands.
- Singapore is a diverse culture, so be prepared for a wide variety of food. Some of it can be very spicy, with lots of curry.

Forms of Address/Introductions/Greetings

- Ethnic Chinese will shake hands. Expect a light handshake, but they may hold for a longer period of time.
- Men and women will shake hands, but the woman will most likely present her hand first.
- Names can be very confusing. Chinese names will have a surname followed by one or two first names.
- Plus the Chinese belong to a dialect group, so in addition to their Chinese names they will have another dialect name.
- Some married Chinese women will use their husband's name and some will keep their maiden name.
- Then to add to all of this, Chinese will have a "Christian name" or "English name" that is totally different from their dialect name, surname, or first names. How you address a person could be completely different from their written or formal name.

- Do not pat a Chinese person on the head or their shoulders. They believe is if you do this, then you are putting out their "fire," and this fire protects them or gives them bad luck.
- Ethnic Malay men will shake hands.
- Malays do not have family names but are called by their given name plus "*bin*" (son of) or "*binte*" (daughter of) followed by their father's name.
- Some Malays that are westernized may drop the "*bin*" or "*binte*" and may even take up English names like the Chinese.
- Muslim men and women traditionally do not shake hands because they do not touch women in public.
- Avoid physical contact with Muslims.
- The younger Muslim generation will shake hands with foreign women, but the more appropriate exchange is bowing the head for greeting or "*salaam*."
- Two women will also use "*salaam*" for their greeting.
- Ethnic Indians will shake hands with member of the same sex.
- The best suggestion when being introduced to a person of the opposite sex is to nod your head and smile. You are safe and it works for all ethnic groups.
- Indians traditionally do not have surnames, so some have taken up the family name that all members of that family will use for generations.
- In addition to the given name they will also have " *Sio*" (son of) or "*Dio*" (daughter of) followed by their father's name.
- Once an Indian woman marries, she generally will stop using the father's name. She will now use her personal name with her husband's name.
- Seniority and respect for the elderly are critical. Make sure when introducing people that the most important person is introduced first.
- If a person enters that is more than a generation older or of higher rank, stand to show respect.
- Make sure that your feet stay flat on the floor instead of crossing your legs when in the presence of higher ranking people or elders.
- Professional titles such as Dr., Mr., or Mrs. should be added to names for courtesy.
- Just ask how they should be addressed or materials sent to them. Remember it is confusing to them also how you should be addressed. Be clear how they should address you.
- If you are meeting and working with people younger than you, then it's appropriate to call them by their first names.
- If the people that you are meeting and working with are older then refer to them by their title and last name.
- "Auntie" or "uncle" is an informal way of addressing people that are middle-aged or older. Be careful because that person you thought was

appropriate to be called these names might not consider themselves to be "middle-aged" just yet.

- You will see couples hugging and holding hands.
- Space will vary with the cultures, but one arm's length is safe.

Appearance/Attire

- Custom office wear is dark slacks, light-colored long-sleeved shirts and ties for men. Coats generally are not required.
- Because of the hot and humid weather, you will see many people in just the shirt and slacks and no ties.
- Some organizations will allow short-sleeved shirts but not all.
- Women will usually wear blouses with slacks or skirts in the office. More formal offices will require pantyhose with a more businesslike attire of pants suits or skirt and jacket.
- Some companies will allow sleeveless blouses. But if so, it's critical that your armpits are shaved. It is considered poor etiquette not to shave.
- Be careful of revealing clothes. They send negative impressions.
- Accessories are simple.
- Make-up is light mainly due to the humidity and hot weather.
- Muslim women wear blouses that cover their upper arms and skirts that cover their knees. They will also wear religious headgear.
- It's better to overdress until you know the dress codes of your associates. It's much easier to take off a jacket or a tie than to come unprepared.
- For a weekend meeting or office work, it is appropriate to come into the office with jeans, polo shirts, and track shoes. But it's inappropriate and unacceptable to wear shorts or Bermudas, round-neck tees, and slippers. Again, err toward business casual rather than going too casual.

Gift Giving

- Government employees may not accept gifts, especially financial gifts.
- Give larger gifts to the whole group, or smaller ones to everyone.
- Thank-you and welcome gifts are appreciated but they need to be small, inexpensive, and not perceived as a bribe.
- Gifts that are good for exchange include chocolates, something from your own country, a gift from your company with a company logo, and brand name gifts. Again, do not create the impression that they look or are expensive.
- Your gift might be refused when it is first offered. They do not want to appear greedy, so offer again and then be pleased that they have accepted your gift. It may take three times before it is accepted.

Be On Your Best Cultural Behavior

- Do not open the gift when it is presented or expect them to open one when presented. They don't want to seem greedy, or in case the gift is poor choice, they don't want to create an awkward situation. Open it at a later time in private.
- Do not offer or bring food to a dining situation. It appears that you think the food that will be served will be inadequate. It would be a tremendous insult.
- Chinese Traditions:
  - You may receive a gift of money in a red envelope as a celebration of their Chinese New Year. It is called "*hong bao*" and will only be new bills in even numbers and even amounts. These are generally given to children and non-government service personnel.
  - More common than "*hong bao*" is to give mandarin oranges. The oranges will come in even numbers, generally two or four, and given when you arrive at the host's home and when you are ready to leave. The host will present the same number of oranges in return.
  - Number 8 is their lucky number and means "get rich." The number 4 is unlucky and means "die." So make sure any gifts you present are in quantities of 8 and avoid 4.
  - Clocks are also to be avoided as gifts. Giving clocks in Chinese is "*song zhong*" and means to "arrange for the burial of deceased parents or an elder."
  - Other items that refer to funerals are straw sandals and handkerchiefs.
  - White, blue, or black paper is to be avoided because those colors signify mourning.
  - Their happy colors for wrapping gifts are red, pink, or yellow.
  - It's important to wrap elaborately.
  - Giving scissors, knives, or other cutting utensils shows that you want to sever your relationship.
  - For baby gifts, never wrap or decorate with a stork because it is the precursor of death.
  - Odd numbers are unlucky so avoid in giving gifts.
  - Flowers are for the sick and funerals, so generally flowers are not good for gifts.
  - The gift could be refused three times before it is accepted. This indicates that the recipient is not greedy.
- Malay Traditions:
  - Malays love to give and receive gifts.
  - If you're invited to a Malay home, bring a small gift for the family. This could include flowers, candies, or toys for their children.
  - Wrap your presents in green or red. White wrapping paper signifies death and mourning.

- During Hari Raya Puasa, the Muslim celebration to bring the end of the month-long fast during the Ramadan, Malays will give green envelopes that contain money.
- You can bring food to a Malay dinner. Make sure it is "*halal*" (their equivalent to *kosher*) with no pork items.
- If the Malay are observant Muslims, then avoid alcohol, perfumes that have alcohol, pork, pigskin products, personal items, toy dogs or gifts with pictures of dogs, images of nude or partially dressed women that might appear in pictures, drawings, or art items.
- Hold your gift until you are departing instead of giving upon arrival.
- Offer and accept gifts with your right hand only. You can accept larger gifts with both hands. Avoid your left hand.
- Indian Traditions:
  - Indians also love to give and receive gifts.
  - They love bright colors and you should wrap their gifts in bright red, yellow, or green wrappings. Avoid white or black wrapping paper.
  - If you give money to an Indian as a gift, make sure it is in odd numbers. Odd numbers are perceived luckier than even.
  - Frangipanis flowers are used for funeral wreaths, so avoid giving them.
  - Avoid giving Hindu Indians gifts of food, mainly any beef.
  - The Hindu Indians do not use cattle products, so this would eliminate any gifts of leather products.
  - Receive and give gifts with your right hand. Both hands can be used for larger gifts.
  - Avoid alcohol unless you are certain they drink alcohol.

Tipping

- Avoid giving tips openly. Instead, just instruct the waiter to keep the change when you are paying the bill.
- If there is a restroom attendant, it is not necessary to leave a tip unless you notice they do have a coin bowl or some form of collecting tips. Then a minimal amount should be left.
- There is a pre-set service charge at the airport and most hotels and restaurants, and tipping beyond that is prohibited.
- It is not necessary to tip taxi drivers and tourists are encouraged by the government not to do so. But the drivers will not refuse your tip if you offer them one. It's best to just round up to the nearest dollar.
- The standard is 10 percent service charge added to the bill in a restaurant.
- A porter in a hotel would receive SG$1 (US$.73).

Gesture Awareness

- Do not jump lines. To queue up for everything is common and to jump ahead in the line is very offensive.
- Give up your seat for a pregnant lady, a small child, elderly person, or challenged person. These people can cut the queue and jump ahead in the taxi line.
- Sucking in air through your teeth is a definite signal of "no."
- The feet are considered to be unclean. Avoid kicking, moving, or touching anything with your foot.
- It's rude to point to a person with your middle finger or forefinger. Instead, use an open palm or your knuckles.
- Pounding your fist into the palm of the other hand is considered to be obscene.
- To get a person's attention, avoid having your palm up and wiggling your fingers. Hold you hand out with the palm down and use a swooping motion with your fingers.
- Turning your head from side to side as considered "no" by Westerners, actually for the Indians is "yes" or they are in agreement.
- Putting your hands on your hips and standing up tall is considered an angry or aggressive position.
- Do not litter or spit. Remember their laws. Even if an official doesn't see you, it is still very offensive to the people that witness it and be ready for some serious offensive looks from them.

Faux Pas

- Smoking is prohibited in most areas, especially air-conditioned venues.
- Make sure cell phones are in silent mode in public areas including a movie or restaurant.
- The crime rate is extremely low and Singapore has very strict enforcement policies.
- Spitting, littering, smoking in prohibited areas, chewing gum, jay-walking, and neglecting to flush the toilet are some of the laws that are strictly enforced. By not obeying you could face a fine or even imprisonment.
- Don't think that because you are a foreigner that their laws will not be enforced. They will.
- For smoking or jaywalking, a sign should be posted, but if in doubt, don't do either.
- Make sure you have some extra tissues if you are traveling and using public restrooms. Some have the usual toilet bowels, but you might still find some with the "squat" style cubicles.
- Good conversation topics can include travel, your plans for the future, arts, economic advancements in Singapore, and Singapore cuisine.

- Conversations to avoid include racial and religious topics, discussions between Malaysia and Singapore, politics, criticizing any aspect of the people of Singapore, and gossiping.
- Follow the lead for conversation if it's a first meeting or if you do not know the other people well.
- Refrain from asking personal questions about age or income. Work related questions are fine.
- Be careful not to cause another person to "lose face."
- It's an insult to bring food to a dining event because it appears that you think the food will be insufficient.
- Do not shout. Speak softly and low.

USEFUL FACTS

President	Sellapan Ramanathan (1999)
Prime Minister	Lee Hsien Loong (2004)
National Name	Republic of Singapore
Size	241 square miles (624 square km)
Population	4,608,167 (2008)
Capital	Singapore
Government	Parliamentary Republic
Currency	Singapore dollar
Religion	Buddhist 43%, Islam 15%, Taoist 9%, Hindu 4%, Catholic 5%, other Christian 10%, none 14%
Language	Mandarin 35%, English 23%, Malay 14%, Hokkien 11%, Cantonese 6%, Teochew 5%, Tamil 3%, other Chinese dialects 2%, other 1%. English is the language of choice for business and politics, but the four national languages are Mandarin, Malay, Tamil, and English.

Ethnicity	Chinese 77%, Malay 14%, Indian 8%, European, and other 1%
Industry	Electronics, chemicals, financial services, oil drilling equipment, petroleum refining, rubber processing and rubber products, processed food and beverages, ship repair, offshore platform construction, life sciences, and tourism
Time Zone	Singapore is eight hours ahead of Greenwich Mean Time (GMT +8 Hours) or 13 hours ahead of U.S. Eastern Standard Time (EST +13). Singapore does not observe daylight saving time.
Telephone Code	International Code: +65 City Code: City Codes are not required
Weather	Singapore is north of the equator, with tropical climate all year long, hot and humid conditions and intermittent showers. Humidity is generally above 90%, with temperatures ranging from 75F to 88F (24C to 31C).
Voltage/Frequency	220 V – 240 V; 50 Hz

 HOLIDAYS/FESTIVALS

1 January	New Year's Day
January/February	Chinese New Year (Chinese New Year is the highpoint of their calendar, with festivities lasting 15 days.)
March or April	Good Friday
April	Feast of the Sacrifice
1 May	Labor Day
May	Vesak Day (The birthday of the Lord Gautama Buddha)
9 August	National Day
October	Hari Raya Puasa (End of Ramadan)

October or November	Deepavali (Most important day for a Hindu and also the Hindu New Year. It marks the coming home of Lord Ram and also the victory of good over evil. The festivities last for the entire month.)
December	Hari Raya Haji (Feast of the Sacrifice)
25 December	Christmas

LANGUAGE TIPS

The majority of people in Singapore speak more than one language. English is the main language, but you will find Mandarin, Malay, Hokkien, and others. *Singlish* is a combination of English and words from Hokkien, which is a Chinese dialect. This informal language is unique to Malaysia and Singapore. It is a shorter and more efficient way to express what you want to say with fewer words. Some of the common words include:

Habis	Finished
Makan	To eat
Chope	To reserve something
Cheem	Difficult
Ang mo	A white person
Rojak	Mixed, a mix of
Liao	Finished, the end

Questions are often ended with distinctive exclamations including ah, lah, ley, and what:

Don't like that, lah?
You are going there, ah?
No parking lots here, what?
It is very troublesome, ley?

Chapter 23: SOUTH AFRICA

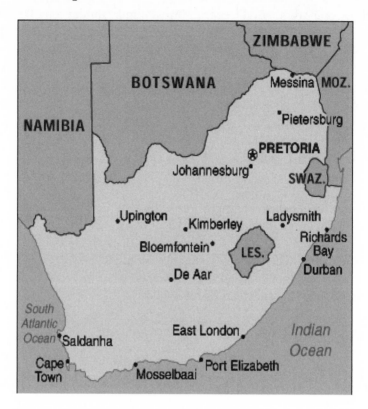

LOCATION/GEOGRAPHY

South Africa is at the southernmost tip of Africa, with the Atlantic Ocean on the west and the Indian Ocean on the south and east. Bordering neighbors are Namibia in the northwest, Zimbabwe and Botswana in the north, and Mozambique and Swaziland in the northeast. Lesotho is within the southeastern part of South Africa. Cape Agulhas, the southernmost point of the country, is in the Western Cape Province about 100 miles (161 km) southeast of the Cape of Good Hope.

 DID YOU KNOW?

- South Africa is the only country in the world that maintains three capitals—Pretoria (administrative), Cape Town (legislative), and Bloemfontein (judicial).
- The world's largest diamond was the Cullinan, which was found in South Africa in 1905. It weighed 3106.75 carats uncut. It was cut into numerous diamonds that now form part of the British crown jewels.
- Vilakazi Street in Soweto is the only street in the world to house two Nobel Peace Prize winners. Nelson Mandela and Archbishop Desmond Tutu both have homes there.
- Archbishop Desmond Tutu coined the phrase "Rainbow Nation" later adopted by Nelson Mandela to describe the country's diversity.
- South Africa is proud of its world-class hospitals. But you should have medical travel insurance from a reputable organization because private health care is available only on a cash basis or upon producing medical travel insurance.
- Tap water is safe to drink but you can easily find bottled water. Only 12 countries in the world supply tap water that is fit to drink. South Africa ranks third overall.
- South Africa is the world's largest producer of macadamia nuts.
- More than 50 percent of the world records for paragliding have been set in South Africa. Paragliding is a competitive flying sport where the pilot sits in a harness suspended by a fabric wing. This is a free-flying, foot-launched aircraft.
- South Africa is the second in the world, after Australia, for wind power, having 280,000 windmills on farms.
- South Africans drive on the left, with speed limits on highways at 120km/h (75 miles/hour).
- The first successful heart transplant was performed in Cape Town in 1967 by Dr. Christian Barnard.
- The largest reptile ever recorded was found in South Africa. The Leatherback Turtle measured 3 meters (9.84 feet) from the tip of its beak to the tip of its tail and weighed 916 kilograms (2,015.2 pounds).

- Four of the five fastest land animals can be found in South Africa, including the cheetah (100 km per hour/62.1 mph), and the wildebeest, lion, and Thompson's gazelle, all of which can move at about 80 kph (49 mph).
- Graca Machel married Nelson Mandela on 18 July 1998, becoming the first woman in the world to have married the heads of state from two different countries. Samora Machel, her first husband and the first president of Mozambique, was killed in a plane crash in 1986.
- South Africa is five times the size of Japan and three times the size of Texas.
- South Africa is the biggest contributor to the world's gold supply and has 80 percent of the world's platinum reserves.
- In 2007 South Africa legalized same-sex marriages, joining Belgium, the Netherlands, Canada, and Spain.

BUSINESS ETIQUETTE

Punctuality

- Punctuality is expected.
- Arrive at least five minutes early for meetings.
- Being up to 30 minutes late is acceptable for social dinners or gatherings.

Meeting Manners

- It's advisable to make appointments as far in advance as possible. Follow up to confirm the meeting and call again the day before.
- An informal approach is customary, with small talk before and during the business meetings.
- South Africans want to know you before entering into a business relationship. Relationship building and networking are important for long-term business and success. Initial meetings are used to establish a personal rapport and to determine if you are trustworthy. This trust is important before negotiations begin.
- Direct eye contact is important.
- Introductions are generally made using first names.
- Keep presentations short, to the point, and filled with exact ideas related to the special circumstances of doing business in South Africa. At times the logistics and financing of the deal can be more important than the actual product or service you plan to sell.
- Plan on a great deal of bargaining, but avoid the hard-sell or being too pushy.

- English is the language for meetings.
- If your company is new in South Africa, a more formal introduction can help you gain access to decision makers.
- Most people in South Africa would prefer face-to-face meetings to telephone calls, letters, or e-mail.
- For more formal meetings, a chairperson will keep the agenda and minutes from previous meetings.
- Larger organizations may offer to send a driver to your hotel to pick you up for the meeting. Accept and sit in the back if possible.
- Women are still striving for senior-level positions in South Africa. Women business representatives should expect possible condescending behavior and more difficulty advancing in business than men. The Old Boys' Network still exists, but some laws are assisting women to be taken seriously as professionals.
- Do not interrupt South Africans while they are speaking.
- Strive for a win-win situation. This harmony will avoid confrontations.
- Decision making may be centered at the top of a company, and decisions are often made after consultation with subordinates, so the process can be slow.
- State delivery dates in contracts because deadlines are viewed as fluid, rather than firm, commitments. Ensure that all the business terms are spelled out, including interim deadlines and performance standards. A lot of their deals are still sealed with a handshake. Be clear on all contract provisions and next steps.
- It's difficult to arrange meetings from mid-December to mid-January or during the two weeks surrounding Easter because these are the prime vacation times. Also try to avoid major Jewish holidays, since there is a large Jewish community.
- Business practices are more similar to those in Europe.

 ## Business Cards

- There is no formal exchange protocol other than respect and professionalism.
- When meeting for the first time, an exchange of business cards will confirm the status and hierarchy between the two companies.
- Store business cards properly instead of just placing them in your pocket.
- Make a comment regarding cards you are presented. You do not need to go into a lot of detail, but a short comment regarding the company, the location of the office or a possible reference to an advanced degree or title.

Meals/Toasts

- Use the continental style of eating, with the knife in the right hand and the fork remaining in the left. Do not switch. If you are left-handed, you will need to adjust.
- Business meetings can be held over breakfast, lunch, or dinner in a good restaurant, but dinners will be more formal and will last longer. Dinners may also take place in a restaurant or in the host's home.
- Always wait for alcohol to be ordered by your host. Alcohol is consumed in moderation in South Africa.
- Be prepared. Meat selections could include ostrich, giraffe, venison, hippo, goat, crocodile, and warthog. You will also find traditional meats, such as lamb and beef. Advise your host in advance if you are a vegetarian.
- *Graze* is the slang word for a meal.
- If you are the honored guest, you should extend a toast. This can be done at the end of the meal right before everyone departs. Just a short, humble message to wish the best health to the host and everyone present.

Entertainment

- If you're invited to a South African's home, arrive on time. They do build in a half-hour allowance, so it is not considered rude if you arrive no more than 30 minutes late.
- Contact the hostess in advance to see if you might bring a dish.
- Arrive with flowers, chocolates, or a good bottle of wine.
- Drinks are served first and sometimes can last as long as the actual dinner.
- Salad is served after the main course.
- Dessert is followed by a cheese course.
- You may move to a separate room for coffee and after-dinner drinks.
- Make an effort to complete the meal and eat everything on your plate. Leaving food on your plate is a poor reflection on the host.
- Also check with hostess about the proper dress. Casual clothes are acceptable and can include jeans or pressed shorts.
- If in a South African home, you should offer to help with the preparation or the cleaning up after a meal.
- A meal in the home of a white South African could include a barbecue by the pool called a *braaivleis* (bray flays – Afrikaans for roasted meat) or *braai* (bray – barbecue).

Forms of Address/Introductions/Greetings

- A handshake is the accepted form of greeting when you arrive and when you leave. Some women will not shake hands but will nod their heads. Wait for the woman to extend her hand.
- Men might kiss a woman they know well on the cheek instead of shaking hands.
- There is a relaxed business atmosphere and you will quickly move into first name exchange if all people are of equal status.
- Introductions are generally handled in order of seniority.
- Exchange good eye contact and a smile. Just don't stare. A traditional African will not look you in the eye during conversation. This is not a sign of arrogance or lack of interest but a sign of respect.
- The traditions of the African culture include using a soft, fingertip handshake to show friendliness. A woman may even bend her knees to show respect, and both men and women will touch their elbow with the other hand.
- You may also encounter a three-movement handshake. It starts with the standard western handshake, followed with gripping of the thumb, and then returning to the standard western handshake.
- Men of the Muslim culture will not extend their hands to women, but a woman can do so to a man. Just remember never to use your left hand to greet or touch anyone. The left hand is seen as "unclean."
- The Hindu culture is more influenced by the West. But a traditional Indian woman greets you by placing the palms of her hands together with a slight bow instead of offering a handshake.
- Women traveling to South Africa for business need to maintain professional status by keeping a moderate distance and not using an over-friendly approach, and they will be treated professionally by their associates.
- The South African culture is generally sociable and friendly.
- Afrikaans family names can be complicated and most South Africans will have several given names. Ask people how they prefer to be addressed if they don't tell you upon introduction.

Appearance/Attire

- Dress is conservative, with business suits for both men and women.
- Avoid wearing their native costumes.
- The safari suit and bush hat should be saved for the game park. Even then you will be labeled as a tourist.

- Casual dress in Johannesburg is dressier. Check with the host or hostess before arriving in jeans or shorts.
- Business dress is becoming less formal in many companies. Dress more conservatively for your first meetings and then dress according to what you see among your counterparts.
- Tropical weight suits are good options. A long-sleeved white or light-colored shirt with a tie is standard for men.
- Short sleeve shirts are for after work or casual meetings.
- Women's clothes standards are changing, but skirts and dresses are still the norm.
- Scarves are very popular for women.
- Sneakers should be worn only in the gym or for sports.
- Some South African women wear a *sari*.
- Muslim men will wear a *fez* or a white skull cap. They must cover their heads for prayer. While Muslim women's dress is more modern than in some other countries, they still cover their heads in public.

 ## Gift Giving

- Gifts are given mainly at Christmas and for birthdays.
- Always bring a gift if you're invited to a South African home.
- Flowers, good quality chocolates, or a bottle of good South African wine are perfect choices.
- Gifts of desk accessories or high quality pens are appropriate to present once a business relationship has been created.
- Proper wrapping shows that you put extra effort into the gift.
- Gifts are opened when they are received.
- If you are picked up at your hotel by a driver from a corporation, a tip is not necessary, but a small gift, like a company pen or something to show your appreciation would be appropriate.
- Do not present gifts with your left hand. Use either both hands or your right hand when presenting and receiving gifts.

 ## Tipping

- Tipping in restaurants is expected, and generally tips are not included in the bill.
- Standard tipping is 10 percent to 15 percent but, of course, this depends on the service provided.
- Porters expect a tip of R5 (US$.65) per bag, but it is not necessary to tip the doorman or desk clerk unless they provide an extra service for you.

- You should also tip your maid/housekeeper, tour guides, delivery person, and the shuttle drivers at the airport if they help you with your bags.
- It is not customary to tip hair salon owners, but you should tip the service provider, such as the person who washes your hair in the salon.
- Taxi drivers generally receive a 10 percent tip.

Gesture Awareness

- It's impolite to point at someone with your index finger wagging. It can be taken as a personal challenge.
- It's rude to talk with your hands in your pockets.
- It's customary for African men to precede women to pass through a doorway.
- Do not pull away from physical contact; it can be interpreted as unfriendliness or lack of trust.
- The reversed "V" or peace sign, with the palm facing inward and the middle and index fingers extended is the same as giving someone the finger in the West, and usually is accented by an upward thrust of the hand.
- While dining, do not point or gesture with your silverware during conversation.
- Do not misunderstand the porters at the airport who may approach you with both hands held in a cupped position. This is a gesture to show humbleness meaning, "The gift you may give me for carrying your bags will mean so much that I must hold it in two hands." It does not represent that they are soliciting a tip.

Faux Pas

- Do not fail to show respect. There is great respect, especially in the rural areas, for elders and ancestors. Showing respect is critical.
- Avoid being pushy or aggressive. Accept that business dealings may be slow in South Africa.
- Always wait to be asked to sit down.
- Don't initiate or participate in racist or sexist conversations.
- Do not interrupt a speaker.

USEFUL FACTS

President	Kgalema Motlanthe (2008)
Deputy President	Baleka Mbete (2008)
National Name	Republic of South Africa
Size	471,008 square miles (1,219,912 square km)
Population	43,786,115 (2008)
Capital	Administrative Capital: Pretoria Legislative Capital and largest city: Cape Town Judicial Capital: Bloemfontein. No decision has been made to consolidate the seat of the government.
Government	Republic
Currency	Rand
Religions	Christian 68% , Muslim 2%, Hindu 1.5%, indigenous beliefs and animist 28.5%
Language	There are eleven official languages, but English is the language of administration and is spoken throughout the country. Other languages are Afrikaans (spoken by descendants of Dutch colonizers and similar to Dutch and Flemish), Ndebele, Northern Sotho, Southern Sotho, Swazi, Tsongo, Tswana, Venda, Xhosa, and Zulu.
Ethnicity	Black 75%, white 13%, Colored 9%, Indian 3%
Industry	Industrial leader for minerals including gold, silver, copper, and diamonds. World's largest producer of platinum, gold, and chromium.
Time Zone	South Africa is two hours ahead of Greenwich Mean Time (GMT +2) or seven hours ahead of U.S. Eastern Standard Time (EST +7). No time zone differences within South Africa. South Africa does not observe daylight saving time.

South Africa

Telephone Code	International Code: +27 City Code: +12 (Pretoria) +21 (Cape Town) +51 (Bloemfontein)
Weather	Mostly semiarid, subtropical along east coast; sunny days and cool nights. Temperatures in South Africa tend to be lower than in other countries at similar latitudes, such as Australia, because of its greater elevation above sea level. Summer is mid-October to mid-February with hot, sunny weather. Autumn is from mid-February to April, with very little rain and warm temperatures. Winter in South Africa is May to July, with crisp days and cold nights. Spring is from August to mid-October, when South Africa is known for the spectacular flowers that blanket the plains.
Voltage/Frequency	220/240 V: 50 Hz

 # HOLIDAYS/FESTIVALS

1 January	New Year's Day
21 March	Human Rights Day
March/April	Good Friday and Easter
March/April	Family Day (Monday after Easter Sunday)
21 March	Human Rights Day
27 April	Freedom Day (The first democratic election was held in South Africa in 1994 and the new constitution took effect in 1997.)
1 May	Worker's Day
16 June	Youth Day
9 August	National Women's Day
24 September	Heritage Day (Celebrates their diverse "rainbow nation")
16 December	Day of Reconciliation (A day to overcome the past and build on a new nation)
25 December	Christmas Day
26 December	Day of Goodwill

LANGUAGE TIPS

Afrikaans	Phonetics	English
Ja/Nee	yaa/ney	Yes/No
Dankie	dang kee	Thank you
Asseblief	a si bleef	Please
Hallo	ha loh	Hello
Jammer	ya min	Sorry
Waar's die...	Vaars dee...	Where's the...
Het jy 'n Kamer?	Het yay i' kaa mir	Do you have a room?
Hoeveel kos dit?	Hu fil kos dit	How much is it?
Hoe gaan dit?	Hu khaan dit	How are you?
Goed dankie en jy?	Khut dang kee en yay	Fine, and you?

Chapter 24: SOUTH KOREA

LOCATION/GEOGRAPHY

Located in Northeast Asia, South Korea occupies the southern end of the Korean Peninsula, which is bordered by China and Russia to the north. (A demilitarized border between South and North Korea was established in 1953.) The west coast faces China across the Yellow Sea. The east coast and southern coasts, both facing Japan, are formed by the Sea of Japan (the East Sea) and the Korea Strait (Tsushima Strait), respectively.

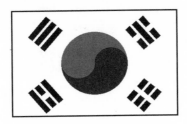

DID YOU KNOW?

- Half of the words that you will find in a Korean dictionary are of Chinese origin but do not belong to the same language family.
- Approximately 1.8 million people of Korean descent live in China, and many with Korean ancestry live in the United States and Japan.
- More than 3.5 million people participate in T'aekwondo in Korea, which is their most popular sport. The World Federation of the sport is located in Seoul.
- Ssirum, a form of wrestling, has been popular since the Three Kingdoms period (57 BC to 668 AD), but unfortunately, the sport is losing its identity and the popularity has decreased tremendously. In the past, the winners of ssirum tournaments were awarded an ox—actually the animal, not a trophy in the shape of one.
- Korea has a "National Living Treasure" designation that protects its culture and heritage through individuals and masters who pass on Korean music, dance, games, martial arts, rituals, and crafts to the next generations.
- Because of high infant mortality, a traditional ritual called Tol was celebrated when a baby reached one year old. The mortality rate has dropped considerably, but this special celebration is still practiced today.
- If you hear the classical piece Boccherini's Minuet in E while riding the train, this is your sign that the train will stop and you need to get off. They will be cleaning this train and you just have to wait for the next one.
- Speaking of music, most doorbells in Korea, chime with "Fur Elise." If you are not familiar with this piece of music by Ludwig von Beethoven, then find it online. You will recognize it instantly.
- Every day more than four million people will be squeezed, smashed, and tightly packed into the Seoul Metropolitan Subway system. It is even worse on weekends.
- There are 115 stations on the Seoul Metro Subway system. All directional signs in the subway system are written in both Korean and English. The voice announcements in the train about upcoming stations are said in Korean and then English.

Be On Your Best Cultural Behavior

- Seoul was the host of the 1988 Summer Olympic Games, which were held in September because of the hot and brutally humid weather.
- The President of South Korea resides in the Blue House, locally known as Cheong Wa Dae, and the site of leadership since 1104 AD.
- Only five percent of the population in Korea is over the age of 65, while 50 percent are under the age of 25.
- Seventy percent of Korea is mountainous, but most of the mountains are not high.
- Cheju hosted three of the 2002 World Cup games and is the largest island in Korea.
- Kim is the most popular Korean surname. Approximately 21 percent of Koreans have this name.
- Cho Kwang-jo, a scholar of Korean history in the 16th century, created a Confucian "village code" that became the basis for the law in small villages and the principles for official use by all Koreans.
- Korea has one of the highest per capita rates of alcohol consumption in the world. Drinking may occur prior to your business or to close a deal. Scotch is the popular drink.

BUSINESS ETIQUETTE

Punctuality

- Punctuality is important and respected. Arriving on time shows respect for the person or group you are meeting.
- Call if you see you will be running a few minutes late.
- You may be kept waiting for your appointment, but it is not a sign of disrespect. Instead it shows how pressured and rushed Korean people are with their time.
- Thirty minutes late for a social gathering is acceptable.

Meeting Manners

- Schedule meetings three to four weeks in advance.
- Expect your first meeting to be a time to get to know one another as opposed to having business discussions. Personal connections are important.
- Third-party introductions could be crucial. Third-party intermediaries could also handle any sensitive matters that may occur.
- Generally the most senior South Korean will enter the room first.
- Meetings will remain formal until trust has been developed.

- Women are achieving great advancements in a highly male-dominated society. They are getting into fields that were previously just for men. But some South Korean men still have a difficult time allowing women to make major decisions. Western women will be accepted in business.
- Be prepared for all your meetings by sending an agenda and any back-up material far enough in advance so it can be reviewed prior to the meeting. This should also include information about your company and any client testimonials that might help to explain your company and provide necessary information.
- Have your materials available in both Korean and English.
- Be informed that Koreans avoid saying "no." So even if they are saying "yes," they may actually be telling you no.
- Avoid asking questions that may need a direct yes or no answer. Phrase your questions to avoid the South Koreans' losing face. Better to give them an option to answer without a direct response.
- Deliver your answers to their questions as directly and concisely as possible. No further discussion or details should be given. This is when "less is more" is better.
- Be careful about the interpretation of contracts. To Westerners a contract is the final step to secure and finalize the deal. But to South Koreans a contract may be just their guide to conducting business. To many South Koreans the relationships developed between all involved are more important than contracts. Be clear about their awareness of the legalities of a contract. Some South Koreans are beginning to understand that contracts are legally binding.
- Business dealings will move slower than in Europe or North America. Be patient and do not rush the final decisions.
- Younger South Koreans will be easier to negotiate with because they are following more Westernized customs.
- At the end of the meeting, you can almost gauge your success or failure. If you receive a low and deep bow, then your Korean associates feel it was a good and successful meeting. If the bow is short and quick, then, chances are, it was not.
- Smoking is still very common in South Korea, so you might have to schedule breaks in your meeting.
- Holidays are generally taken from mid-July to mid-August, so plan in advance for your meetings and travels. Time is also taken over the major holidays.

Business Cards

- Exchange business cards when meeting for the first time.
- Come with plenty of cards because you will exchange them frequently.
- Your title should be clearly stated on your card. Status is very important during your dealings.
- The business card is extremely formal and a sign of how you will treat people and their business.
- Stand and then offer and accept cards with both hands.
- Read cards carefully before putting them away. Once you have read the cards, you can place them in your portfolio or business card case.
- Your cards should have your language on one side and the other side translated into Korean.
- Never write on their business cards in their presence.

Meals/Toasts

- Allow your host to show you to your seat. The seat of honor is the seat facing the front door. If you are seated there, then you should protest slightly.
- The eldest will always be served first. They will also start the eating process.
- If there is a great difference in age, then the younger or lower status person will offer a drink to the most honored or older person. They will offer a glass with two hands or support the right hand with the left. Depending on their status, the person receiving the glass will likely accept it in the same manner. Once this procedure is completed, then the person giving the drink will pour it into the glass of the receiver.
- Rice is their main and traditional dish in Korea, but this is followed by *kimchi,* a spicy vegetable dish made mostly of cabbage. There are more than 200 variations of *kimchi.*
- Noodles may be substituted for rice.
- Never point with or pierce your food with your chopsticks.
- Return your chopsticks to the table after a few bites and when you take a drink or stop to talk. As you place them on the chopstick rest, do not cross them.
- Avoid using your hands to pick up any food. Even when eating pieces of fruit, use a toothpick to pick them up.
- If you are eating food with bones or shells, then place them on an extra plate or on the table.
- If you have no idea what you are eating, you can ask. You might not like what you hear, but you should try a little bit of everything.

- Do not read anything into the silence you may experience during a meal. Generally there is little talk during meals. South Koreans prefer to concentrate on their food during the meal and then talk afterward, while they are enjoying coffee or tea.
- If conversation is exchanged during the meal, stay away from business talk unless your host brings it up first.
- Also allow your host to be first. Allow them to either serve you food on your plate or to tell you to serve yourself. Either way, don't start serving or eating before the host.
- Make sure you always place the food on your plate first. Don't take it from the serving dish or bowl and place a bite directly in your mouth.
- Try to use chopsticks. Practice ahead of time, but if all else fails, you may ask for forks or knives in a restaurant. A spoon will be provided for soups or dishes with noodles.
- Some of their foods can be very spicy and can be similar for breakfast, lunch, and dinner. The younger generation is moving away from the hot breakfast of rice and soup and going for a simpler start of their day. But generally, soup and *kimchi* are served at all three meals.
- If offered second helpings, you should refuse the first offer. Some will refuse up to three times before they accept. You also need to finish everything on your plate.
- To show that you are finished eating, place your chopsticks on the chopstick rest or on the table. Do not place them parallel across your rice bowl. If you're confused, just watch your host.
- Offer to pour other people's drinks and do not pour your own. Not pouring another person's drink is offensive Women will pour only men's drinks and not another woman's drink, but a woman can pour her own. If you want a refill, then you need to drink all of it to signal you would like more.
- Etiquette is to pass or accept food or drink with your right hand while your left hand supports your forearm/wrist.
- If you invite, then you pay the bill. But as a guest, you should also offer to pay the bill. If two people are dining, then the younger person generally pays for the older person.
- If you're invited to go drinking after dinner, then accept and go. Stronger relationships are developed in these more informal social gatherings.
- *Gun-bae* is the most common South Korean toast. When you raise your glass to toast, make sure you do it with your right hand. To show more respect to the person being toasted, support your right arm with your left hand. Be careful about draining your glass, because your host feels this is your cue to request a refill.

Be On Your Best Cultural Behavior

Entertainment

- If you're invited for a meal, always try to accept. You should also reciprocate the meal within a reasonable amount of time or on your next trip.
- Dinner is the largest meal of the day and usually takes place between 7 p.m. and 9 p.m. (1900 and 2100). Most entertaining will take place in restaurants and bars. To be invited to a home is an honor.
- Generally, spouses are not invited to dinner meals in restaurants. These business meals and entertaining are considered part of the negotiations.
- It is still common in Korean homes and restaurants to eat at a low table, sitting on cushions that are placed on the floor. Men will traditionally sit cross-legged and women will sit with their knees bent and legs together to one side. If you get uncomfortable, you can stretch your legs out in front of you under the table. Then you can go back to your original sitting position.
- During a social gathering, wait to be introduced.
- When you are leaving a social gathering, it is important to say goodbye and bow to each person individually.
- If you are invited to a South Korean home, it is common for people to meet and travel there together. Before entering the home, remove your shoes.
- The host will pour drinks for the guests in front of them; the hostess does not pour drinks.
- At times the hostess may not even join the party for the meal. She may stay in the kitchen to prepare the meal. She may then join everyone at the end of the evening for singing and drinks.
- Good topics of conversation include their cultural heritage, economic success, and international accomplishments; sports, especially the Olympics and soccer; hobbies; and kites.
- Topics to avoid include local and national politics, the Korean War, Socialism, Communism, the host's wife, and other personal family matters.
- Do not wander around the home to take your own self-guided tour, not even into the kitchen. Generally, the entertaining will remain in a few rooms.
- At the end of the evening, your host will probably accompany you to your car. They believe it is insulting to tell you good-bye or good night inside their home.
- A thank-you note should be sent the day after you've enjoyed a visit to a home.

Forms of Address/Introductions/Greetings

- Greetings in South Korea follow more formal rules of protocol.
- Most South Koreans will shake hands after the bow. They want to keep their culture alive but incorporate the new.
- If you are of lower status, then you bow to the higher. But the person of higher status generally initiates the handshake. If you are shaking hands, don't make it a firm one. It can be a solid handshake but avoid squeezing.
- Professional women will shake hands. Western women will probably need to initiate the handshake with Korean men, unless he is of higher status and then he will initiate.
- The person that initiates the bow will say *man-na-suh pan-gop-sumnida*, which means, "pleased to meet you."
- As you bow, say *an nyung hah sae yo* (the phrase for "Hello. How are you?"). Do not bow too fast and not too slow.
- If shaking hands with an elder, use both hands. It's good to compliment them on their good health.
- When shaking hands, most people support their right forearm with their left hand.
- To greet or say good-bye to an elder, stand with your legs straight and together. Place both arms stiffly by your side, keep your back straight and bend from the waist. Keep your head down and do not look at the elder.
- Eye contact can be confusing. Generally, eye contact indicates attentiveness to the other person, but in South Korea it is difficult for them to maintain direct eye contact with a higher or more authoritative person. Even some men will avoid direct eye contact with a woman. Direct eye contact will be avoided between junior and senior business associates.
- Titles are used to address people, and some will use title and their family name. You may be asked to address them by their first name, but wait until instructed to do so.
- Names can be confusing to Westerners. Koreans have the family name and then a given name. At times a given name may also include a part of the family/generation heritage. It can be confusing. Family names generally have just one syllable.
- Married women keep their maiden names. If you do not know a woman's maiden name, then she can be referred to as Mrs. with her husband's family name.
- Provide a detailed introduction about yourself if this is the first time you are meeting a person.

Appearance/Attire

- Business attire is conservative.
- Men wear dark suits with white shirts and conservative ties.
- Women dress conservatively, with subdued colors, for the initial meeting. As time progresses and you are comfortable with the relationships, then brighter colors can be worn.
- Consider the dinner arrangements and sitting on the floor. Tighter and shorter skirts would not be appropriate for women.
- Shorter skirts or sleeveless tops are considered inappropriate and in poor taste for business settings.
- You will see shorts and sleeveless shirts for their outings, but you still want to start conservatively.
- Jewelry for men consists of a watch and a wedding ring.
- Men will need to leave their jackets on during meetings unless the most senior South Korean removes his.

 Gift Giving

- Gift giving is very important to the South Korean culture, so always come prepared.
- If you are being presented with a gift, then refuse it a couple of times before you actually accept. Not to accept the gift is extremely insulting to the person that is presenting it to you.
- When receiving a gift from an elder, always use both hands to accept.
- Use both hands when presenting a gift.
- Some good gifts ideas for a first exchange in business could include a gift from your company displaying your logo or something from your country.
- Do not present expensive gifts but do look for good quality. Koreans will feel they need to reciprocate with gifts of similar cost. If they cannot return a similar gift then "loss of face" will result.
- If you think the gift you receive is too extravagant and possibly a bribe, you can return it stating that your company's policy will not allow you to accept such an expensive a gift. You should still show appreciation and thanks but regret you cannot accept such generosity.
- If you are presenting gifts to several people in a company, make sure that the gift of greater value is given to the senior person. The rest of the gifts may all be similar, which is probably a safe move. Or a tasteful gift to the entire team that could possibly be displayed is acceptable.
- If you're invited to a home, bring a gift of fruit, good quality chocolates, or flowers. Also crafts from your home country are a great idea.

South Korea

- If you know that the host or hostess smokes or drinks, gifts of imported liquor, coffee, or cigarettes are always appreciated.
- Since the number four is unlucky, do not present gifts in multiples of four.
- Giving a gift of seven items is considered lucky.
- Avoid scissors and knives as gifts.
- Gifts of cash are very popular for weddings, holidays (for children), birthdays, and even funerals. Cash gifts should be placed in an envelope.
- You can wrap gifts in yellow or red because they are royal colors, but do not sign your card in red.
- Use bright colors for the gift wrapping but avoid green, white, or black paper.
- When presented with a gift, do not open it. Gifts are opened privately unless you are a very good friend.

Tipping

- If you see a "no tipping" sign, then obey and do not tip. If you go ahead and tip, it is considered offensive.
- Service charges are automatically set in upscale restaurants and hotels.
- Tipping is not necessary unless you feel the service was exceptional and deserves an additional tip. In that case, 10 percent of the bill is appropriate.
- Taxi drivers do not expect to be tipped, but they certainly appreciate a gratuity. Most companies will allow drivers to keep the change left when you pay your fare. If they offer assistance with your luggage, then 10 percent of the fare is appropriate.

Gesture Awareness

- Do not touch, pat on the back or their arm, or backslap a Korean who is not a close friend or relative.
- Pass and accept with your right hand while your left hand supports your wrist.
- To get the attention of a person, extend your arm palm down, move your fingers in a scratching motion. Never use your index finger to motion to a person or to get them to come to you. It's considered very rude.
- Always cover your mouth if using a toothpick or yawning.
- Never use your index finger to point.
- Be careful of using large hand motions or facial expressions while you are talking. These gestures are frowned upon.

Faux Pas

- Heavy fines can be imposed for littering, spitting, or smoking in public places. Eating is legally allowed in public places but is frowned upon.
- Saving face is very important so all criticism should be done in private.
- Feet should not touch another person or object. They are considered dirty. Men should always be aware that the soles of their shoes are always pointing down. Do not cross your legs in front of a higher person in an open sitting arrangement.
- It is considered vulgar to blow your nose in public. If your nose does start to run or you need to blow it, turn away from the table and quietly take care of it. It is better to leave the table or move away from the table.
- Remember not to pick up food with your fingers. Fruit is cut and eaten with a fork or a toothpick.
- To remain modest is critical. If you are given a compliment, you can state that you are not worthy or just say "thank you." You can extend compliments, but be careful of singling out one person when you have been working with a team of people.
- Do not confuse Korea with other Asian countries, especially Japan, regarding their history or culture.
- As the evening of a social event progresses, you may see (and hear) your host getting up to sing a song "*karaoke*." If you are invited, then you need to go and sing your best. Even if you can't carry a tune, make it fun, keep it simple, and give it your best. It's considered rude to refuse to participate.
- Drinking is a key element in many business and social dealings. There is a swing now with the younger generation toward moderation and concentration more on quality than quantity.

 ## USEFUL FACTS

President	Lee Myung-bak (2008)
Prime Minister	Han Seung Soo (2008)
National Name	Republic of Korea
Size	37,911 square miles (98,189 square km)
Population	49,232,844 (2008)
Capital	Seoul

Government	Republic
Currency	Won
Religion	Protestant 20%, Catholic 7%, Buddhist 26%, Confucianist 1%, other 1%, no affiliation 45%
Language	Korean is the official language, and English is widely taught.
Ethnicity	Homogeneous except for approximately 20,000 Chinese
Industry	Agriculture, semiconductors, wireless telecommunications equipment, automobile production, steel, ships, petrochemicals. and computers
Time Zone	South Korea is nine hours ahead of Greenwich Mean Time (GMT +9) or 14 hours ahead of Eastern Standard Time (EST +14). South Korea does not observe daylight saving time.
Telephone Code	International Code: +82 City Code: +2 (Seoul)
Weather	The winters in South Korea can be very cold but with dry air from north China and Siberia. The summers are warm, with winds from the east and south bringing warm, moist air from the Pacific Ocean. Precipitation occurs year-round, with the most rain from June to September and snow from November into early May.
Voltage/Frequency	220 V; 60 Hz

HOLIDAYS/FESTIVALS

1 January	Solar New Year
Febraury	Seollal (First day of the solar New Year and one of the most important holidays, lasting three days with time spent visiting families and enjoying food and traditional games.)
1 March	Independence Movement Day
5 April	Arbor Day/Day of Trees
1 May	Labor Day
5 May	Children's Day
12 May	Buddha's Birthday
6 June	Memorial Day
17 July	Constitution Day
15 August	Liberation Day
September	Chuseok (Harvest Moon Festival and referred to as Thanksgiving Day)
3 October	National Foundation Day
25 December	Christmas Day

LANGUAGE TIPS

Korean Phonetics	English
An nyong ha se yo	Hello
An nyong-hi kye se yo	Good-bye (when you're leaving)
An nyoong-hi ka se yo	Good-bye (when another leaves)
Ko map sum nida	Thank you
Kam sa ham nida (formal)	
Ne/A ni yo	Yes/No
Choe song ham ni da	Sorry
Ol mayeyo	How much is it?
Hwa jang shi ri odi yeyo	Where are the toilets?
Odi-e' in nay o	Where can I find the ...?
Yeogiseo naeryeo jusaeyo	Stop here, please.

Chapter 25: SPAIN

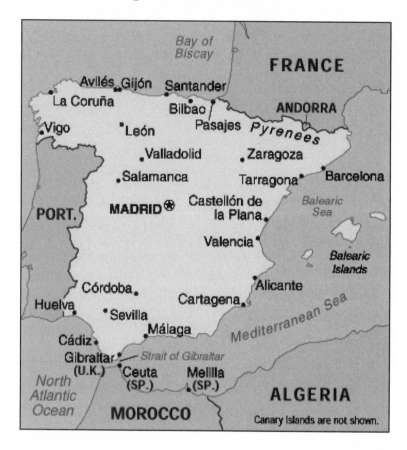

LOCATION/GEOGRAPHY

Spain occupies the majority of the Iberian Peninsula, which it shares with Portugal, in southwest Europe. To the northeast of Spain is France. Only ten miles (16 km) south, at the Strait of Gibraltar, is Africa. The Bay of Biscay is to the north and the Mediterranean Sea is to the east of Spain. On the east coast in the Mediterranean are the Balearic Islands and 60 miles west of Africa are Spain's Canary Islands.

 DID YOU KNOW?

- In 1561, King Philip II established Madrid as the capital.
- According to the Guinness Book of Records, the Madrid restaurant Botin is the oldest restaurant in the world.
- If you take a ride on the high-speed train, The Ave, that connects Madrid to Seville, Cordoba, and Ciudad Real, you are guaranteed your money back if The Ave is delayed more than five minutes.
- Barcelona hosted the 1992 Summer Olympic Games. Before the games, the seaside was the site of factories and a port, but it was totally rebuilt in time for the games to feature beaches, restaurants, and bars.
- Malaga, Andalucia, is the birthplace of Pablo Picasso (1881) and is also the chief Mediterranean seaport and a popular resort city in southern Spain.
- El Greco was actually from Crete, but he settled in Toledo, Spain.
- The Latin dance, *flamenco*, originated in Andalucia.
- Gibraltar has a one-kilometer (.62 miles) border with Spain. This small colony is considered part of Britain and is located on the southern tip of Spain. Gibraltar is known for its "Rock," inhabited by Barbary apes. The British say they will leave the Rock of Gibraltar only when the apes do.
- Approximately 10 million people visit the Canary Islands each year.
- Pamplona may have the "Running of the Bulls" and Valencia may have oranges, but Bunol hosts La Tomatina, the world's largest vegetable fight. Twenty thousand people and 90,000 pounds of tomatoes collide. After about 30 minutes, participants head to the river to wash away the saucy mess.
- Spain did not have a role in either World War I or World War II.
- In 2005, same-sex marriages became legal in Spain.
- Since 2006, smoking has been banned in all workplaces, bars, and restaurants.
- Saint Josemaria Escriva de Balaguer from the Aragonese town of Barbastro created the famous cult Opus Dei in 1928. This cult was featured in Dan Brown's The Da Vinci Code.
- Spain is one of the last remaining refuges for the European wolf. Their population is estimated at 2,000.

Be On Your Best Cultural Behavior

BUSINESS ETIQUETTE

Punctuality

- Spaniards may not practice punctuality for business meetings, but they do expect that you will arrive on time.
- Arrive at your scheduled appointment time, but be prepared to wait 15 to 30 minutes for your contact to meet with you. Don't take it personally; it is not meant to be rude, but you might want to come prepared with something to read or do while you wait.
- Call with an explanation if you are delayed or will arrive late.

Meeting Manners

- Most offices are open Monday to Friday from 9 a.m. to 1:30 p.m. (0900 to 1330) or 2 p.m. (1400) and then will reopen at 4:30 p.m. (1630) or 5 p.m. (1700) until about 8 p.m. (2000).
- Always make appointments well in advance and follow up by confirming by letter, fax, or e-mail just before the appointment.
- Typically, Spanish is the language of meetings, but some large companies conduct business in English and Spanish. Check ahead to see if an interpreter is needed.
- Most Spaniards have 30 days of paid vacation per year and generally will take this time off in August or around Easter. Avoid scheduling meetings over these periods and at Christmas.
- The *siesta* still remains an important part of Spaniards' day, but Spaniards' working hours are becoming more "Europeanized." Some are taking shorter breaks and most offices do not close completely during the day. Bigger stores and shops remain open through the entire day and close at 9 p.m. (2100).
- Even though the working day generally starts at 9 a.m. (0900), people don't usually get down to business until after visiting and coffee. So generally, 9:30 a.m. or 10 a.m. (0930 or 1000) is more common for early appointments. The best initial meeting time in the office is generally mid-morning.
- When you arrive for your appointment, present your business card to the receptionist to advise your contact that you have arrived.
- Lunch generally starts between 1 p.m. and 2 p.m. (1300 and 1400) and can be a very quick, casual meal at a local café or bar or can last several hours in a fine restaurant. Workers may stay at the office until 7 p.m. or 8 p.m. (1900 or 2000) or later.
- Business can be conducted over meals, but this should be arranged in advance. Spaniards consider eating as a social activity. Breakfast

meetings are not very popular and should not be scheduled before 8:30 a.m. (0830) Spaniards will go home for lunch, so the best time for a business meal might be a late dinner. If the day includes dinner, the working day may continue beyond midnight.

- The meeting and decision making is not hurried but a more gradual, detailed procedure that involves consideration from various levels within the company.
- Individualism is particularly predominant in management and may not favor group decisions or team orientation. The individual in highest authority makes the final decision.
- Spaniards generally expect that the person or people who are negotiating will have the authority to make final decisions.
- It's to your advantage to maintain good relationships with all counterparts in all positions for complete success.
- Spanish business culture requires a sense of self-dignity, consideration, and diplomacy.
- Be prepared for personal questions about your family life and background to establish a strong relationship. Spaniards prefer to be familiar with people in business. Personal contacts enable the negotiation process to advance more quickly and successfully.
- Trust and personal feelings play a major role in the final decision-making process.
- Women are gaining senior management positions, but there are still relatively few women at high levels. Businesswomen traveling to Spain will be treated with respect, but dressing and behaving in a professional manner are essential. Many Spanish men still feel the need to be in control in all situations. This macho and chauvinistic behavior toward women known as machismo has changed drastically over the last few years.
- Men are usually willing to accept a lunch or dinner invitation from a businesswoman. However it is difficult for women to pay for a man's meal. Spanish men expect to pay. Women should speak to the maitre d'

Business Cards

- Have plenty of business cards to exchange at first meetings.
- Always include your official business position and if you have a PhD.
- Spanish people are impressed with titles, so never eliminate from your card.
- Cards should be printed in your language on one side and Spanish on the other.

- Present your card with the Spanish side facing the recipient.
- Social cards are still exchanged at social gatherings. Joint cards are given by married couples with the husband's name first (just tradition), followed by the wife's, their address, telephone and, if they prefer, the e-mail address. These are printed in script type and follow the correct etiquette. You should also have a social card to exchange at these occasions. Can be easily printed for you in Spain.

Meals/Toasts

- Most business meals will be handled in restaurants, bars, or hotels, not homes.
- The person who extends the invitation pays the bill. If you have been invited out, you should reciprocate at a later date, being careful not to give the impression that you are simply repaying your hosts. Women need to handle payment in advance or make arrangements to handle the bill to avoid any conflict about who is paying.
- The best way to experience Spanish food is to follow the example of the Spanish themselves and *graze*. A wide range of small plates will generally accompany drinks. Rarely is there a menu, but you will most likely receive olives, raw and cooked vegetables, cured and cooked meats, cheeses, fish, and shellfish. *Tapas*, a variety of appetizers, snacks, or finger foods, are often served.
- A popular lunchtime sandwich, consisting of a long bread roll filled with ham and cheese, is called a *bocadillo* (bock a di yo).
- Make sure you eat continental style, with the knife in your right hand and fork in your left. Keep both hands above the table at all times.
- No bread and butter plate is used. Bread is set directly on the table. Restaurants generally charge for bread by the piece.
- Eat everything on your plate. It's considered bad manners to leave and waste food. Accept a second helping only if you are sure you can finish it.
- When finished with the meal, place your knife and fork side by side on the plate. If they are crossed or at opposite sides of the plate, it will be assumed that you have not finished and would like more to eat.
- Spain is a wine-drinking country, especially with meals. Spain is known for its sherry from Jerez de la Frontera. Sangria should be taken in small quantities because it contains a large amount of brandy.
- If you want a draught beer, you should order a *cana* (small) or *tubo* (large at 300 ml). If you simply ask for a *cerveza*, you will receive a more expensive bottled beer.
- Spain follows the traditional European seating arrangement, with the host and hostess sitting at opposite ends of the table, the male guest of honor seated to the right of the hostess, and the female guest of honor

placed at the right of the host (provided the host is a male and the hostess is a female).

- Dinner is served from 8:30 p.m. to 11 p.m. (2030 to 2300). Many restaurants and bars are open continuously throughout the day, offering *tapas*, appetizers, and meals.
- Women should not dine alone in a restaurant or bar at night. It is acceptable to do so at lunch.
- When making a toast, the host or hostess simply raises his or her glass and says, "*Salud!*" Guests do the same in response. Attempt to give a toast in Spanish. Be brief when toasting. It is acceptable for women to give toasts.

Entertainment

- Being invited to a home is rare and would constitute a mark of true friendship. At times an invitation is extended only to show politeness and you can decline. If they ask again, you should accept and appreciate the honor. You may be invited to the home for drinks before proceeding to a bar or restaurant.
- It is common for Spaniards to be late by 15 to 30 minutes for social events. But they will never be late for a bullfight.
- If you want to include your spouse for the meal that you are hosting, you must first extend an invitation to your Spanish contact's spouse. If the spouse accepts, then it is permissible to include your own spouse.
- Meals are considered a social activity, so don't assume you will discuss business. Allow your counterpart to initiate any business discussion.
- The nightclubs in Spain will stay open until 3 a.m. or 4 a.m. (0300 or 0400) in the morning, particularly from Thursday to Sunday. Some establishments will be open until dawn.

Forms of Address/Introductions/Greetings

- Initial business introductions are always formal, with a brief but firm handshake. Maintain eye contact while saying *buenos dias* (bway-nohs dee-ahs), meaning good day, or *buenas tardes* (bway-nahs tard-ays), meaning good afternoon/evening, depending on the time of the day, to both men and women.
- Men generally continue to shake hands for all occasions. Women embrace and kiss. You will also see women meeting men with a kiss. In a more personal setting, men will hug or pat each other on the back as well as shake hands.
- Spaniards will stand close in conversation and may even pat your arm or shoulder as they are talking. Do not move away. Doing so is very offensive to the Spaniards.

- First names are traditionally reserved for family, close friends, and children.
- It is always correct to use the basic title of courtesy (*Senor* for Mr., *Senora* for Mrs., *Senorita* for Miss) followed by the surname.
- It's advisable to use titles such as Professor, but professional and/or academic titles are not normally used when addressing Spanish executives.
- Spaniards have two surnames, with their father's first surname and their mother's first surname. You should use both unless or until it is clear that your colleague uses only one. The same applies to compound first names.
- *Usted* (oo-sted) should be used when addressing a counterpart in Spanish unless you are invited to the use the more informal *tu*.
- Younger Spaniards may use first names and *tu* from the beginning in business situations, at least with their peers, but still will use *usted* for elders or superiors.
- The old-fashioned culture is still observed, and modesty is valued above assertiveness. Spaniards convey a dignified image in public or formal settings but become relaxed in private.
- Spaniards are amusing and entertaining, with humor playing an important part in both business and personal situations. Banter is acceptable but not with sarcasm or anything that might offend. Respect and trust is very important in dealing with Spaniards. Avoid any disrespectful remarks about their traditions, customs, or practices.
- Topics of conversation can include your home country, travels (especially in Spain), Spanish art, architecture, and pre-20th century history, Spanish traditions (*flamenco*), Spanish wines and sherry, sport (especially football/soccer), bullfighting, politics (but with care and if you understand), and family (especially your host's children).
- Topics to avoid are bullfighting if you disagree with your counterpart about it, religion, the Spanish Civil War and WW II, Franco, Basque separatism, and Catalan regionalism, Gibraltar, questions of a personal nature (especially during initial introductions), and machismo and feminism.

 ## Appearance/Attire

- Spaniards are extremely top-quality and dress-conscious and will perceive your appearance as an indication of your professional achievement and relative social standing.
- Men should wear dark woolen or linen suits and silk ties with white cotton shirts.

- Women should wear well-cut suits, pant suits, or business dresses of high-quality fabrics. Approval is given for designer clothes and brand names.
- Spanish women do not draw attention to their physical sexuality, so when traveling to Spain women should dress professionally and modestly. Dress conservatively, avoiding bright or flashy colors.
- Dress is elegant even for casual occasions.
- Shoes are the most important part of dress. Shabby or run-down shoes can ruin a nice impression.
- The summers can be extremely hot, so lightweight suits are advised. Men can be seen outside with their ties loosened and their jackets over their shoulders.
- Shorts are not acceptable in public. The dress code for entering a church is extremely important and it's disrespectful to display excessive bare flesh.
- Better restaurants enforce a "business casual" dress even in the hot months of July and August. Smart casual does not mean wrinkled t-shirts, cheap jeans, and sneakers.

Gift Giving

- Chrysanthemums are used for funerals. Other flowers to avoid are dahlias, white lilies, and red roses. Do not give a bouquet of 13 flowers.
- Purple and black combined can be very distasteful, since these are the colors associated with the processionals during Holy Week.
- Gifts are not normally exchanged at business meetings but can be given at the successful close of a deal.
- If you receive a gift, you should open it immediately in front of the giver.
- If and when you offer a gift, it should be of high quality and wrapped in quality paper. Use logo gifts only if they are tasteful and of good quality.
- Be careful of extravagant gifts that could be perceived as bribes.
- Coffee-table books from your home country are always welcome, along with desk items, art, and music.
- University or sports team shirts and caps are good for children if you're invited to a home.
- A bottle of fine brandy or whisky will work if you came unprepared with gifts from your home or company.
- Chocolates, dessert items, or flowers (being careful on the selection of flowers) are great items to take if invited to a Spanish home.
- Spanish companies traditionally give their employees a hamper or basket of food and drink at Christmas. (Families and friends exchange presents on the Feast of the Epiphany, 6 January.)

 Tipping

- There are no real official standards for tipping. Locals tip very modestly if at all.
- It's polite to leave a small tip of five percent for a waiter in a restaurant and change for the bartender, and it's common to tip toilet attendants and hotel staff.
- The easiest and most common way to figure a tip is to just round up the bill to the nearest euro.
- Tipping is not obligatory and not leaving a tip is not insulting as it is in the United States. Waiters are paid a salary that they can live on, but tips are appreciated.
- Taxis are metered and usually have a fixed fare, but a gratuity of 10 percent is appropriate.

 Gesture Awareness

- The OK symbol, joining the thumb and index finger, is very vulgar in Spain.
- When summoning someone (waiter), turn your palm down and wave your fingers or entire hand.
- Avoid yawning or stretching in public. It's considered very disrespectful.
- Do not confuse their impassioned body language for anger. When they are angry, you will know it.
- Never touch, hug, or back slap a Spaniard you do not know well, unless a friendly Spaniard touches you first.
- Spaniards speak a lot with their hands. Never mimic them.
- Women need to be aware of eye contact. Returning a man's gaze may be interpreted as flirting or showing interest.

 Faux Pas

- Assertiveness and superiority are not respected. Spaniards prefer a more modest approach to business negotiations.
- Make sure you completely understand the correct greeting and proper usage of their names. The Spaniards have two, with their father's first surname and their mother's surname. Normally the father's surname is used on its own.
- Avoid at all costs causing loss of face by criticizing, embarrassing, or misunderstanding. Spanish culture places great emphasis on personal pride.
- Don't be insulted if you are interrupted while talking. They are just genuinely interested.

USEFUL FACTS

Ruler	King Juan Carlos I (1975)
Prime Minister	Jose Luis Rodriguez Zapatero (2004)
National Name	Reino de Espana Kingdom of Spain
Size	192,819 square miles (499,401 square km)
Population	40,491,051 (2008)
Capital	Madrid
Government	Parliamentary Monarchy
Currency	Euro (formerly peseta)
Religions	Roman Catholic 94%, others 6%
Languages	Castilian Spanish 74% (official nationwide), Catalan 17%, Galician 7%, Basque 2% (each official regionally)
Ethnicity	Castilians 74%, Catalans 16%, Basques 2%, and Galicians 7%, and small percentage of the nomadic Spanish Roma (Gypsies) or Gitanos
Industry	Agriculture, manufacturing, mining and construction services, textiles and apparel, food and beverages, metals and metal manufactures, chemicals, ship building, automobiles, machine tools, tourism, clay and refractory products, footwear, pharmaceuticals and medial equipment
Time Zone	Spain is on Greenwich Mean Time (GMT) or five hours ahead of Eastern Standard Time (EST +5). Spain observes daylight saving time.
Telephone Code	International Country Code: +34 City Code: +91 (Madrid)

Weather	Hot and clear summers in the interior; more moderate and cloudy along the coast. Cloudy and cold winters in the interior. Partly cloudy and cool along the coast. Mediterranean climate on the coast, continental climate with mild to hot summers and cold winters in the plateaus and valleys to the east.
Voltage/Frequency	220 V; 50Hz

HOLIDAYS/FESTIVALS

1 January	New Year's Day
6 January	Epiphany
March/April	Holy (or Maundy) Thursday
March/April	Good Friday and Easter
1 May	Workers' Day
25 July	Saint James Day
15 August	Assumption of the Virgin
12 October	National Holiday (Hispanic Day)
1 November	All Saints' Day
6 December	Constitution Day
8 December	Immaculate Conception
25 December	Christmas Day

LANGUAGE TIPS

Spanish	Phonetics	English
Mucho gusto/ Encantado	Moo-choh goo stoh/ en-cahn-tah-doh	Nice to meet you. Pleasure to meet you. (male)
Igualmente	Ee-guahl-mehn-tay	Same here
Senor/Senora/Senorita	Sayn-yor/Sayn-yor-ah/ Sayn-yor-ee-tah	Mr./Mrs./Miss
Como se llama usted?	Koh-moh say yah-mah oo-sted	What is your name? (formal)
Como te llamas?	Koh-moh tay yah mahs	What is your name? (informal)

Me llamo…	May yah-moh...	My name is…
Si/No	See/Noh	Yes/No
Vamos!	Bah-mohs	Let's go!
Hasta manana	Ah-stah mahn-yahn-ah	See you tomorrow
Aqui	Ah-kee	Here

Please see other chapters of Spanish-speaking countries for additional words and phrases.

Chapter 26: SWEDEN

LOCATION/GEOGRAPHY

Sweden shares the Scandinavian Peninsula with Norway, its neighbor to the west. Sweden is surrounded on its other sides by the Baltic Sea, the Gulf of Bothnia, and two other bodies of water called the Kattegat and Skagerrak. Finland is to the east, and Denmark, Germany, and Poland are to the south. One-tenth larger than California, Sweden is the fourth largest country in Europe

DID YOU KNOW?

- Smorgasbord is a famous Swedish traditional buffet.
- Saunas are enjoyed, and there's even a protocol to follow. Times are reserved for men separate from women, and it's fine to enjoy without your bathing suit. Some people follow a sauna session with a dip into a cold stream, a shower, or even a snow bath.
- North of the Artic Circle, the sun never sets for part of the summer. This is called the "midnight sun." In the winter, the nights are unending and the season is called "polar nights." In the artic north of Sweden, you will be able to see the display of the Aurora Borealis (the Northern Lights) during the winter months.
- Holiday celebrations fall on the Eve of the holiday, instead of the actual day.
- Alfred Nobel (1833-1896) invented dynamite and was the founder of the Nobel Foundation. We will also know him for the Nobel Prize, which was partly funded with the revenue from his oil production business in Baku. The annual Nobel awards celebration is held in Stockholm's City Hall.
- Carl Von Linne was a Swedish botanist and naturalist from the 16th century who introduced the scientific method of naming flora (plants) and fauna (animals).
- Anders Celsius, astronomer who lived from 1701-1744, invented the thermometer.
- Other names you may recognize call Sweden home. These include the performing group ABBA and companies including Ericsson, IKEA, Saab, and Volvo.
- Are you familiar with Pippi Longstocking? Pippi Langstrump, as she's known in Sweden, is a fictional character in a series of children's books that were first published in 1945 by Swedish author Astrid Lindgren.
- Five weeks is the minimum vacation time per year.
- To toast comes from an old tradition of *skal* which is a greeting. As people entered they were met with shouts of *skal* (skoal), the bowl of the welcome drink to represent friendship. The first letters of the welcome or greeting is how the word got its name. *Sundheit* for Good Health; *Karlet* for Friendship; *Aruger* for Long Life and *Lycka* for Happiness.

BUSINESS ETIQUETTE

Punctuality
- Be punctual for both business and social events.
- If you are running late, phone ahead and have a good reason.
- "Fashionably late" is not appropriate.

Meeting Manners
- Schedule appointments at least two weeks in advance.
- Confirm the time and location in advance.
- The best time of the day for meetings is from 9 a.m. to 10 a.m. (0900 to 1000) and 2 p.m. to 4 p.m. (1400 to1600).
- Avoid canceling or changing the time and place of meetings.
- June, July, August, Christmas holiday time (22 December to 6 January), and late February through early March are popular holiday times, so plan your travels and meetings accordingly.
- Most Swedes speak English, so most meetings will be handled in English.
- Your proposal should be well prepared and highlight the experience and knowledge of your company.
- The first meeting might be spent evaluating your company and what you bring to the table.
- A detailed agenda with facts and figures is critical. Stick to the agenda and the start and finish time as outlined on the agenda.
- The Swedes prefer to-the-point and well outlined details that are easy to understand. State-of-the-art, highly technical presentations are not necessary.
- A decision will take several meetings and a consensus. Teamwork and compromise are critical to reach a decision. Hierarchy is important, but even lower management may play a role in the decision-making process.
- Women and men are both members of the team in the process and decisions.
- Emotions do not belong in the negotiations. Remain controlled.
- Compliment the whole group as opposed to individuals.
- Time is critical, so very little chitchat will be conducted before or during a meeting.
- Procedures are enforced, and they believe following procedure is the most effective way of accomplishing a program or project.

Business Cards

- Appropriate to have one side of your card translated to Swedish. If you are from an English-speaking country, most Swedes do speak and understand English.
- Have plenty of cards.
- Titles and your education are not necessary on your business cards.
- There is no particular protocol, other than respect, for exchanging cards.

Meals/Toasts

- Breakfast meetings are not a local custom, but are common for traveling businesspeople.
- Lunch and dinner meetings are common. Spouses may be invited to dinners but not to lunches. Business generally is not discussed, so allow your Swedish associates to initiate the business conversation. If they start the discussion, then it is fine to continue.
- Reservations should be made in advance for luncheon meetings. Select a more formal restaurant.
- The honored guest will sit at either the head of the table or in the center. The most important guest will be seated to the left of the hostess and the female guest of honor sits to the right of the host.
- Men will stand when a woman enters the room. Both men and women will stand when older people enter or leave a room.
- Continental eating is the standard, keeping the knife in the right hand and the fork in the left. To signal that you have completed the meal, place the fork and knife diagonally across your plate with the handles of the silverware at the 4 o'clock position.
- Do not start to eat until you have been instructed by the host to do so.
- Pass foods and all dishes to the left. Taking the last serving from the platter is considered rude.
- Make sure you keep your hands above the table. Just rest your wrists on the top of the table.
- Bread is the only food that you would pick up with your hands.
- Leave a little food on the plate so you do not receive any more. If you want something more to drink, then lower your glass to half full. It will be refilled.
- Coffee breaks happen twice a day at 10 a.m. (1000) and 4 p.m. (1600).
- Alcohol is available for lunch and dinner meals. Drinks for dinner are usually regional beers or wine.
- Smorgasbord is famous as a Swedish tradition. Make several trips to sample different foods. Proper etiquette is to sample everything and not fill up your plate on one trip. Each trip will require a clean plate.

- The most common toast is *skal*, (pronounced "skoal"). Do not take a first sip until the host has offered the first toast. The host will say "welcome" and then you can begin to drink your wine.
- You can then follow up with a toast after the host has made the initial one.
- Always keep good eye contact during a toast. Start by looking at everyone, take your drink, make eye contact again, and place the drink back on the table.
- If numerous people are being toasted, then look at each individual as you make the toast.
- *Tack for maten* (thank-you for the food) is said by the male guest of honor at the end of the dinner party to thank the host or hostess.

Entertainment

- Invitations to a Swedish home are not extended early in a business relationship.
- If dinner is served in a home, it is generally between 6 p.m. and 7:30 p.m. (1800–1930).
- For weekend dinners in a home, the usual start time is at 8 p.m. (2000).
- The traditional dinner has four courses—fish, meat, salad, and dessert.
- Coffee is served after the meal and not during. Generally everyone moves to the living room for coffee.
- Meals can be either more relaxed or formal in a home. Just make sure you know the proper dress for the evening.
- Do not wander around the house from room to room. In Swedish homes, some areas are off-limits to guests.
- Arrive on time if invited to a home, and bring a gift of chocolates, a bottle of wine, or flowers.
- Wait to be seated. There may even be place cards.
- Tradition is to remove your shoes when entering a Swedish home.
- When you are ready to leave a Swedish home, wait until you reach the doorway or are actually outside before you put your coat on. Doing it while still in the home and talking sends a rude sign that you can't wait to leave.
- If you have been a guest in someone's home, the very next time you see them, it is important to thank them again immediately.
- If you invite someone for a meal, then you will pay. Rank could make a difference. Making arrangements in advance to handle the bill is the professional way to ensure you will pay.
- If you are hosting, consider arranging transportation or taxi service for your guests following the meal.

Forms of Address/Introductions/Greetings

- Shake hands with everyone. Bypass the group wave. It is not acceptable.
- The handshake between men is quick and firm, but a little easier between men and women or two women.
- Some men may wait for a woman to extend her hand to them, but it's more common for either to initiate the handshake.
- Men will remove their gloves when shaking hands with another man.
- You will even still see a man tip his hat to a woman and even take it off while speaking with one.
- Women will be introduced first when in a group.
- There's no closeness, backslapping, or touching on first introductions.
- Air kissing on both cheeks can replace a handshake after your business or social relationships have been established.
- Eye contact is good and direct during introductions. Make sure you maintain this contact while talking with people.
- First names are very appropriate initially in the relationship. Titles are not important.
- Generally, the Swedish people are comfortable at two arms' lengths personal space.
- Body language and hand gestures need to be kept to a minimum.
- Avoid private conversations in public areas.
- Swedes will be impressed if you speak any Swedish, but chances are, they will switch to English immediately.
- Swedes are quiet people, so keep your emotions to a minimum and use a soft, almost monotone voice.
- Third-party introductions are common. If not the case, then move around the room introducing yourself with handshakes and stating your name.
- *God dag* (Good Day) is the Swedish greeting, along with the handshake and good eye contact.
- Use a handshake to end your conversation.

Appearance/Attire

- Women traveling and doing business in Sweden, should dress professionally and remain professional at all times.
- Conservative dress is appropriate for business appointments.
- Men will wear suits and ties. Khakis and other informal clothes are not appropriate for men in the business setting.
- Women will also be in business attire with suits, skirts and blouses, or dresses.

- The latest fashions and well-dressed style are standard for Swedes.
- Sneakers and jeans can be seen as informal wear on the streets, but you won't see them being worn to work.
- Informal social gatherings may not require a coat and tie for the men, but dress will not be as casual as jeans, sneakers, or t-shirts.
- Shorts and t-shirts can and only should be found during the summer in a relaxed atmosphere.
- Equality is important in Sweden, so most will dress on an average level, with nothing too elaborate or flashy.

 ## Gift Giving

- Wait until you receive a gift before you send one or give one to a business associate.
- Sending a holiday card to thank them for the business throughout the year is appropriate. Allow enough time for cards to reach them in time for the holidays.
- An invitation to a social event or dinner party merits a thank-you note or gift.
- Flowers can be brought with you to the dinner party, but make sure they are unwrapped before presenting them to the hostess.
- Do not present chrysanthemums or white lilies. Both are used for funerals.
- Red roses and orchids are on the romantic side, so also avoid them.
- Send and present flowers only in odd numbers, which is an old European tradition
- Appropriate gifts if invited to a Swedish home could include flowers, wine, cake, or chocolates. Children love to receive candy.
- Fine liquor or wines from the United States are great gifts, since they are very expensive in Sweden.
- Gifts are more appropriate at the end of business dealings. Just make sure the gift is not expensive or considered a bribe. Books about your home country, desk accessories, or a gift that you know the recipient will enjoy and appreciate are your best bets.

 ## Tipping

- Tips are usually included in the total price at a restaurant. But an additional 7 percent to 10 percent is expected.
- Tipping for special services by hotel staff is not expected, but you can decide based on the service they provide.
- A fixed amount may be assessed for porters and cloakroom attendants.

- You should modestly tip doormen at hotels and restaurants.
- A 10 percent tip is appropriate for taxi drivers, or at least round up the fare that is shown on the meter.
- It's best to catch a taxi at designated taxi stands. You can also arrange a taxi at your hotel, but a hotel surcharge may be added to the fee.

Gesture Awareness

- Keep your hands out of your pockets while you are speaking. Keep them at your side when standing.
- Women should never cross their ankle over their knee. Men can do this, but not women.
- Tossing your head means "come here."
- Make eye contact to get the attention of the wait staff. It's impolite to wave or call out to them.

Faux Pas

- No gum chewing, slouching, or leaning against a wall in public.
- Men should remove their hats when talking with women. Even tipping your hat is common when passing someone you know.
- Nude sunbathing is common. Don't stare.
- Avoid personal questions. Avoid, "So, what do you think?" Even that is too personal.
- Do not fill in the holes in a conversation. Swedes comfortably handle silence.
- Do not compare the local regions against one another. Swedes have pride and will take offense.
- Don't fail to understand the differences between Finland, Norway, Sweden, and Denmark.
- Don't stretch the truth.
- No profanity at any time. It is considered very offensive.
- Conversation topics to avoid include criticizing the Swedish government, economy, or culture; family; income; paying compliments to people that you just met; the Olaf Palme assassination; personal background; anything as it relates to rank, status, and showiness; comparing social welfare systems; complaining about high costs of living in Scandinavia; or criticizing the Swedish sense of humor. Good conversation topics include travel, the Swedish culture, hockey, fine art, Swedish history, current events, vacations and holidays, soccer and other sports, music, outdoors, nature, and politics (if you are sure what you are talking about).

USEFUL FACTS

Sovereign	King Carl XVI Gustaf (1973)
Prime Minister	Fredrik Reinfeldt (2006)
National Name	Konungariket Sverige Kingdom of Sweden
Size	158,927 square miles (411,621 square km)
Population	9,045,389 (2008)
Capital	Stockholm
Government	Constitutional Monarchy
Currency	Krona
Religion	Lutheran 87%, others include Roman Catholic, Orthodox, Baptist, Muslim, Jewish, and Buddhist
Language	Swedish is the official language of Sweden, with a small minority speaking Sami and Finnish. English is their second language. Swedish is also one of the official languages of Finland.
Ethnicity	Swedes with Finnish and Sami minorities; foreign-born or first-generation immigrants: Finns, Danes, Yugoslavs, Norwegians, Turks and Greeks,
Industry	Iron and steel, precision equipment, electrical and telecom equipment, wood pulp and paper products, processed foods, motor vehicles, pharmaceuticals
Time Zone	Sweden is one hour ahead of Greenwich Mean Time (GMT +1) or six hours ahead of U.S. Eastern standard Time (EST +6). Sweden observes daylight saving time.
Telephone Code	International Code: +46 City Code: + 8 (Stockholm)

| Weather | The north of Sweden is within the Artic Circle, so it has a cold climate. The winters are generally long and very, very cold. The south of Sweden has much milder climate but still cold winters and cool, partly cloudy summers. |

| Voltage/Frequency | 230 V; 50 Hz |

HOLIDAYS/FESTIVALS

1 January	New Year's Day
5/6 January	Epiphany Eve/ Epiphany
March/April	Good Friday/ Easter Sunday/ Easter Monday
30 April	Walpurgis Night/Birthday of the King (King Carl XVI Gustaf's birthday)
1 May	May Day
The sixth Thursday after Easter	Ascension Day
Seven Sunday after Easter	Whitsunday
6 June	Constitution Day and Flag Day (Anniversary of adoption of the 1809 constitution. Shares the date with Flag Day that commemorates 6 June 1523, when Gustavus I ascended to the throne.)
Friday falling October 30-November 5	All Saints' Eve
Saturday falling October 30-November 6	All Saints' Day
14 December	Saint Lucia's Day
24/25 December	Christmas Eve/Christmas Day
26 December	Boxing Day
31 December	New Year's Eve

LANGUAGE TIPS

Swedish	**Phonetics**	**English**
Hej	Hay	Hello
Adjo/Hej da (informal)	Ad-juuh/Hay doo	Good-bye
Ja/Nej	Yah/Nay	Yes/No
Snalla	SNELL-la	Please
Tack	Tock	Thank you
Var sa god	VAHR sha good	You're welcome
Ursakta	Oor-sayk-tha	Excuse me
(getting attention)		
Forlat (begging pardon)	Fur loot	Excuse me
Talar du engelska?	Taahlar doo	Do you speak English?
Ayngelskah		
Jag forstar inte	Yag fur stoor eenta	I don't understand
Var ar toaletten?	Wahr ahr tooalathan	Where is the toilet?

Chapter 27: SWITZERLAND

LOCATION/GEOGRAPHY

Located in central Europe, Switzerland borders Austria, France, Italy, Liechtenstein, and Germany. The tallest peak in Switzerland, Dufourspitze, at 15,203 feet (4,634 m), is near the Italian border. The largest lakes in the country—Geneva, Constance (Bodensee), and Maggiore—share the French, German-Austrian, and Italian borders. The Rhine is the principal river..

DID YOU KNOW?

- Switzerland is one of the most crowded countries in Europe. Two thirds of the country is not populated because of the mountains. Most of the population lives between Geneva and Zurich.
- Because of its location, the Swiss people are a mixture of the nationalities that surround the country. German, French, Italian, English, and several other languages are spoken, and the majority of the population is multilingual.
- Emmentaler, or as we know it, Swiss cheese, is the country's oldest cheese, dating to the 15th century. It is a cow's milk cheese and is made in giant wheels that weigh more than 200 pounds. The holes in Swiss cheese are a product of gas bubbles that form during the manufacturing process when the bacteria that produce the texture and flavor of the cheese also produce carbon dioxide.
- Switzerland did not become a United Nations member until 2002.
- Switzerland was neutral in both the World Wars but today every "fit" man serves in the army and stays in the reserves.
- Sixty percent of the Swiss population works in the service industry.
- The Pope is protected at the Vatican by Swiss Guards.
- Henri Nestle, a Swiss pharmacist, started in business developing and marketing milk for babies. Today Nestle is known for milk chocolate.
- The women of Switzerland did not have the right to vote until 1971.
- The World Health Organization and the International Red Cross are headquartered in Switzerland.
- The first Swiss in space was Claude Nicollier; he joined the shuttle Atlantis in1992.
- Brian Jones and Bertrand Piccard were the first balloonists to circum-navigate the globe non-stop. It took them 19 days, 21 hours, and 55 minutes to travel 29,000 miles in their balloon Breitling-Orbier 3 in 1999.
- In case you decide to use the Swiss ATM and you see "CHF," it stands for the Swiss franc. CHF is the official ISO code for the currency of Switzerland and Liechtenstein.

- Twenty-five Nobel Prize winners, including Albert Einstein and Wilhelm Rontgen, who discovered X-rays, graduated from Zurich's technical college.
- The Romans founded Zurich in 58 BC as a customs post. Today Zurich is the world's largest gold marketplace.
- In 2002, Switzerland legalized the use of marijuana, but sales are still illegal.

Punctuality

- Arrive on time and not early. The Swiss are extremely punctual and expect that of their associates.
- Arriving even a few minutes late for a meeting is a bad way to start. If you arrive 10 minutes late, the Swiss might make you wait 10 additional minutes for them.
- If you're invited to a social event, then 15 minutes grace period is allowed in the German areas, but the Italian- and French-speaking areas will give you up to 30 minutes to arrive fashionably late.

Meeting Manners

- Come prepared with your purpose, goals, and future plans with that company. You'll give a bad first impression without proper documentation and information.
- It's common to schedule morning meetings as early as 7 a.m. (0700). People in management will even arrive an hour before their employees.
- Appointments are mandatory. Agendas are necessary and will be followed completely.
- Consensus decisions are the goal. Once the agreement or contracts have been reached, the Swiss will deliver as outlined.
- It is difficult to schedule appointments during the months of July and August because of annual vacations.
- Women are progressing, but few hold high-level positions. Female associates working in Switzerland will be treated with respect but must always act and look professional.
- The German Swiss will get right down to business at the start of the meeting, while the French and Italian Swiss will be a little more relaxed in the start of the meeting, perhaps beginning with refreshments and a little chitchat.
- Humor is not part of their business meetings. Side jokes or trying to make the meeting more light-hearted is not the style or accepted practice.

- The Swiss are conservative and not receptive to risks and will take their time with detailed information to reach decisions, accept new ideas, or come to final decisions.

Business Cards

- Bring plenty of business cards.
- Present your card to the receptionist and/or secretary upon arrival for your meeting. It can be used for their files and as a reference for the person you are meeting.
- Put academic credentials or business qualifications on your business card. Definitely include your title and rank within your company. This is a critical part and could even be highlighted in a different size or font.
- Especially if your company is older and more established, you might include the founding date of your company.
- Make sure you check on the common language of your meeting associates and whether it is necessary to have your business card and other meeting materials translated into German, French, or Italian.

Meals/Toasts

- Allow two hours for lunch, which generally is between 12 p.m. and 2 p.m. (1200–1400).
- The Swiss will "do lunch." Lunch and dinner are the most likely times for business meals.
- Dinner is earlier in Switzerland than in some European countries. It could begin at 6:30 p.m. (1830) and generally most restaurant guests will be gone by 10 p.m. (2200). Even finding a fast food restaurant open at 11 p.m. (2300) could be a challenge.
- Dinners are more for fine dining and tend to be more formal. Spouses are generally invited to the evening meal. Business should not be discussed at these meals unless your host brings up the subject.
- Do not come in and just take a seat. Wait for your host or hostess to show you to your seat. The guest of honor is seated in the middle of the table on the side that faces the door.
- Do not start to eat until everyone is served.
- Often meals will be served family style in platters from which you serve yourself. Do not insult your host/cook by not taking any of the food; taking a small portion of each thing is appropriate.
- You should finish everything on your plate, so you do not insult your host or cook. Be careful in taking a second helping. You are expected to eat it all.

- Because of the mix of German, Italian, and French Swiss, you will be eating a mixture of their cuisine. Two Swiss specialties include *fondue* and *raclette*. *Fondue* is cubed bread on skewers dipped into melted cheese mixed with wine and/or *kirsch*. The other cheese specialty is *raclette*, which requires a special grill that is placed on the table. A block of cheese is melted on this grill, then diners scrape it off and eat it with potatoes, vegetables, or meats
- Wrists should stay on the table during your meal. It's bad manners to have them on your lap or your elbows on the table.
- To rest during your meal, cross your fork and knife on your plate to signify that you are just taking a break but are not finished.
- When you have completed the meal, place your silverware parallel to one another at an angle across the right side of your plate. You might be served more from your host if you do not show you are finished with your meal.
- Cocktails and other mixed drinks are not common before the meal. You may be offered a pre-dinner aperitif of wine, vermouth, or Campari. You may be offered red or white wine during the meal. Coffee will be offered at the end of the meal with after-dinner drinks.
- If you invite, then you pay. If you and your colleague often meet over meals, then arrangements should be determined about who should pay or you may alternate inviting and paying.
- Toasting is a little different for each area. The German-speaking Swiss will say "*prost;*" the French-speaking will say "*votre sante*" or just "*sante;*" and the Italian-speaking Swiss will say "*salute.*"
- Once the host has offered the toast, make sure you look at him directly and return the toast in the local language. Clink your glasses with everyone at the table, and then take your first sip.

 ## Entertainment

- It is an honor to be invited to a Swiss home. When you are invited, it is important that you arrive on time and make sure you come with gifts.
- Flowers, chocolates, or a bottle of fine wine, whisky, or brandy are all good gifts to bring to your host.
- People have their own small vineyards and produce their own wines or receive bottles from the family plot. To be invited in a *carnotzet,* which is an underground cellar where men will meet, is a tremendous honor and you should not refuse.
- The guest of honor will take the seat in the middle of the table, on the side that faces the door, so do not just come in and take any seat at the table. Your host will seat you.

Forms of Address/Introductions/Greetings

- The handshake is the standard greeting. Shake hands on arrival and again at departure.
- Kissing is also common between both men and women for the French and Italian Swiss. The more formal German Swiss will kiss only with close friends. Hugging or embracing one another is unusual even for women.
- Stick with shaking hands with your associates until you feel your relationship has advanced to the next level.
- Try your languages by greeting acquaintances with *gruezi* for the German-speaking areas, *buon giorno* in the Italian areas, and *bonjour* for the French. It is appreciated.
- Always stand while you are being introduced. If you are in a situation with a group of people, it is ideal if you can wait for a third person to initiate the introductions.
- Don't be surprised, especially in more rural areas, to see a man raise his hat as he passes a friend or acquaintance.
- Use professional or courtesy titles followed by surname when addressing adults. You may be given permission to use their first names, but if not, then continue with the more formal address.
- The sequence of names is the same as in North America, with the first name followed by the surname.
- For the German-speaking, use *herr* to address a man and *frau* to address a woman.
- In French-speaking areas, use *monsieur* for the man and *madame* for the women.
- For the Italian-speaking areas, use *signore* and *signora*.
- *Fraulein, mademoiselle,* and *signorina* are used to address female children, teenage girls, and younger or unmarried women.
- A lot of Swiss names will be hyphenated. If that is the case, then both names are used.
- Avoid asking questions about age, occupation, marital status, religion, or anything that could be perceived as personal. They will not ask you personal questions either.

Appearance/Attire

- Over the past few years, the dress codes have softened, and business casual and even casual is accepted in many companies, even incorporating a "dress-down" Friday.

- For your meetings, at least the initial ones, you should wear business, conservative dress. The Swiss believe if you look good, then you will make a good effort in your business dealings.
- Dark business suits for men are still the norm for upper management and or for meeting foreign businesspeople.
- Women can be found in suits, skirts, or pants suits or taking on the more casual look.
- Jewelry should be simple but elegant, even including the Swiss watch.
- The Swiss German style is a wild and colorful combination of clothes. You would definitely be noticed.
- One thing that is important to many Swiss is the appearance and look of your shoes. Make sure they are well polished to set a good impression. Never wear running shoes for a meeting or event.
- Have a sweater, light raincoat, and umbrella year-round.
- On weekends, as the Swiss travel to the mountains to enjoy a music celebration or festival, some people wear the full folkloric dress of their region.

 ## Gift Giving

- It's better to wait to the end of negotiations before any gifts are exchanged.
- Your Swiss associate should give the first gift, so you will know how to return the appropriate gift. Come prepared with a variety of gifts for all occasions. Good suggestions include a bottle of wine, whisky, or brandy. A coffee table book or something from your country always works.
- Do not present an expensive gift. It will look like a bribe.
- If you're invited to a Swiss home, then a gift will be needed, followed by a handwritten thank-you note to the hosts. Gifts could be flowers and/or good Swiss chocolates.
- Try to find chocolates from a specialized shop making high-quality products. The Swiss are known for their wonderful chocolate, and just presenting a bag or box of chocolates is the same as stopping at a convenience store in the United States and grabbing a last-minute gift. Never give Belgian chocolate as a gift to the Swiss.
- But do not bring chrysanthemums, white lilies, or red roses to a Swiss home. The first two denote death and the third, romance. Ask a florist for assistance.
- If you use the service of a tour guide or interpreter, then a nice gift would be more appreciated than a tip.
- Avoid knives, scissors, or any other sharp objects. These are inappropriate gifts and are perceived as symbols of severing a friendship or close bond.

Tipping

- Tipping is not necessary because by law a 15 percent service charge is included in hotel and restaurant bills.
- Generally, the locals will round up their payment.
- If you were provided excellent service, then an additional tip of one to five francs per meal is appropriate.
- You can pay in euros in most cities, but your change will come to you in Swiss francs.

Gesture Awareness

- Especially when you are talking, keep your hands out of your pockets.
- Do not sit with your ankle on the other knee.
- Avoid slapping your colleague's back.
- Use your whole hand to point. It's considered an obscene gesture to point with only your index finger.
- Pushing and shoving in queues is not uncommon.

Faux Pas

- Don't ask personal questions or questions about specific facets of someone's job.
- Conversations you want to avoid include World War I and II and the neutral role of Switzerland, the Swiss military, money and Swiss banks, or losses to Italy in the 2004 Olympic Winter Games.
- Do not litter.
- Chewing gum is considered vulgar, especially by the elders.
- Don't walk against a red light. Traffic regulations are strict and violations can result in a fine and/or imprisonment.

USEFUL FACTS

President	Pascal Couchepin (2003)
Vice President	Hans-Rudolph Merz (2007)
National Name	Schweiz/Suisse/Svizzera/Svizra
Size	15,355 square miles (39,769 square km)
Population	7,591,400 (2008)

Capital	Bern
Government	Federal Republic
Currency	Swiss franc
Religion	Protestant 42%, Roman Catholic 41%, Islam 4.3%, Eastern Orthodoxy 1.7%, none 11%
Language	The four official languages in Switzerland are German, (with many dialects), French, Italian, and Romansch (less than 1%). English, Serbo-Croatian, Albanian, Portuguese, Spanish, and others languages are also spoken.
Ethnicity	German 65%, French 18%, Italian 10%, Romansch 1%, other 6%
Industry	Machinery, chemicals, watches, textiles, precision instruments
Time Zone	Switzerland is one hour ahead of Greenwich Mean Time (GMT +1) or six hours ahead of Eastern Standard Time (GMT +6). Switzerland observes daylight saving time.
Telephone Code	International Code: +41 City Code: +31 (Bern)
Weather	Even though they are surrounded by mountains, the temperatures in the plains can reach up to 86 F (30 C) in the summer and it can get hot in the mountains. The temperatures in the winter generally never go below 41 F (-5 C), except for the mountain areas. As you trave through the various areas, the conditions can change drastically from sunny and bright to cold and dreary.
Voltage/Frequency	220 V; 50 Hz

HOLIDAYS/FESTIVALS

1 January	New Year's Day
2 January	Berchtold's Day (Honors Duke Berchtold V, the founder of Bern)
February (first Sunday)	Homstrom (Celebrates the end of winter)
Late March/April	Good Friday, Easter Sunday and Monday
April (first Thursday)	Glarus Festival
30 April	May Day Eve
1 May	Labor Day
May/June	Ascension Day (40 days after Easter Sunday)
May/June	Whit Sunday and Monday (10th and 11th days after Ascension)
1 August	National Day/Independence Day/Confederation Day
September	Federal Fast (Second Monday, except in Geneva, where the Genevan Fast is celebrated on the first Thursday of September. These two dates are occasions of feasts, not fasts.)
25 December	Christmas Day and St. Stephen's Day
26 December	Boxing Day

LANGUAGE TIPS

Swiss German/German	Phonetics	English
Ya/Nein	Yah/Nine	Yes/No
Bitte	Bit-uh	Please
Danke	Dahn-kuh	Thank you
Bitte schon	Bit-uh shern	You're welcome
Entschuldigen sie	Ent-shool-de-gen-zec	Excuse me
Axgusi	Ax-scu-see	
Guten tag	Goot-en tahk	Hello
Gruezi	Grit-zee	
Gruss Gott	Groos got	
Auf Widersehen	Auf vee-der-zane	Good-bye
Ufwiederluege	Oof-vee-der-lawgah	
Tschuss (familiar)	Choohs	
Habensie ein Zimmer?	Ha-ben zee ine tsimmer	Have you any rooms?
Wieviel Kostet das?	Vee-feel cost-et dahs	How much does it cost?
Das ist schon	Dahs is shern	It's beautiful
Nehmen Sie...(credit cards)?	Nay-men zee...	Do you accept (credit cards) ?

Be On Your Best Cultural Behavior

Chapter 28: THAILAND

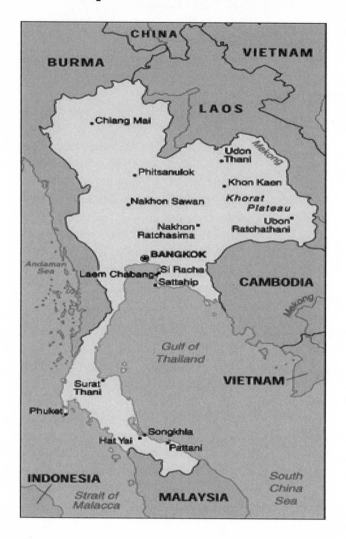

LOCATION/GEOGRAPHY

Thailand is located in Southeastern Asia and borders Myanmar (Burma) on the west, Laos and Cambodia on the east, and Malaysia on the south. The Andaman Sea and the Gulf of Thailand form the coasts of Thailand.

 DID YOU KNOW?

- Until 1939, Thailand was known as Siam.
- Thailand has the distinction of being the only Southeast Asian country not to be taken over by a European power.
- Rice is Thailand's most important crop, with exports of 6.5 million tons of milled rice every year. Thailand is the largest exporter of rice in the world, the second largest tungsten producer, and third largest tin producer.
- The national sport is Thai boxing. It is a martial art with a very long history and is related to Kung Fu or Silat.
- The King of Thailand is an American citizen. Rama the Ninth was born in the United States and took the throne when his brother was assassinated. He is the only monarch of a foreign country to be born in the United States. He is also a best-selling author of nonfiction scholarly books that are popular with Thai people. All the profits of these books are given to charity.
- Monsoons blow from the southwest from April to October, bringing heavy rains. The rest of the year will have a dry wind blowing from the northeast.
- Tin is the most important mineral found in Thailand. Also mined are diamonds and tungsten, and there are large crude oil resources.
- The highest waterfall in Thailand and one of the highest in Asia is Tee Law Su Waterfall. The longest river is the Mekong River, which forms a border between Thailand and Laos.
- The first Thai alphabet was created by King Ramkhamhaeng, who ruled at the end of the 13th century.
- You can find the largest reclining Buddha image in the temple, Wat Po. But the tallest Buddhist monument in the world is in the town of Nakhon Pathom. It is 127 meters (387 feet) tall.
- The most important means of transportation is by canals and waterways. Look for the floating markets where produce is sold from boats.
- Traffic jams can be endless, so many offices provide staggered start and finish times for work days. They may start or finish at 10 minutes before the hour or at unusual times.

Be On Your Best Cultural Behavior

- *The King and I*, with Yul Brynner and Deborah Kerr (1956) and the remake *Anna and the King of Siam,* with Jodie Foster (1999) were both banned in Thailand because they distorted the country's history and made a mockery of their monarchy.

BUSINESS ETIQUETTE

Punctuality

- Punctuality is expected, but your travel can be delayed by the incredible traffic. Plan well. Call your counterpart if you see you are running late because of traffic.
- When setting up your meetings, try to avoid the heavy traffic times in the beginning and end of the day.
- If you are invited to a meal as part of business, always arrive on time. If there are several people joining you, then try and arrive as a group.
- If you are invited to a Thai home, arrive as close as possible to the designated time.

Meeting Manners

- Arrange your meetings one month in advance if possible and then confirm the day of your appointment.
- If meeting with government officials or the royal family, be prepared for a briefing by your host or your own organization.
- It's advisable to send a list of attendees and credentials in advance so the Thais will have an understanding of the status of each person attending and can plan accordingly.
- Agendas and materials should be coordinated in advance.
- Upon entering the room for the meeting, remain standing until instructed where to sit.
- Presentations, slides, printed material, proposals, and contracts can all be in English, especially if you are meeting in Bangkok. In more remote or rural areas, other arrangements might need to be made to have translations in Thai. Just be careful not to get too complicated or use any slang and cause embarrassment to the Thais. British and American speakers normally can be understood if they remember to speak clearly and slowly. Other nationalities' accents may not be as easily understood. It's best to check ahead of time to have a good understanding what is the most comfortable and accepted procedure to follow for your presentations. You don't want to go so slow that you are insulting and put them to sleep.

- Come prepared with material for each person in attendance and bring a few extra copies for staff that might not be able to attend but will need to review the material. Again, check if English is acceptable or if your material should be in both Thai and English.
- Chitchat at the beginning or end of the negotiating process is critical. The Thais will need to like you to do business with you. If you are invited to activities such as dinner, golf, or other social events, accept the invitation and consider it a better opportunity to get to know them and to strengthen your business relationship.
- If necessary, hire an interpreter.
- It helps to have your slides avoid a lot of text but use colorful photographs and bullets that describe your product and presentation.
- Don't expect decisions to be made immediately. Generally, a few days will pass after the Thais have consulted with other people before they will make their final decision. If you feel it's necessary, offer to provide additional material or to meet again.
- Be aware of the small details that the Thais might be focusing on. This could be an indication that there are larger problems that need your attention. Remember the Thais do not want to lose face or confront you, so take notice of these little signs. You will need to ask questions—but not specific questions—to try to ascertain the needs or wants of your Thai associates. Avoid causing them to lose face, but try to get to the core of their concerns.
- Body language and facial expressions are important because Thais believe these speak more than actual words.
- The process of negotiations and final decisions can be slow. Do not encourage them to proceed at a faster pace, because Thais do not like confrontations. Be calm with all proceedings.
- It's best if you avoid planning your trips around the Thai New Year, or *Songkran*, which takes place in early April. Most staff will be on leave.

 ## Business Cards

- Business cards are exchanged in the first meetings to help identify the key people.
- Have your name, position, and the standard business information of address, Web site, e-mail address, and phone and fax numbers.
- Exchange your card with the most senior person/oldest person first if at all possible. The host of the meeting generally will start the exchange of cards. If this does not happen, then you might just wait until the end of the meeting and include your card with other printed materials.

- Make sure your business cards are of high quality. This does make a difference.
- Have Thai on one side and English or your native language on the other. Make sure to use your right hand and to present, with the Thai side facing the recipient.
- Before placing your counterpart's card on the table or in a business card holder, take a few seconds to look at it and make a comment about something that is on the card.
- Include all special titles like Dr., Ph.D., or any other special qualifications on your card.

Meals/Toasts

- Business dinners and lunches usually will take place at restaurants.
- Allow your host and most senior members to take their seats first. Do not sit until they are in their seats; you will most likely be instructed where to sit.
- Allow the Thais to place your order. They enjoy their food and are very proud in making selections. If you have religious restrictions or have allergies, you need to tell your hosts and make suggestions to them.
- The food most likely will be placed in the middle of the table for your selection, and a plate of steamed white rice will be placed in front of each person. It may seem to be a large amount of food for the meal, but it would be considered bad form if the host did not order enough food. Try not to leave a lot on your plate. Always eat your rice.
- If soup will be served with the meal, a bowl will be set in front of you. Do not use this bowl for anything other than the soup.
- A communal plate is set for every three to four people for any scraps from shell fish or other foods. You could ask for a plate if none is provided.
- In a more casual atmosphere, diners will serve themselves. In a more formal or upscale restaurant, allow the wait staff to serve you. If you are serving yourself, remember to return the serving spoon to the appropriate dish. Be extremely careful that the spoon does not touch your rice or put some of the rice back into the main serving dishes.
- Thais normally eat with a spoon and fork. The Chinese will use chopsticks for their food and noodles. Use the spoon, which is held in your right hand, for putting the food into your mouth. Use your fork, held in your left hand, to push the food onto the spoon.
- If eating sticky rice, which is a northern Thai delicacy, then eating with your fingers is acceptable. Use only your right hand and do not lick your fingers.
- Avoid placing several different dishes with the rice on your plate. Place the rice on your plate and then a small amount of a particular dish.

When you have completed that, then you can add something from a different dish. This also helps in not leaving a lot of food on your plate. It's considered very impolite to leave food, at least large amounts, on your plate at the end of the meal. Just pace yourself and take small amounts.

- If food is too spicy for your taste, you can ask for some a little less spicy.
- If food is passed from one diner to another during the meal, then just follow their lead.
- It's common for toothpicks to be available at the table at the end of the meal. Just make sure you cover your mouth while using a toothpick.
- Alcohol will be in abundance for the dinner meal. You usually will not find it served at lunch. Pace yourself with the alcohol because the wait staff will constantly fill your glass.
- Beer is a popular drink, but it's difficult to find a light beer. You will also notice that ice is added to beer. This could be helpful because their local beers have a bitter taste.
- If you want to host the meal and pay for it, make arrangements to have the bill presented to you away from the table at a set time. This will avoid any embarrassment when the Thai guests want to pay. Generally the host or the oldest or most senior person will pay.
- Their common and most popular toast is *Chai Yo*, which means "good luck."

Entertainment

- If you are just joining Thai staff for a quick lunch at the local food market, then all could just pay their own.
- You can eat anytime of the day, especially in Bangkok. The general time for meals is 7 a.m. (0700) for breakfast, 12 p.m. (1200) for lunch and between 6 p.m. and 8 p.m. (1800 and 2000) for dinner.
- The family and hierarchy are extremely important. Early in the relationship, personal questions will be asked to place you within a hierarchy so they know how you should be treated. This status is determined by the way you are dressed, your age, job, family name, education, and social connections.
- If you are invited to a Thai home, check whether your hosts are wearing shoes. If they are not, then remove your shoes before entering the home.

Forms of Address/Introductions/Greetings

- The handshake is one form of greeting but the *wai* is their common and traditional form. Follow the lead of the host to know which is most appropriate. It's unlikely you'll ever do both. Generally, the Thais will *wai* one another and then shake your hand. If they present a *wai* to you, then return this greeting to them. But the *wai* does have strict protocol rules you should follow:

- Raise both your hands, with palms and fingers together, your elbows in at your waist, and hands pointing upward as if you were praying. Lightly touch your body with your hands somewhere between your chest and forehead. The usual height is the same as your chin.
- This sign can be used for greeting and as a sign of respect. The height of the hands and how low the head comes down to meet the thumbs of both hands demonstrate respect and courtesy.
- The person who is younger in age or status will be the first to offer the *wai*. This can be done while you are sitting, walking, or standing. The senior person will return the *wai* with their hands around the chest area. Some older people will not *wai* younger people. A nod is a common sign of acknowledgement.
- If you are the junior person and the senior person is seated, then move to their level by either bowing your head while you make the *wai* or actually stoop to be closer to their level or lower.
- If you are at a distance from the person, then don't be disappointed if the *wai* is not returned.
- Do not *wai* children, taxi drivers, maids, waiters, or other service staff.
- During a social gathering, allow your host or hostess to introduce you to their guests. This provides an understanding of your status and who should perform the *wai* first and how low the head should be bowed.

- A first name is generally used instead of the surname. But this is accompanied with the honorific title of *Khun* before the name. This can be used for both men and women instead of Mr., Mrs., or Ms. You would be addressed as *Khun* Steve (first name) or *Khun* Andrea. Also many Thai are given a nickname, and after a relationship has been established, you may be asked to call someone by a nickname. These nicknames are generally one syllable words and can be Thai or English words, colors, fruits, or just a shortened form of their first name. Even if addressing by the shorter version of the name, use *Khun* before this nickname.
- If they later revert to the Mr. or Mrs., then don't be surprised if you become Mr. Steve instead of your surname.
- Titles are not usually used except for a doctor. Then it is Dr. with their first name. All other professions will still use *Khun* and the first name.

Appearance/Attire

- The standard dress is still conservative business suits for the office in Thailand. Jackets can be carried over your arm until you reach the office.
- Even with the heat, most offices require a shirt and tie. Most men will wear a long-sleeved shirt. Outside of Bangkok, you will find that many companies require just open-neck shirts with collars and no ties. Visitors still will wear a shirt and tie.
- You will see that most men will wear an undershirt, or "*singlet*." Outdoors, it helps prevent sweat stains from the tremendous heat, and indoors, it helps them withstand the freezing air conditioning in the office buildings.
- Skirts are better than pants for women. There are still some rules requiring women to wear skirts in some government offices and schools. Skirts should be below the knees. The women may also wear matching jackets to help withstand the cold temperatures in their offices.
- Thailand is still conservative, and wearing sleeveless tops is not recommended. It's best to have a jacket to cover your arms.
- Be ready to remove your shoes when entering a person's home. And make sure your shoes are highly polished.
- To enter a temple, dress conservatively. Women should have on a long skirt or slacks (trousers) covering their knees; shoulders should be covered; and avoid wearing sandals.
- Check the dress code if invited to a Thai home. You could confer with other invited guests.
- Clothing is important and Thais judge your status by your appearance. Remember it can be very hot and humid, so a change of clothes is advisable. Body odor can be a challenge at the end of a long day.

Gift Giving

- Before presenting gifts in the office, make sure you understand their procedures.
- If you want to present a gift to an individual, choose something small and inexpensive from your home country.
- Your gift probably will not be opened in front of you. It will be set aside and opened after you have gone. The Thais do not want to be embarrassed or lose face. If you are presented a gift, then follow this same practice.
- A tradition at New Year's is to present gift baskets with fruits (tinned), cookies, whiskey, and other items they would enjoy. Present on behalf of your company.

- A good idea for the entire office is to bring in food for the staff and just leave it in the kitchen. Do not announce to everyone that you placed the food there for all of them. Be humble.
- Avoid all sharp items, such as knives and scissors, and mirrors as gifts. Never give handkerchiefs or perfumes to business acquaintances.
- If you are invited to a Thai home, a gift is appreciated but not expected.
- Make sure gifts are wrapped attractively because appearance matters. Add color or more bows or ribbons.
- Flowers, fruit, or good quality chocolate are appropriate gifts.
- Avoid marigolds or carnations because they are associated with funerals.
- Avoid wrapping gifts in green, blue, or black because these are colors associated with mourning. Yellow and gold are the royal colors and are excellent for wrapping gifts.
- Red wrapping paper should be used only if presenting a gift to a Chinese Thai.
- For weddings and ordination parties, money is the usual gift.
- Be careful not to compliment Thais' possessions too much or they may feel they need to give it to you. Be more general in all that you compliment, saying, "Your home is beautiful," or "Your home is decorated beautifully."

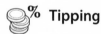 ## Tipping

- If a service charge is included, then a tip is not expected but is appreciated and is becoming customary.
- When tipping, generally it is 10 percent of the bill.
- If you pay cash, when your change is returned, it is provided in smaller bills to allow for your tip.
- A tip between 10 and 50 baht (US$.30 and US$1.50) is appreciated.
- Public taxis are metered, so rounding off the fare is the general tip.
- A bellman could be tipped 10 or 20 baht (US$.30 or US$.60) for assisting with your luggage.
- Salaries for the majority of the workers in the hospitality and service industries are generally low, so they depend on tips.

 ## Gesture Awareness

- To hail a taxi, keep your hand horizontal with the fingers facing down. Holding your hand with the fingers up is very rude.
- During a business meal, do not blow you nose at the table, but excuse yourself and go to the restroom. Spitting, nose blowing, and nose picking

is common in public. There have been campaigns to try and fix these public displays, but little progress has been made.

- Avoid stepping over anything, especially food or someone's work, or touching anything with your feet. Do not point your feet at someone or something.
- Also do not touch someone on the head or pass things over their heads. During a presentation, do not pass papers, a microphone, or any material over a person's head.
- Pointing with your finger is rude. Use your whole hand to gesture to an object or a specific area you want to point out.
- If you want a person to come toward you, extend your hand with the palm down and gently motion all your fingers toward you.

 Faux Pas

- Be respectful in areas that do not allow photos. Abide by the requests of signs in temples and even if there are not any, still be respectful. Pay particular attention if monks are worshipping.
- Remove your shoes when you enter a temple and do not sit with your feet toward the Buddha. Sit either cross-legged or with your feet tucked behind you.
- Since feet are considered the lowest and dirtiest part of the body, do not point to things with your feet, hold doors open with your feet, or point them at the Buddha images.
- The head is the highest part of the body, so do not point at or touch anyone's head. Never touch a monk.
- The King and his family are held in high esteem, so never say anything disrespectful about them. If you see a coin that has dropped on the ground, remember the King's image is on this coin and it's a tremendous insult to touch it with your feet.
- An old custom that is not as practiced as before is to step over the threshold rather than stepping on it. This simple gesture would still be appreciated, both at temple doors and homes.
- Avoid conversation about the monarchy or national security. Thais do enjoy talking about your country if they have ever visited there or like hearing stories about what you have experienced in Thailand.
- You can cross your legs, but be careful of pointing or exposing your feet toward a person.

USEFUL FACTS

Ruler	King Bhumibol Adulyadej (1946) (Rama the Ninth)
Prime Minister	Chaovarat Chanweerakul (2008)
National Name	Kingdom of Thailand
Size	197,595 square miles (511,771 square km)
Population	65,493,298 (2008)
Capital	Bangkok
Government	Constitutional Monarchy
Currency	Baht
Religion	Buddhist 94%, Muslim 4.6%, Christian, less than 1%, Hindu less than 1%
Language	Thai, English (secondary language of the elite), ethnic and regional dialects
Ethnicity	Thai 75%, Chinese 14%, other 11%
Industry	Tourism, textiles and garments, beverages, tobacco, cement, light manufacturing such as jewelry and electric appliances, agricultural processing, computers and parts, integrated circuits, plastics, furniture, automobiles and automotive parts
Time Zone	Thailand is seven hours ahead of Greenwich Mean Time (GMT +7) and is 12 hours ahead of Eastern Standard Time (EST +12). Thailand does not observe daylight saving time.
Telephone Code	International Code: +66 City Code: +2 (Bangkok)

Weather	Thailand has tropical weather, with rainy, warm and cloudy southwest monsoons from mid-May to September, and then dry, cool northeast monsoon from November to mid-March. The southern isthmus is always hot and humid.
Voltage/Frequency	220-240 V: 50 Hz

HOLIDAYS/FESTIVALS

1 January	New Year's Day
February	Chinese New Year's Day (Date depends on the lunar calendar)
February	Makha Bucha Day/Magha Puja Day (Date changes but always on full moon day on the 3rd lunar month, Makha. This commemorates the gathering to meet Lord Buddha nine months after his first enlightenment.)
6 April	Chakri Memorial Day (Crowning Day of King Rama I, the first king of the Chakri dynasty)
13-16 April	Songkran Festival (Celebrates the lunar new year with water)
1 May	National Labor Day
5 May	Coronation Day
19 May	Visakha Bucha Day/Visakha Puja/Buddha Day (Celebration of the Lord Buddha's birthday, enlightenment, and death)
Mid-July	Khao Phansa Day (Buddhist Lent Day)
12 August	The Queen's Birthday (Also Mother's Day)
23 October	Chulalongkorn Memorial Day (Rama V honored)
5 December	The King's Birthday (Also Father's Day)
10 December	Constitution Day
31 December	New Year's Eve

LANGUAGE TIPS

Thai Phonetics	English
Khap khun	Thank you
Mai ao khap khun	No, thank you
Sawat dii	Hello
Sabai dee rue	How are you?
Sabaay dee	I'm fine
Khaw thoht	Excuse me
Karuna	Please
Mai Khao jai	I do not understand
Poot passat Thai mai dai	I cannot speak Thai
Chai/Mai chai	Yes/No

Chapter 29: TURKEY

LOCATION/GEOGRAPHY

Turkey borders the Black Sea between Bulgaria and Georgia, and the Aegean Sea and the Mediterranean Sea between Greece and Syria. Turkey also borders on Armenia, Azerbaijan, Iran and Iraq. Ninety-seven percent of Turkey is in Asia and three percent is in Europe.

 DID YOU KNOW?

- Muslims are to pray five times a day at dawn, noon, afternoon, sunset, and evening. The exact times will appear daily in the newspapers.
- The Muslim holy day is Friday, but not practiced in Turkey.
- Smoking is common and a law was passed to ban smoking in offices, but this is not taken seriously. Bus companies, movie theaters, and some shopping malls are trying to enforce this regulation.
- In 1922, the Ottoman Empire ended and the Republic of Turkey was founded. Mastafa Kemal Ataturk was the president of the Republic.
- The Bosporus, also known as the Istanbul Strait, forms the boundary between the European part of Turkey and Anatolia, the Asian part. Turkey is at times referred to as the "bridge between East and West" because it straddles the two continents of Europe and Asia.
- The highest mountain in Turkey is Mount Ararat. It is believed that Noah's Ark may have landed there.
- The largest lake in Turkey is Lake Van. It is reported to have a sea monster.
- The currency of Turkey is the lira. It is also used in Malta. Before converting to the Euro in 2002, Italy and the Vatican also used the lira as currency.
- Even though people always think of The Netherlands as the home of the tulip, it is the national flower of Turkey. Actually, several hundred years ago, tulips were introduced to The Netherlands from Turkey.
- Two of the Seven Wonders of the Ancient World were located in Turkey— the Mausoleum at Halicarnassus and the Temple of Artemis.
- Would you believe Santa Claus comes from Turkey? Bishop Nicholas (later becoming Saint Nicholas) lived in Turkey in the 4th century.
- More than a million people a day visit Beyoglu. In this district on the European side of Istanbul, you will find bars, discos, cafes, clubs, and many restaurants. The famous Istiklal Avenue reaches from Taksim Square to Tunel in this district.

Be On Your Best Cultural Behavior

BUSINESS ETIQUETTE

 Punctuality

- You should always be on time and it is expected, but plan on waiting for your Turkish counterparts.
- Appointments should be made at least one to two weeks in advance by telephone, and pre-arrangements are necessary.

 Meeting Manners

- Appointments need to be made in advance and confirmed with a letter or e-mail. Follow up with a phone call a few days before your meeting.
- The Turks want to get to know you and work with people that they know and respect.
- Take the time to build a personal relationship.
- Relationships can be established in the office, over a meal, or at social functions.
- Start with small talk and avoid going straight into business. Watch their pace and follow.
- Long-term relationships are built on trust, how well they like and want to deal with you. All of this is so important before you ever get to the business part of your deals.
- Courtesy is important in all that you do with the Turks.
- Avoid trying to schedule your appointments during *Ramazan* (Ramadan).
- Also avoid traveling and scheduling appointments during June, July, and August. Many business people will take this period to spend with their families.
- Have all your materials printed in both English and Turkish.
- Have your presentations extremely well prepared, complete, and ready to go with handouts of charts, graphs, and all necessary material. Your proposals must show how your business will be a benefit to all.
- Even though they now have national companies and corporations, many Turkish businesses are still family owned and run.
- Decisions may be slow, with decisions ultimately being made by the head of the family or the head of the company. Be prepared to make some concessions throughout the negotiation process. Build this into your early planning.
- Do not pressure the Turks or set deadlines. Be patient.
- The Turks like power, influence, honor, and respect, and nonmonetary incentives can be just as important to them as financial benefits.

Business Cards

- There is no formal ritual for the exchange of business cards, but use both hands when you exchange or accept cards.
- When you arrive for a meeting, have your card ready to present to the receptionist or secretary.
- It's a nice gesture to have one side of your card printed in Turkish.
- You may not receive business cards from Turkish associates. They may not extend their cards to you unless they are sure they want to establish a business relationship.

Meals/Toasts

- It is common to smoke during meals. They may even take a break for a drink and a cigarette.
- Turkish coffee or tea will be served at the end of the meal, along with pastries.
- Their Turkish coffee is a national drink and you should at least sample it. You have choices of no sugar, a little sugar, or sweet. It is sipped and melts into your taste buds, so do not gulp.
- Alcohol may accompany the evening meals. The local favorite is called *raki* (rak-uh).
- The bottom of the cup of Turkish coffee will be full of grounds, so do not drink the last drop.
- Turks enjoy making a toast while raising their glasses and saying *serefe* (sharafa) which means "cheers."

Entertainment

- Most dinners will take place in restaurants.
- The host will pay for the meal. Turks do not follow the custom of sharing a bill or each paying for yourself.
- It is nice to make the offer to pay for your meal, but your host will not accept.
- The best advice is to thank them for the meal and then return the favor a few days later in a restaurant of your choice. Be sure to speak with the restaurant manager in advance to make clear you will be paying for the meal and that payment from the other guests should not be accepted.

Forms of Address/Introductions/Greetings

- A firm handshake is the customary greeting.

- It's not always customary to shake hands when you are departing, but it's occasionally practiced.
- Friends and relatives will greet with one or two kisses on the cheek.
- To show respect for elders, kiss their right hand and then place your forehead on the hand.
- The most common way to address a Turkish person is to call a man by his first name followed by *bey* (bay). A woman would also be addressed by her first name and followed by *hanim* (ha-num).
- Use titles such as Doctor or Professor, lawyers, engineers. Senior ranking staff should be addressed properly.
- *Efendim* (literally "my master") will be used to address a person with whom you are not familiar. This could be a secretary, a taxi driver, the waiter, doorman, or a person in a store or shop.
- If not met by a person when entering a room for a business meeting, always go to the most elderly or most senior person first.
- When you enter a social event, just meet the person closest to you and then work you way around the room or table counterclockwise.
- The Islamic greeting of Asalamu *alaykum* (peace be upon you) or *Nasilsiniz* (How are you?) is the most common and nicest way to greet people. They appreciate your knowing and sharing this greeting with them. Often times they may even help you to pronounce these words.
- Personal space is close, so be prepared for them to stand close to you during conversation. Do not back away.
- Be patient in your initial conversations. The Turks may ask a lot of questions that do not seem relevant, but this is part of their process.
- Good conversation could include their own country because the Turks are very proud of their country. They also enjoy sharing their culture and history. You can even ask about their job, role, and company. The men love their football (soccer) and will go on and on about their favorite team.
- You may ask questions about their family, and they love to talk about their children.
- Good eye contact is a sign of sincerity.

Appearance/Attire

- Their business dress is conservative, including a suit and tie.
- Women will dress in professional business dress.
- In the summer, because of the extreme heat, ties may be eliminated and just a shirt and slacks for men may be appropriate. Follow the example of your Turkish counterparts.

- In the more rural areas outside the big cities, conservative dressing is more likely. Women should refrain from showing their legs or arms, nor should their clothes be tight-fitting.
- Shorts should not be worn by men or women.

Gift Giving

- Gifts are not appropriate during business relationships.
- Dining out with your associates is more appropriate than gifts.
- If you do present a gift, then a gift from your own country is appreciated.
- Turkey is a Muslim country, so the normal gift of a bottle of wine could be completely inappropriate. Make sure your associates drink before presenting a gift of alcohol.
- If you are invited to a home, then a gift is needed. *Baklava* or pastries are good ideas, along with decorative items for the home. Make sure you bring gifts of candy or sweets to the children.
- Be careful if you bring flowers to the hostess of the home. It's better to let a florist assist with your choices.

Tipping

- Tipping is generally very modest.
- The person receiving the tip would like to receive it in lira but will accept any currency, provided it is given in bills/notes. Avoid giving non-Turkish coins just because coins cannot be easily exchanged into lira.
- Service charges are generally added, but an additional tip may be given for exceptional service.
- An additional 5 percent to 10 percent is given in restaurants, and in upscale restaurants a tip of 10 percent to 15 percent is given even if the service charge is added.
- Porters and service attendants are usually given 1 to 2 lira (US$.80 to US$1.60) depending on their service and assistance.
- Tour guides are tipped 6 to 12 lira (US$5 to US$10).
- Airports, bus stations, and train station have an official tariff for their porters and it will be posted. An additional US$.75 per bag is sufficient.
- If you have a Turkish bath (*hamam*), the attendants will line up to "bid you farewell" and they all expect a tip if their services have been good. They should be given 15 percent of the total price of the services, to be shared among them.
- Taxi drivers usually do not receive big tips, but the fare is just rounded up to a convenient amount. You can provide more if they assist with your bags.

Be On Your Best Cultural Behavior

Gesture Awareness

- To show or signal "no," raise your head slightly, tip it backward, and close your eyes. To show "yes," just nod your head upwards.
- To hail a taxi or bus, stretch out your right arm and move your wrist inward repeatedly.
- To show that something is good, hold your hands up with the palms outward, and then slowly bring the fingers into your thumb in a grasping motion.
- To make the fig gesture, clenching your hand into a fist and placing your thumb between the first two fingers, is extremely rude.
- It is acceptable to hold hands with a person of the opposite sex in cities and at the beach resorts. It is still frowned upon in rural Turkey and the East.

Faux Pas

- Ask permission first if you want to smoke. Smoking or eating on the streets is not acceptable.
- Always ask permission before you take a photograph. This is especially true of an individual or in a mosque.
- Topics to avoid include their political history, EU membership, the Cyprus issue, Turkish-Kurdish relations, and discussions of Islam.
- Never enter a mosque wearing shoes. You will find a rack where your shoes must be placed. It is important that your feet are clean and not tracking in mud, dirt, or dust.
- Men should not wear shorts and should always have on a shirt or t-shirt to enter a mosque.
- Women should be covered, including their hair, when entering a mosque. A scarf can be provided if you do not have one.
- Showing the sole of your shoe to someone is a major act of offense. Do not even point at someone or something with your shoe. They consider the sole of your shoe dirty. When sitting across from a person, keep your legs together or crossed.

USEFUL FACTS

President	Abdullah Gul (2007)
Prime Minister	Recep Tayyip Erdogan (2003)

National Name	Turkiye Cumhuriyeti
Size	297,591 square miles (770,761 square km)
Population	71,892,807 (2008)
Capital	Ankara
Government	Republican Parliamentary Democracy
Currency	Turkish Lira
Religion	Islam (mostly Sunni) 99.8%, Christians, Jews and others 0.2%
Language	Turkish (official), Kurdish, Dimli, Azeri, Kabardian
Ethnicity	Turkish 80%, Kudish 20%
Industry	Mining (coal, chromite, copper, boron), textiles, food processing, autos,electronics, petroleum, steel, construction, paper, and lumber
Time Zone	Turkey is two hours ahead of Greenwich Mean Time (GMT +2) or seven hours ahead of Eastern Standard Time (EST +7). Turkey observes daylight saving time.
Telephone Code	International Code: +90 City Code: +312 (Ankara)
Weather	Hot and dry summers with mild and wet winters for the Aegean and Mediterranean coasts. The Black Sea coast receives the heaviest rainfall. Eastern Turkey has more brittle weather, with extremely cold winters and heavy snowfalls, while their summers are very dry and hot.
Voltage/Frequency	230 V; 50 Hz

HOLIDAYS/FESTIVALS

1 January	New Year's Day
23 April	National Sovereignty and Children's Day
1 May	Spring Day
6 May	Hidrellez (Feast days)
19 May	Ataturk Commemoration and Youth & Sports Day
27 May	Freedom and Constitution Day
1 July	Navy and Merchant Marine Day
30 August	Victory Day
29 October	Independence Day
November	Ramazan Bayramy (End of the fast of Ramadan)
17 December	Rumi's Birthday (Birthday of Mawlana Rumi)

LANGUAGE TIPS

Turkish	Phonetics	English
Hos Geldiniz	Hosh gel din iz	Welcome
Hos Bulduk	Hosh bull duk	It's nice to be here
Merhaba	Mare-ha-BA see	Hello
Hoscakal	Hosh-cha-kal	Good-bye
Nasilsin?	Ne-sel-sin	How are you?
Iyiyim, sen nasilsin?	E-im, sen ne-sel-sin	I am fine, and you
Tesekkur ederim	Te-sh-qu-err ed-err-im	Thank you
Birsey degil	Beer-shey di-eel	You're welcome
Lutfen	Lut-fen	Please
Sizi anlamiyorum	Si-ze ann-la-ma-yor-um	I don't understand
Afedersiniz, tuvalet nerede?	Aff-ed-dar-san-iz toy-vu-let nar-rey-de	Where is the washroom?

Chapter 30: UNITED ARAB EMIRATES

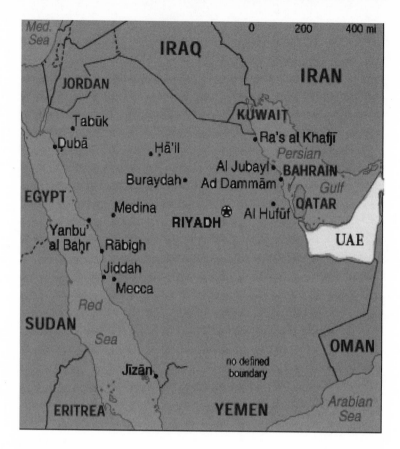

LOCATION/GEOGRAPHY

The UAE is located in the southeast of the Arabian Peninsula across the Persian Gulf from Iran. Bordered by Saudi Arabia on the Southeast and Oman on the Southwest, UAE is composed of seven emirates.

DID YOU KNOW?

- Two of the three tallest hotels in the world can be found in Dubai. The tallest, at the moment, is the Rose Tower, standing at 333 meters (1,093 feet), with 72 floors. The third tallest is the Burj Al Arab, located on a man-made island and shaped like a sail.
- According to a 2003 Human Rights Watch report, because of all the major construction, 90 percent of the country's 1.7 million workers are migrants.
- The UAE is a Muslim country and Islamic law is enforced.
- Dubai has the largest population and is the second largest emirate by area, after Abu Dhabi. The smallest emirate is Ajman.
- Fujairah is not desert terrain as are the other emirates but is predominantly mountainous terrain.
- The Mall of the Emirates, one of the largest shopping centers in the world, features ski slopes and lifts, a toboggan run, equipment to rent or buy, and an indoor temperature of 23F (-5C).
- The Palm Islands of Dubai are the largest artificial islands in the world and can be seen from space. Estimates say they will have a population of approximately 500,000 upon completion.
- Dubailand, once completed, is projected to be twice the size of Disney World in Orlando.
- The local weekend in UAE has changed from the traditional Thursday and Friday to Friday and Saturday. Schools and local businesses have changed over to the new weekend.
- January-February is a good time to visit if you like to shop and look for bargains. During the Dubai Shopping Festival, you can find tremendous discounts, from their malls to the small shops.

BUSINESS ETIQUETTE

 Punctuality

- It is better to make your appointment for "early morning" or "late afternoon" rather than specific hours. The importance of courtesy and hospitality can cause delays and prevent a strict schedule.
- Relationships and people are more important in UAE than strict schedules and punctuality. You still need to arrive on time for all appointments, but your UAE counterpart may arrive late.

 Meeting Manners

- Brochures or other promotional literature need to be of good quality and full color and should always be printed in Arabic.
- It has been said that the best location for a meeting is in a hotel lobby. It may decrease the interruptions you will receive in an office environment from people or phones. Plus, it shows the interest of your counterparts if they take the time to come to the hotel.
- There is a strong hierarchy in business in the UAE. Many companies are owned and run by one person who is powerful and will make most of the decisions. Nepotism is common.
- Businesses in the UAE open at approximately 9 a.m. (0900). They will close for most of the afternoon and reopen late afternoon to mid-evening.
- Prayer times are printed in the daily papers because exact times will change throughout the year. Observe these times when trying to make appointments. A Muslim prays facing Mecca, and the timing will vary according to the position of the sun. The five times of prayer are *Fajr,* between dawn and sunrise; *Dhuhr,* about a half hour after midday; Asr, mid-afternoon; *Maghrib,* immediately after sunset; and *Isha,* one and one-half hours after sunset. Friday is the Islamic holy day.
- If you don't mind taking a chance, it is often better to show up to see a person rather than booking an appointment. This really does work well, but be ready to wait and hope for an opening in the schedule so they can see you. Just as a back-up, have a letter that you can leave with the secretary if you cannot be seen or get in for an appointment.
- If you know someone, you are expected to drop by for an impromptu social call if you are in the area.
- Secretaries in the UAE usually do not have the authority to make appointments for their bosses.

- Expect the business proceedings to be extremely slow. Be prepared to bargain. Disagreement is fine, but allow your UAE associates to state their opinions in the discussion. Focus on exchanging good ideas and suggestions, not winning your point.
- Over the past several years, foreign enterprise has been welcomed. Many businesses are foreign-owned and operated.

Business Cards

- Business cards are exchanged but are not a high priority.
- If you do exchange business cards, you should have them printed in Arabic along with your native language.
- It's important not to show favoritism or that one language is less than the other, so print the translation on the same side of card, not on the reverse side, or use a separate card for each language.

Meals/Toasts

- Building relationships is an important part of doing business in the UAE. Accepting invitations to meals or social events will be a good start to building trust and understanding.
- Be careful with scheduling meals during prayer times or major Islamic holidays. These are extremely important times and require respect.
- It's important to remember not to eat with your left hand. Do not pass or offer food with your left hand; it is considered very rude.
- The chance of your being invited by a ruler for coffee is pretty slim, but you never know. The coffee custom: If you are received by a ruler in a private meeting or audience, the ruler will ask you if you would like some coffee. You should refuse. The ruler will even try to insist, but you must continue to refuse. This custom goes back to the Bedouin tent, when a visitor could be using his host's only cup by accepting. If coffee or anything else is physically offered, then you should accept and there are no restrictions.

Entertainment

- The locals will entertain at home and will accept an invitation to a hotel or restaurant.
- Women in the UAE are involved in the business and professions but in traditional social gatherings could still be separated.
- If invited to a meal, do not misunderstand that it is to clinch the deal. In fact, it could be the groundwork to soften the blow of not getting the job.

- Since there are so many different forms of greeting, it is safe to allow your counterparts to initiate the greeting and then follow their lead.
- Firm embraces, kissing on both checks, and walking hand-in-hand are common and do not carry any sexual implications.
- Men will generally shake hands with all men present but not with women. If a man knows the woman well enough to touch her at all, he is a blood relative and knows her well enough to kiss her. But you will see some younger men that will exchange a handshake or even a hug in some instances with a woman associate from the United States or other countries. Eliminate any embarrassment or disrespect by allowing them to make the initial step. Some UAE women will instantly extend their hand, so be ready to reciprocate.
- Among family and friends within the Islamic culture, they will shake hands, touch on the shoulder, and kiss on the cheeks and nose.
- The standard greeting is *As-salam alaikum*, which means "peace be upon you." The reply to this greeting would be *Wa alaikum as-salam*, or "and upon you be peace."
- Upon arrival at a reception, the visitor should stand in the doorway and say the greeting. Once the visitor receives the reply, he may enter the room.
- First names denote more familiarity than in the West. There is no real equivalent of Mr., although the Hashemite noble title *Sayyed* is used in correspondence.
- Using bin, ben, or ibn before a name, especially a middle name, means "son of." *Bint* (daughter of) is the female form.
- A man is known to his friends as *Abu* (father of), followed by the name of his (usually eldest) son. Females may be addressed as *Umm* (mother of).
- Members of ruling families are addressed as His/Your Highness (*Samu al-Emir*). Ministers and ambassadors have the designation of "Excellency."
- Titles for Doctor, *Shaikh* (chief), *Ustadh* (professor), and *Mohandas* (engineer) are used. *Shaikh* is applied only to the first name and never the surname.
- If the visitor does not receive a reply, the phrase may be repeated. Continuous failure to reply means that the visitor is not welcomed and should not enter.
- Shoes should be removed if the room is carpeted. Leave them outside to avoid bringing in impurities and making the carpet ritually unclean for prayer.

- Once you are inside the room, shake hands with the most senior person first. This person may or may not be the host.
- Then make your way around the room in a counter-clockwise direction, shaking hands with each person before taking your seat and joining the conversation.
- You should not change the subject of conversation except by invitation or if the conversation should logically come to you or provide an opportunity for you to speak.
- If the attendance is larger than 50 people, or if the seating presents a challenge to move around, then it is acceptable to shake hands with the host and wave a greeting to the others.
- Crossing your legs once you are seated is acceptable but do not direct the sole of the foot to an individual. This is a "go away" gesture.
- Cultivating your relationships is of the utmost importance. Having a connection in the UAE can be critical for initial introductions and necessary connections.

 ## Appearance/Attire

- Local standards should be observed with modest dress.
- It is inappropriate and, in some places, even illegal for foreigners to wear the local garb or native clothing.
- Appropriate dress for men is shirt and trousers during the day with collar and a tie in the evening.
- Bush suits are popular and appropriate for the climate.
- Men should avoid wearing jewelry, especially around the neck.
- Women do not have to dress as modestly as in other parts of Arabia but still should be careful not to offend by wearing anything too revealing. Where the Islamic law is rigorously enforced, clothes should cover the tops of the arms and legs. You will eliminate all stares if your shirt or dress has sleeves and you wear nothing too revealing or tight. Avoid shorts and mini-skirts.
- Wear cotton or linen because of the hot and humid weather.
- Sandals are great and you will see "skimpy" bathing suits on the beach, but showing too much skin when not at a resort or on the beach is inappropriate.
- The bottom line for women is to dress appropriately, with longer skirts or slacks and be respectful of their culture by covering your arms and legs. You will see all variations, but the important part is to respect their standards.

Be On Your Best Cultural Behavior

Gift Giving

- Gifts are not necessary. If they are presented, they will be held and opened in private.
- Do not give alcohol, pork, or pork skin products, and be careful with any art gifts that might involve a partially clad or naked woman.
- The mixture of nationalities can be very tricky. You might give a gift of perfume to a Dubaian but not to an Egyptian.
- Traditional perfume is the most appreciated gift for Arabians. A man displays his status by his scent, but do not give perfumes that contain alcohol.
- Perfume should be given to women only by other women or close relatives.
- Gifts must be the best you can afford. If you present a carpet as a gift, for example, it should be handmade.
- Never buy gold jewelry or silk garments for men. These items are considered more typical and suitable for women than men in Islamic culture.
- Platinum is most acceptable but can be confused with white gold. Silver is safer, but must be hallmarked by a government authority as opposed to just bearing a maker's mark.
- Avoid giving personal items, knives, toy dogs, or gifts with pictures of dogs.
- Be careful about admiring an item. Your host could feel obligated and present this to you. It would be impolite to refuse this gift.

 Tipping

- Tipping in a restaurant or hotel is common. A service charge may be added to the total bill, but if it is not, 15 percent is the standard.
- It's not customary to tip taxi drivers, but do not expect them to have the change for anything larger than AED 50 (US$13). Come prepared with smaller notes.

 Gesture Awareness

- Eat and gesture with your right hand. The left hand is used for hygiene.
- Pointing at another person is offensive.
- Be careful if you must cross your legs. It's safer not to cross them to avoid directing the sole of your foot toward an individual. It means "go away" and is offensive.
- The thumbs-up gesture is offensive to some, so avoid it.
- Do not stare at people while they are praying or walk on or step over their prayer mats.
- It is considered offensive in the UAE to touch anyone's head.

United Arab Emirates

Faux Pas

- Avoid eating, smoking, and drinking in public areas during *Ramadan*. All Muslims will fast from sunrise to sunset and these customs should be respected in public.
- The welcome kiss on the cheek is about as far as you want to go with public affection. Public displays can offend people around you and may even cause you to be noticed by the police.
- Loud speech and laughter are considered vulgar. Any form of indecency or profanity in Dubai could result in action from the police.
- There is a zero tolerance policy toward drunk driving and other drink-related incidents.
- Avoid flattery. Genuine praise is appreciated but over flattering is suspect.
- Be careful and respectful about taking photographs. Ask permission if you want to photograph a person or several people and avoid secure areas like government or official buildings, military areas, airports, docks, and telecommunications equipment.
- Be careful of your reading material upon entering the UAE. Books and videos could be checked and anything unacceptable will be retained at customs.

USEFUL FACTS

President	Sheikh Khalifa bin Zayed al-Nahyan (2004)
Prime Minister	Sheikh Muhammad ibn Rashid al-Maktoum (2006)
National Name	Al-Imarat al-'Arabiyah al-Muttahidah
Size	32,278 square miles (83,600 square km)
Population	3,100,000 approximately (2008)
Capital	Abu Dhabi
Government	Federation formed in 1971 by seven emirates and called the Trucial States. Each emirate has a separate ruler in addition to the President and Prime Minister.

Currency	UAE dirham
Religion	Islam 96% (Sunni 80% Shiite 16%), Christian, Hindu, and other 4%
Language	Arabic (official), Farsi, English, Persian, Hindi, Urdu
Ethnicity	Emiri 19%, Iranian and other Arab 23%, South Asian 50%, other expatriate (includes East Asian and Westerners) 8%
Industry	Hospitality, petroleum and petrochemicals, fishing, aluminum, fertilizers, cement, ship repair, construction materials
Time Zone	UAE is four hours ahead of Greenwich Mean Time (GMT +4) or nine hours ahead of U.S. Eastern Standard Time (EST +9). UAE does not observe daylight saving time
Telephone Code	International Code: +971 City Code: +2 (Abu Dhabi)
Weather	Best time to visit for perfect weather is October to May. You will encounter very hot and humid weather June to September. The highest recorded temperature was in 1969, with a world record temperature of 167 F (75 C). The humidity often reaches 100 percent in the winter.
Voltage/Frequency	220/240 V; 50 Hz

HOLIDAYS/FESTIVALS

1 January	New Year's Day
Varies	The Day of the Sacrifice—Eid ul-Adha
Varies	Islamic New Year—Ra's Al Sana Al Hijria
6 August	Accession of the Ruler of Abu Dhabi (Observed in Abu Dhabi, the capital of UAE)
2 December	National Day varies End of Ramadan
Other public holidays:	Christmas, Mouloud, Leilat al-Meiraj, Id al-Fitr

LANGUAGE TIPS

Arabic Phonetics	**English**
Marhaba	Hello
Ya hala	Hi
Ahlan wa sahlan	Hi /Welcome
Masa El Khair	Good evening
Ma'assalama	Good-bye
Shloonik Insha'lla zany	How are you?
Kam	How much?
Affwan	Excuse me
Na'am/La	Yes/No
Shukran	Thank you

Chapter 31: UNITED KINGDOM

The island of Rockall not shown.

LOCATION/GEOGRAPHY

The United Kingdom of Great Britain and Northern Ireland is located off the northwest coast of Europe and is surrounded by the Atlantic Ocean, the North Sea, the English Channel, and the Irish Sea. The UK consists of the island of Great Britain, which includes England, Scotland, and Wales, as well as the portion of Ireland known as Northern Ireland. There are also several island groups and hundreds of small islands.

DID YOU KNOW?

- The first sovereign to call Buckingham Palace home was Queen Victoria (in 1837).
- Prior to 1857, when the first Divorce Court was established, it was common practice for men to actually take their unwanted wives to market like any other possession and trade them.
- The Romans constructed the first London Bridge in approximately 60 AD. There have been at least five different versions since then. A recent London Bridge was purchased by an American in 1971 and shipped in pieces to Lake Havasu City, Arizona, to be used as a tourist attraction.
- Public lavatories originated at the Great Exhibition, which was held at Hyde Park in 1851. They were so successful at this event that public toilets were installed in London.
- The first ship to come to the aid of the *Titanic* was the British ship *Carpathia*.
- Founded in 1849 and boasting seven floors and 300 departments, Harrods of London has an average of 35,000 customers a day pass through its doors. You will find 300,000 people there on 1 January looking for the best sales.
- In 1766, James Christie held his first auction in London. His first sales included chamber pots, a set of sheets, and other items that are just a little different from the luxurious items sold now at the famous auction house, today called Christie, Manson, and Woods.
- The oldest man buried in Westminster Abbey was Thomas Parr. He was 152 years old and left the advice, "Rise early, go soon to bed, and if you don't want to grow fat keep your eyes open and your mouth shut." He died in 1635.
- Britain's largest horse race is the Grand National, which is held in Liverpool in April. This steeplechase may not be the most prestigious or highly regarded to win, but it is the most popular with the public.
- There are more than 6,000 restaurants, 1,200 hotels, 3,500 pubs, 30,000 shops, 200 museums, 100 theaters, 600 cinema screens, and 300 markets in London.

- The phrase "mind your P's and Q's" is from English ale that was and is drunk in pints and quarts. If things got a little out of control, the innkeeper would remind drinkers to mind their own pints and quarts and to settle down.
- Tea, which is England's national drink and more popular than coffee, was first sold as a medicinal beverage.
- Over the years, Northern Ireland has had violent conflicts regarding the unification of Northern Ireland with the Republic of Ireland and the battle over whether they are British, Irish, or both. The people from Northern Ireland are entitled to both British and Irish citizenship. Political and religious (Irish Catholic versus British Protestant) violence has abated in recent years.
- The Queen may not enter the House of Commons because she is not a commoner.
- The playwright William Shakespeare (1564-1616) and writer Charles Dickens (1812-1870) are still two of the most popular British writers.
- Ben Jonson (1573-1637), another famous British writer, is buried upright in Westminster Abbey's Poet's Corner. He died in debt and couldn't afford a proper gravesite.
- Dr. Patrick Steptoe invented the in vitro fertilization procedure, successfully delivering the first "test-tube" baby, Louise Brown, in 1978.

BUSINESS ETIQUETTE

Punctuality

- Punctuality is very important in all business situations.
- You will find the Scots to be extremely punctual.
- To show respect, telephone if you see you will be a little late.
- Allow yourself plenty of time for travel to your meeting.
- If you're invited to a restaurant, arrive on time. If you're invited to a home or social event, it is acceptable to be 10 to15 minutes late.

Meeting Manners

- Appointments should be made in advance and confirmed upon arrival in the UK. Never just show up without calling.
- Things are changing with the younger generation, moving away from the standards of more formality and working only with companies they know. Younger business people do not stress long-term personal relationships before establishing a working relationship or the necessity of an intermediary for a business connection. But that being said, there are still traditions, and final decisions are up to the most powerful.

- Networking and relationship building is necessary.
- Be prepared for meetings that follow an agenda. The agenda should be sent in advance to the attendees of the meeting to allow time for review and recommendations or changes prior to the meeting.
- If a senior member is present, most of the discussion will come from that senior member.
- Very little chitchat will occur before the meeting starts. Avoid a lot of compliments and praise.
- Stay to the point, avoid exaggeration, and use professional and well prepared materials. Have facts and figures to back up all your claims.
- Hard-selling is not well received.
- The British are very direct and may come across as blunt. They will speak their minds and will say "no" if they feel it's appropriate and required.
- Businesswomen are completely respected but should appear professional at all times. Show knowledge of your field and dress conservatively.
- Follow up your meetings with a written summation and your next steps.
- July and August are big holiday months, so be careful in planning your travels or business meetings. Easter is a popular time for a holiday and there are two bank holidays in May. Many businesses will completely close down between Christmas and New Year. However, the UK has the lowest number of holidays in Europe.

Business Cards

- Business cards are exchanged during initial introductions with little to no formal ritual.
- Not much attention is paid to business cards other than a quick glance and then they are put away.
- Still the usual courtesies need to be adhered to, presenting your name facing the recipient and avoiding writing on the cards or placing them in your rear pocket.

Meals/Toasts

- The best advice is to follow the lead of your host.
- Continental is the style of eating, with the knife held in the right hand and the fork in the left while eating.
- Always stay standing at the table until invited to sit down. You might be shown to a specific seat.
- Avoid putting your elbows on the table.
- To show that you are not done eating, cross your fork and knife on your plate with the fork over the knife. To show that you are finished eating, lay your knife and fork parallel across the right side of your plate.

Be On Your Best Cultural Behavior

- Curry is the most popular food in Britain, while fish and chips are the common and popular fast food.
- It's common practice in a pub to pay for a round of drinks for your group.
- If you extend the invitation to a meal in a restaurant, then you pay.
- Toasts are given at formal meals. "Cheers" is the common greeting when offering a toast.

Entertainment

- The British do some business entertaining in their homes, but most entertaining is restaurants and pubs.
- Lunch is the best and most productive time for a business meal. Dinner meals are reserved for more social get-togethers.
- Lunch is generally between 12 p.m. and 2 p.m. (1200 and 1400), and dinner is between 7 p.m. and 11 p.m. (1900 and 2300).
- High tea can be a substitute for dinner and generally falls between 4 p.m. and 6 p.m. (1600 and 1800) in the more upscale hotels.
- Avoid discussing business until your guests or hosts bring up the subject, unless the meal or function was intended to be a working session.
- Topics to avoid are religion, the monarchy, and the Royal family; partisan politics; the European Union and Brussels; the euro; the Middle East; personal questions about background, religion, occupation, or class; race; immigration; and sex.
- Good topics of conversation include the weather, sports (especially football/soccer), British history, culture and literature, art, popular music, current affairs, and food and drink, particularly real ale.
- Beer is the popular drink for informal get-togethers. Beer may be served at cellar temperature and may even seem flat, but you can find your preferred taste with varying brews and strengths. "*Bitter*" is the most common style and easily found. UK beer can be much stronger than American beer.

Forms of Address/Introductions/Greetings

- A handshake is the most common form of greeting for both men and women.
- Shake hands when you meet and again when you are leaving.
- Allow enough personal space when greeting people. Generally this is a little more distance than experienced with North and South Americans and with Southern Europeans.
- Some formality may be noticeable at first. It may take a little longer to build a relationship or friendship, but once it has been established it will be solid and last over time.

- Have good eye contact when first meeting, but avoid long, direct eye contact. It can make some people feel uncomfortable.
- Exchanging kisses is becoming more standard but is not appropriate initially in business situations. Let the relationship grow and also allow them to take the first steps.
- Protocol is still important during introductions. Understand the procedures of introducing a lower ranking person to higher and younger to older. If people are of similar age and rank, then introduce the one that you know better.
- Younger people will immediately move to using your first name, but with older British, you need to wait until invited to move to a first-name basis.
- Most people will still use the titles of Mr., Mrs., or Miss with their surnames.
- Keep your correspondence more formal until they move toward more informality.

Appearance/Attire

- The normal style of dress is conservative for both men and women. The traditional pinstripe is still a popular style of suit.
- Some companies have adopted "smart casual" dress for their entire week or for "dress down" Fridays.
- The Scots will not be wearing kilts to work. These are saved for special occasions such as a Highland wedding or special social gatherings.
- Some upscale restaurants and hotels may still require jackets and ties for men and dresses for women.

Gift Giving

- Giving or receiving gifts is not a major part of the British business culture, and they may even feel embarrassed if a gift is presented.
- At the end of the discussions or a finalized deal might be the time for a gift. This could include silver, gold, or an item that is inscribed with the name and date.
- It doesn't need to be an expensive gift but something that was chosen with thought to the recipient's interests. A book or good quality pen is always a nice gift for a business exchange.
- Inviting a collegiate to a meal, the theater, or opera is a good way to show thanks or to reciprocate for a gift.
- Always be prepared with gifts to present to others in case you should receive a gift from them. Have something that could easily be tucked in your briefcase, wrapped and ready.

- If you are invited to a home, bring a box of good chocolates, a good bottle of wine, or flowers.
- Be careful about presenting alcohol as a gift unless you know the person's taste and know it is one of their favorite spirits. Your host will probably not open your bottle of wine when presented. This is not because they are unappreciative but because they probably have already selected the wine for the evening and yours will be enjoyed later. If a good bottle of champagne is presented, that may be chilled and served after your meal.
- If you are a guest in a home, a handwritten note is a kind gesture and should be sent immediately after the event or dinner.
- Be careful of the usual flowers to avoid in Europe including red roses, white lilies, and chrysanthemums.
- When gifts, other than the bottle of wine, are presented or received, they are opened.

 Tipping

- A service charge of 10 percent to 15 percent is generally always included in your hotel and restaurant bills. You can leave an additional tip by presenting cash directly to the staff that provides the service.
- A small tip is appropriate for hotel staff that provide services, which may include the porter for bags he may handle; a concierge if he or she helps with tickets, a restaurant reservation, or setting up a tour; or a doorman who assists with securing a taxi. Present the tip by just placing it in their hand while you extend a handshake of thanks.
- If there is no table service, then tipping is not necessary. You may say to a server, "Have a drink on me" or "Get yourself a drink." The server will then add the price of a drink or just keep the money. By doing this when you place your first drink order, you usually will secure better service and you don't need to do further tipping.
- A 10 percent to 15 percent tip or a couple of pounds, whichever is greater, should be provided for hairdressers, porters, and others that provide services.
- Taxi drivers expect 10 percent to 15 percent or a couple of pounds, again whichever is greater.

 Gesture Awareness

- The "V" sign of raising the index and middle fingers with the palm inward is considered vulgar and offensive. Winston Churchill's version to signify peace or victory was made with the palm facing outward. It is not seen or used as much nowadays.
- If you want to indicate the number two with your fingers, then use your thumb and first finger.

- Keep all hand and gestures to a minimum.
- When in a bar or pub, don't whistle, tap your coins on the bar, or wave your money in the air to get the attention of the bar staff. Just wait for your turn and they will take care of you.

Faux Pas

- Wait patiently and do not cut in line. If there is a queue, go to the back.
- Smoking is banned in most public areas, so don't light up without checking.
- Avoid putting pens or pencils in your shirt or jacket pocket.
- Avoid wearing striped ties because they may represent an institution, club, or military regiment of which you are not a member.
- Privacy is important, so if you're invited to a home, do not just take off for your own tour of their home nor should you ask if you could take a tour.
- The terms "English" and "British" should not be confused as meaning the same. British people live in the UK and are from England, Scotland, Wales, or Northern Ireland. But the English are people from England; Scots, from Scotland, Welsh, from Wales; and Irish, from Ireland.

 ## USEFUL FACTS

Sovereign	Queen Elizabeth II (1952)
Prime Minister	Gordon Brown (2007)
National Name	United Kingdom of Great Britain and Northern Ireland
Size	93,278 square miles (241,590 square km)
Population	60,943,912 (2008)
Capital	London
Government	Constitutional Monarchy and Parliamentary Democracy
Currency	Pound sterling

Religion	Christian (Anglican, Roman Catholic, Presbyterian, Methodist) 71.6%, Muslim 2.7%, Hindu 1%, other 1.6%, unspecified or none 23.1%
Language	English, Welsh, Scots Gaelic
Ethnicity	White (primarily British) 92.1%, Black 2%, Indian 1.8%, Pakistani 1.3%, Mixed 1.2%, other 1.6%
Industry	Agriculture, machine tools, electric power, equipment, shipbuilding, aircraft, motor vehicles and parts, electronic and communications equipment, metals, chemicals, coal, petroleum, paper and paper products, food processing, textiles, clothing, consumer goods and tourism
Time Zone	The United Kingdom is Greenwich Mean Time (GMT) or five hours ahead of U.S. Eastern Standard Time (EST +5). The United Kingdom observes daylight saving time.
Telephone Code	International Code: +44 City Code: +20 (London)
Weather	The United Kingdom enjoys a temperate climate, but expect clouds and rainfall year-round. The temperatures can vary considerably, but rarely fall below 23 F (-5 C) or go much above 86 F (30 C). You will find drier weather in the east and warmer in the south. Occasional snowfall will occur in winter to early spring, but it is not common.
Voltage/Frequency	230 V; 50 Hz

HOLIDAYS/FESTIVALS

1 January	New Year's Day
2 January	Bank holiday – Scotland
25 January	Burns' Night (Scotland) (Robert Burns, the Favorite Son of Scotland was a poet and a national icon.)
17 March	St. Patrick's Day

February/March	Pancake Day or Shrove Tuesday (Traditionally held after Shrove Monday (or Collop Monday) and before Ash Wednesday. A day when all rich foods like eggs, butter, and fat are made into pancakes and eaten so they are not left in the home during Lent. In the United States, celebrated as Mardi Gras.)
March/April	Good Friday to Easter Monday
23 April	St. George's Day (Patron Saint of England)
1 May	Bank holiday (Scotland)
May	Spring bank holiday (Britain)
12 July	Orange Day, Battle of Boyne (Northern Ireland)
Early August	Summer bank holiday (Scotland)
Late August	Summer bank holiday (Britain outside Scotland)
5 November	Guy Fawkes Day (England) (A day of Thanksgiving to Guy Fawkes for stopping the destruction of the British Houses of Parliament with explosives.)
25 December	Christmas
26 December	Boxing Day, St. Stephen's Day

LANGUAGE TIPS

Although English is the main language, here are some differences that might help you understand a little better:

UK English	United States English
Fortnight	Two weeks
Pants	Underwear
Trousers	Slacks
Trainers	Tennis shoes or sneakers
Off license (offie)	Liquor store
Motorway	Freeway
Bonnet (of a car)	Hood
Boot (of a car)	Trunk
Torch	Flashlight
Petrol station	Gas station/filling station
Level crossing	Railroad crossing
White coffee	Coffee with milk
Mince	Hamburger meat
Lift	Elevator
Queue	Line
Pissed	Drunk (not mad or angry)
Fag	Cigarette

Be On Your Best Cultural Behavior

Chapter 32: UNITED STATES

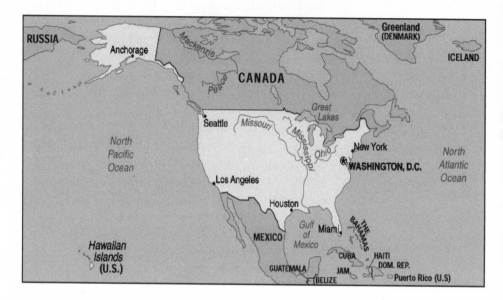

LOCATION/GEOGRAPHY

The United States is bordered by Canada to the North and Mexico to the South. It is the third largest country both in size and population. The Atlantic Ocean and the Gulf of Mexico form the United States' eastern and southeastern coastlines, while the Pacific Ocean is to the west. The Great Lakes to the north and the Mississippi, Missouri, and Ohio rivers are major inland waterways. The states of Alaska and Hawaii are separated from the mainland.

DID YOU KNOW?

- The International Boundary between Canada and the United States is the longest common border in the world that is not militarized. These are the only two countries that border three oceans—the Atlantic, Pacific and Arctic.
- Almost half of U.S. residents live the Eastern time zone; almost 30 percent live in the Central time zone; about five percent live in the Mountain time zone; 15 percent live in the Pacific time zone; and less than one percent live in any other time zone.
- Alaska is as large as 21 of the smallest states combined.
- The nickname "Big Apple" for New York City is from an early swing dance that originated in a South Carolina club called The Big Apple.
- The only state not to have a rectangular flag is Ohio. It is a pennant.
- The federal government owns 32 percent of all the land in the United States.
- Point Roberts, Washington, is divided from the rest of the state by British Columbia, Canada. So if you want to travel to or from Point Roberts to the rest of the state you must go through Canada and through Canadian and U.S. customs.
- The state with the most people per square mile is New Jersey.
- All the U.S. Interstate Highways moving north-south are numbered sequentially, starting from the west, with odd numbers. The interstates that go east-west are numbered sequentially, beginning from the south, with even numbers.
- Italian born (1454) explorer and cartographer, Amerigo Vespucci, gave his name to America. He died in 1512 from malaria.
- At 6,194 feet (9,968 meters), Mount McKinley is the highest point in the United States. The Mississippi-Missouri is the longest river, and Lake Michigan is the largest lake.

BUSINESS ETIQUETTE

Punctuality

- Punctuality is very important in all business situations.
- A lot of social events follow a come-and-go concept, so you can arrive and depart at your convenience.
- Traffic can be a challenge in some busy cities, so allow enough time to avoid delays.
- A phone call is necessary if you are running late or stuck in traffic.
- If you're invited to a meal or a seated event, you will need to arrive on time.

Meeting Manners

- The general work week is Monday through Friday from 8 a.m. to 5 p.m. (0800 to 1700) or 8:30 a.m. to 6 p.m. (0830 to1800).
- Appointments should be made in advance, with a confirmed meeting time and place that is convenient for all. When cancellation is necessary, notice should be given as soon as possible.
- Appointments are generally set up during the week but can also be arranged for special outings or dinners over weekends.
- Most meetings will take place in an office, a hotel meeting room, or a restaurant.
- Generally, business meetings or dinners do not take place in homes, but occasionally invitations are extended to show a gesture of goodwill.
- Americans are creative and are risk takers and look for new ideas to get things done quicker and more efficiently.
- Saving face is not as important in the United States as in some countries, but obvious insult or undermining a person is not acceptable.
- United States businesspeople will tend to rush and look for decisions to happen quickly. Businesspeople can be very persistent. Business moves at a fairly fast pace.
- Businesspeople are very direct and will disagree and say "no."
- Silence becomes uncomfortable for many people, so Americans may just continue to talk to fill the silence.
- Ethics are important.
- It is not uncommon for young executives to own a company or to be the president or chairman of the board.
- Meetings will start with small talk and then proceed to a written agenda or set plan.
- Budgets and financial plans are generally followed closely. Some companies can deviate, but most have a set goal or cap to their programs.
- There is give-and-take while negotiating to final decisions.

United States

- Contracts can be reached quickly. An oral agreement is made and then agreed upon with legal contracts.
- Decisions have various steps. Many managers are given the authority to decide on certain contracts or decisions up to a point or financial level. For decisions or costs that affect the overall budget or bottom line of the company, then more discussion or approval must be obtained.
- Most people in the United States speak only English, so interpreters will be needed for other languages.

Business Cards

- Business card exchange is handled on the first meeting. Cards are exchanged freely and frequently.
- No formal protocol has been established. A sign of respect would be to stand and present cards with your name facing the recipient.
- Read the cards to confirm names or other pertinent information. Place the cards in a portfolio or your chest pocket. Do not place their cards, or your own, in your wallet and then place in your back pocket.
- Generally cards in the United States carry a company logo and name, the name of the person, address, e-mail address, Web site, phone, fax, and perhaps a cell phone number. If a person has a title or other certifications, they may also be displayed on the card. Generally, if a person has received a doctorate degree, it is noted on the card. Some will also include master's degrees.

Meals/Toasts

- If you invite someone out for a business meal, then you will pay.
- If necessary, make arrangements in advance to handle the bill so no discussion or misunderstanding takes place at the end of the meal.
- If a woman is the host, then prior arrangements to handle the bill will show a sign of professionalism and will eliminate argument over who will pay at the end of the meal. Arrive early and make the necessary arrangements with wait staff, maitre d', or hostess before the arrival of your guests.
- It is fine to refuse a drink or food.
- You can finish all that is on your plate if you desire. It might look a little nicer to leave a bite or two.
- If you're invited to a home, then bring a gift to the host. It's not necessary to bring children gifts, but a game, toy, or some electronic device would be appropriate.

Be On Your Best Cultural Behavior

- Toasts in the United States are brief and happen at the beginning or end of the meal. Generally, the host will give the first toast while standing.
- If you are receiving the toast, then do not touch your glass or drink to yourself. Just a nice smile, nod and thank-you are sufficient.
- If a toast is given in return, the best time is between the entrée and dessert.
- Some people will clink their glasses, which is an old tradition. It isn't necessary, but go with the flow. Never stand and clang on a glass with your knife or another piece of silverware. Just raise your glass and ask for attention.
- Keep the glass at eye or shoulder level. Don't raise the glass high above your head. The drink will surely come down on someone in the vicinity.
- "Cheers" is used for simple toasts or as a signal to begin eating.

 ## Entertainment

- Breakfast meetings are common and can start as early as 7 a.m. (0700).
- Lunch generally falls between 11:30 a.m. and 2 p.m. (1130 and 1400) and can last one and one-half hours. In the United States, lunch is generally a lighter meal.
- Meetings may occur over the weekend at brunch, which generally is 11 a.m. to 2 p.m. (1100 to 1400).
- Wine and alcoholic drinks generally are reserved for evening meetings and meals. Some companies have strict policies forbidding alcohol during lunch or any other business functions. Follow the lead of your host.
- Dinner is generally the main meal of the day and can start as early as 6 p.m. to 8 p.m. (1800 to 2000).
- Business is not generally conducted on Sundays, but appointments can be made if travel arrangements fall over the weekend.
- Many conventions (congresses) or conferences will take place over the weekend or may begin on Sundays.
- Meals are generally eaten "American" style, with switching of hands and silverware. The fork is held in the right hand for eating. To cut, the knife is placed first in the right hand to cut, and then set at the top of the plate with the blade facing in, and the fork in the left hand. The fork is then transferred to the right hand to eat. If a person is left-handed, this procedure is done in reverse. Some will use the continental style, not switching the knife and fork.
- If eating "American" style, the hand you are not using to eat remains on your lap. The continental style has both hands visible and the wrists resting on the table.

- If the meal is held in a home, it's common to give guests a tour. Guests should not just start to wander and look for themselves.
- Always call in advance, and never invite yourself to a business acquaintance's home.

Forms of Address/Introductions/Greetings

- The standard greeting for both male and female is a firm handshake with two to three shakes or a few seconds. Some might do a double shake by placing the left hand on top of the right to show a little more affection. Those are a little harder to break and get your hand away.
- A nice smile as you look them directly in the eyes with a "hello" works the best. Repeat people's names in your greeting.
- It's customary and acceptable to approach people and introduce yourself.
- The personal space is two and one-half feet to three feet apart.
- Business acquaintances will also frequently exchange one kiss (air kiss) to the right cheek when they know one another better.
- Introductions are generally exchanged by saying the higher ranking person's name first. Other factors to consider are age and gender, with men being introduced to women and younger people being introduced to older.
- In the United States, most people have a first, middle, and last name. Most will be introduced by their first and last names.
- Americans go quickly to a first name basis, but refer to a person initially by using the last name. You most likely will be told to call your counterparts by their first names.
- Titles of Dr., Mr., Mrs., and Ms. are still used in more formal situations.
- Pay attention to how the person is introduced. If the name is Jonathan, don't shorten to Jon or change Rebecca to Becky. Use the name given to you and not a shorter version.
- If someone has a name that you are not sure how to pronounce, ask them to repeat or clarify.

Appearance/Attire

- To be safe, arrive at your first meeting in conservative business dress. Follow your counterparts' lead for any subsequent meetings.
- Many companies have moved into business casual dress. Ask what they mean by business casual. It's always better to go for a professional look.
- On the East Coast, people will be a little more formal, while the West coast is more relaxed.

- The business look for women is still a suit of either skirt or pants. A casual look of slacks and top may be acceptable. It helps to accessorize to add a little flair to the outfit.
- Outside of work, dress is much more casual and you will see all ages in jeans, shorts, t-shirts, open-toed shoes, and baseball caps. Remove hats or caps when you enter a home, place of business, restaurant, church, or building.

Gift Giving

- Gifts are not expected for business meetings. If it is an ongoing business relationship, gifts may be exchanged in the very beginning or at the end of a deal.
- Gifts are often given when initially meeting a new customer to show that you want to work with them.
- Gifts do not have to be expensive and may carry the company's logo or be from your country. Also, make sure gifts are not perceived as a bribe instead of just a nice gesture of a working relationship.
- Gifts are presented either unwrapped or in a gift bag with just a ribbon or simple wrapping.
- Gifts are generally opened when they are presented.
- The biggest time for exchange of gifts is during the holiday season from Thanksgiving to Christmas. Then wrappings and gifts become a little more elaborate.
- If you visit a home, always bring a gift with a nice card. It can be a bottle of good wine (if the host drinks wine), chocolates, or a gift that would interest your host. Flowers can be sent the next day to show appreciation.
- If you visit a home with children, it is nice to bring the children a gift but is not necessary. It could be something from your company or country, a DVD, or an electronic device that is appropriate for their age.
- Always follow up with a handwritten thank-you note when you receive a gift.

Tipping

- Fifteen percent is the normal tipping for restaurants and providing gratuities for good service rendered. For more upscale restaurants, a 20 percent tip or more is given.
- A hair dresser will receive 15 percent of the total bill and an additional tip of US$1 to several dollars is presented to the person that washes your hair. Even if the hair dresser owns the shop, a tip generally is still provided.

- Hotel tipping can be endless. A good standard for bellmen is US$1 per bag or US$2 for the first bag and then US$1 for every additional bag. Determine your tipping range depending on the frequency of your visits to that hotel and service provided.
- US$1 to US$2 is provided for everyone that handles your bags. If the doorman takes bags from the taxi and carries them to the front desk, then tip the doorman. If your bags are taken from the front desk to your room by another bellman, that person is also tipped.
- The airport skycaps should also be tipped US$1 to US$2 for each bag. Some airlines are now charging fees for your luggage. Understand each carrier's policies and the procedures to handle these extra handling fees. This is not a tip. A tip should be presented if you use the services of a skycap in addition to these mandatory fees.
- Housekeepers are provided tips daily for the service they provide in cleaning your room. The standard is US$1 to US$2, but if several people are occupying the room, then several extra dollars could be provided. This money should be left on the bed daily due to their shift changes, and it's not necessary to place it in an envelope or to leave a note.
- Valet parkers, shuttle drivers, tour guides, and other services providers also expect tips. The amount of the tip is up to you and can depend on the service they provide. For a quick service or delivery, US$1 to US$5 is generally acceptable. If their service is more involved, then 15 percent to 20 percent of the overall bill may apply.
- Taxi drivers will generally receive 15 percent of the fare and an additional US$1 for each bag if they assist with your luggage.

Gesture Awareness

- Point with your index finger to show a location, but avoid pointing at a person.
- To call someone, wave all the fingers or just your index finger with the palm facing out.
- The OK sign, made by forming a circle with your thumb and index finger, is acceptable. This indicates that everything is fine.
- The thumbs-up sign is very common to show approval, and thumbs down shows disapproval or disagreement.
- To wave good-bye, just move your entire hand from side to side with the palm facing outward.
- A nice backslap shows friendship or congratulations.
- Direct eye contact and a smile are gestures of hello and are used frequently even just passing people on the street.
- Shaking your head up and down signifies yes. Shaking from side to side means no.

- Showing your middle finger with your hand in a fist is an insult.
- Shaking your fist at someone is also rude and indicates anger.
- Winking could be misunderstood as a flirtatious gesture.
- To hail a taxi, raise your hand with your index finger extended.
- To motion for someone to stop, place your hand up with fingers and thumb together completely facing the person and make a halt sign.

 ## Faux Pas

- Do not give a woman a gift of perfume or clothing; it will appear too personal and inappropriate.
- Do not wave your napkin, snap your fingers, or scream out "waiter" to get attention in a restaurant or bar.
- Do not smoke without first checking to see if permitted or asking if anyone minds.
- Conversations to avoid initially include politics, religion, or controversial topics.
- Avoid ethnic or religious jokes.

 # USEFUL FACTS

President	Barack Hussein Obama (2009)
Vice President	Joseph Robinette Biden, Jr. (2009)
National Name	United States of America
Size	3,537,418 square miles (9,161.923 square km)
Population	303,824,646 (2008)
Capital	Washington, D.C.
Government	Federal Republic
Currency	Dollar
Religion	Protestant 52%, Roman Catholic 24%, Mormon 2%, other Christian 2%, Jewish 2%, other or unspecified 2%, unaffiliated 12%, none 4%

Language	English 82%, Spanish 11%
Ethnicity	White 65%, Hispanic 13%, Black 12%, Asian 4%, American Indian and Alaska Native 1%, Native Hawaiian or Pacific Islander 0.2%, other 5%
Industry	Computers, telecommunications, consumer goods, medicines, agriculture and tourism
Time Zone	The United States has six time zones and Eastern Standard Time is five hours behind Greenwich Mean Time (GMT -5). Except for the states of Arizona and Hawaii and the territories of American Samoa, Guam, Puerto Rico, and the U.S. Virgin Islands, the U.S. observes daylight saving time.
Telephone Code	International Code: +1 City Code: +202 (Washington, DC) If dialing to the United States from another country, you would dial 00 + 1 + area code + telephone number. If dialing from state to state within the United States, only the 1 + area code + telephone number (10 digits total) will be needed.
Weather	The United States offers every type of climate from hot deserts to snowy mountains to warm coasts. The climate of the United States is temperate. It is generally cooler in the North and warmer in the South, whatever the season.
Voltage/Frequency	120 V; 60 Hz

HOLIDAYS/FESTIVALS

1 January	New Year's Day
15 January	Martin Luther King Day (Celebrated on the nearest Monday)
Third Monday in February	President's Day
March/April	Good Friday and Easter
Last Monday in May	Memorial Day (Celebrating fallen war veterans)
14 June	Flag Day
4 July	Independence Day
First Monday in September	Labor Day
Second Monday of October	Columbus Day
11 November	Veteran's Day
Fourth Thursday in November	Thanksgiving Day
25 December	Christmas Day

LANGUAGE TIPS

English is the main language spoken in the United States, but each part of the country has is own colloquialisms. Here are phrases or words that might be confusing:

American English	European
Downtown	Center of the city
Bottled water	Mineral water
Pants, slacks	Trousers
Candy	Sweets
Cookie	Biscuit
Gasoline, gas	Petrol
Diaper	Nappy
Stroller, baby carriage	Pushchair, pram, buggy
Parking garage	Car park
Tennis shoes, sneakers	Trainers
Bathroom, restroom	Water closet, WC
Checking in/checking out	Arriving at a hotel/departing
Elevator	Lift

Chapter 33: VIETNAM

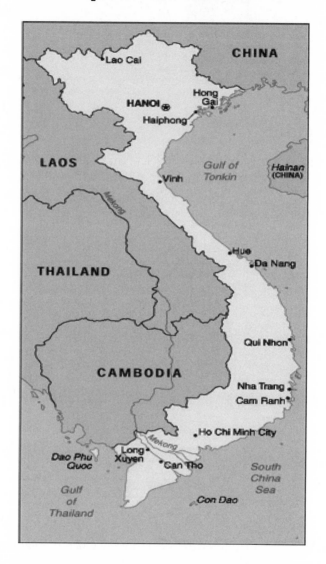

LOCATION/GEOGRAPHY

Vietnam is located in the southern and eastern part of the
Indochinese peninsula in Southeast Asia. The South China Sea is along
its entire east coast. Vietnam is bordered by China to the north and by
Laos and Cambodia to the west.

DID YOU KNOW?

- Myth or not, every small house in Vietnam is said to have a television. Supposedly, the purpose of making televisions affordable for everyone was to reduce the population growth rate. Presently the population density for Vietnam is 224.5 persons per square km. It's projected that Vietnam will have 100 million people by 2020.
- The Perfume River is located in Hue and runs along the walled Royal Citadel. This was Vietnam's old capital, and the Emperor presided there until 1945.
- Rice is the biggest export, and Vietnam is the second biggest exporter of rice in the world.
- A large part of the Vietnamese economy is now tourism. As a visitor to Vietnam, you should take a ride on a three-wheeled rickshaw that is called a *cyclo*.
- Tigers are still found in the northern areas of Vietnam, and elephants and monkeys throughout the highlands.
- Visit Hoi An for custom-made clothes and shoes completed in just hours.
- The Mekong specialty dish is elephant ear fish. It really is a fish.
- Now the official name is Ho Chi Minh City, but from 1954 to 1975, Saigon was the capital of South Vietnam. When it was captured in 1975 by the North Vietnamese, it was renamed in honor their late leader, Ho Chi Minh.
- Hanoi is the capital, but prior to this name, it had many. Hanoi was the capital of North Vietnam from 1954 to 1976. Once Vietnam was reunited, it became the nation's capital.
- The Mekong is the 12th longest river in the world and empties into the South China Sea.
- The most popular form of transportation is their railways. Bicycles are common and cars just get stuck in their big traffic jams.
- The teachings of Confucius, which is a system of behaviors and ethics that stress the obligations of people toward one another, influence the Vietnamese.

- The family is crucial and it's common for three generations to live together in one home. Since the family is the father's responsibility under Confucian tradition, he will provide food, shelter, and clothing and make the important decisions.

BUSINESS ETIQUETTE

 Punctuality

- Strict punctuality in business is necessary and expected.
- They do understand and can be flexible if situations occur that are out of your control, such as traffic, excessive rain, or washed-out streets.
- Punctuality among friends is much more relaxed.

 Meeting Manners

- Connections are critical, and finding a reliable and credible local representative plays a major role. Before you contract with a local consulting firm, ask for references and verify their actual connections, knowledge of your market, and experience.
- A written introduction or a pre-arranged meeting set by a go-between will have the best results.
- Do your research before your trip to Vietnam. Be aware of their marketplace, your target markets, and the right connections to the companies with which you wish to work.
- Long-term commitments are needed to be successful in this country.
- Face-to-face meetings are still the best to build a relationship of trust.
- Make your appointments at least several weeks in advance.
- Vietnamese women receive equal pay for equal work, but men are still the bosses.
- If you plan to operate a local office in Vietnam, it takes time. The government is working to make this process easier. It's important to have a dependable local company or representative. These contacts need to know the market, the negotiating skills, and the best way to open doors for you.
- Always contact your embassy and chamber of commerce in your home country and also in Vietnam. These offices can cut out many steps by providing the business information and contacts you need.
- Be modest in your dealings. Even if given a compliment, be polite and deny it.
- Your materials should be presented in Vietnamese. Most Vietnamese are studying English or other foreign languages but are generally more

comfortable with their own language. Confirm in advance how materials should be presented.

- Translators also will be needed. Come prepared and ready for all meetings and discussions. Hire an interpreter so your material is delivered the way you want to present it. Make sure you meet in advance with the interpreters so they have a complete understanding of you and your company.
- If senior officials are introduced or are a part of the meeting, then keep chitchat to a minimum because this opportunity may not present itself again. If meeting with middle- or junior-level officials, then more talk is necessary to build a lasting relationship.
- Most of the decisions are made by committee. Do not rely on only one person to express your concerns and interest.
- Vietnamese value "saving face" and will avoid any unpleasantness. You may be told "yes" or "no problem," when it may actually mean there is a big problem and they don't mean yes. This is when a local partner may be very important.
- There could also be silence when someone is in disagreement with another. This silence will prevent loss of face.
- The negotiation process can be very slow, with decisions going through many channels and much red tape.
- Be careful what you say through phone calls, fax lines, e-mails, and telephones. The government plays a key role with both security and competitive business.

Business Cards

- Business cards are generally exchanged during the first meeting. They are considered part of an important and necessary opening ritual.
- Using both hands to receive and present cards, with a slight bow to show respect, is their custom.
- Make sure you take a few moments to read a card before you rush to put it in your pocket.
- Try pronouncing each person's name and acknowledging their titles. You are showing people that it is an honor and great opportunity to meet them.
- Have a large supply of cards and promotional material. If you leave home without your cards or you completely run out and cannot present a card, it comes across that you are not legitimate or are trying to hide something, and this could create an extremely negative first impression. Come prepared.

- Manners are relaxed and casual, with the use of a fork, spoon, or chopsticks and rice bowls.
- Do not come in and take a seat. Always wait until you are showed to your seat.
- Allow the elderly to sit before you take your seat.
- If a businesswoman from another country is dining with a Vietnamese man, make arrangements to dine in a public place and insist on hosting. If the Vietnamese man hosts, then the woman is obliged to reciprocate with a meal of equal value.
- Wiping utensils with their napkins is a standard practice before starting a meal.
- Keep the chopsticks on the table or use a chopstick rest after you begin to eat or at the end of the meal.
- Keep the rice bowls close to your mouth while eating. It is considered idleness if you do not.
- While eating soup, hold the spoon with your left hand.
- When you pass anything, make sure you pass with both hands.
- You may finish all food on your plate and it's considered polite to do so.
- When you have completed your meal, rest your chopsticks on top of your rice bowl.
- The Vietnamese generally eat breakfast very early, have a longer lunch, and then eat an early evening meal. Many noodle shops and storefronts will remain open for the younger and later crowd.
- If presented with food or drink, you should taste or drink at least a small amount. It's considered impolite not to at least try.
- You can use a toothpick, but just make sure you completely cover your mouth. You may even find toothpicks on the table.
- Be careful. A small dish or shaker of white crystal could be monosodium glutamate (MSG) rather than salt or sugar.
- Tea most likely will be offered at a reception or meeting. This ritual form of hospitality should always be accepted and never refused.
- Domestic and imported beers are available. Rice wine is popular, but other wines are available, including fruit wines. Water from the tap should be avoided even though it has been filtered and sterilized. You will need to boil again if you want to drink it. Choose bottled water or other bottled beverages.
- Toasting at banquets or dinners is common. If cognac or whiskey is served at the meal, it's customary for individuals to drink only after a toast is made. To return a toast is standard practice.
- For toasts, the glass should be held in the right hand and supported by the left.

- Their common toasts are *tram phan tram (cham fum cham)*, meaning "empty your glass 100 percent" and *chuc suc khoe (chook sa koi-ah)*, "good health."

Entertainment

- Some Vietnamese men feel uncomfortable socializing with foreign women. In a social setting, they may seat women so they are next to one another during meals or gatherings.
- Family meals may still be eaten around a central banquet on the floor.
- The host may serve the guests, but it's more likely that everyone is invited to start helping themselves from the food that is placed on dishes in the center of the table.
- You will find hundreds of traditional dishes, but rice and noodles are the staple foods and are served with most meals.
- A good topic of conversation is the sport of soccer (football). Vietnam has one of the most popular and successful soccer teams in Southeast Asia.

Forms of Address/Introductions/Greetings

- Men and some women will shake hands at the start and end of meetings. Initially, you might want to let the woman extend her hand first or follow her lead with a slight bow or nod.
- Many times they will shake your hand with both hands.
- Vietnamese will come in close to talk and may engage in friendly touching, patting, and hand-holding.
- To say, *"xin chao"* (seen show) plus a person's given name and title will put you miles ahead of your competition. This greeting of hello will be appreciated.
- There is nothing sexual about men and women, or two people of the same sex, walking arm in arm or holding hands. If a person of the same sex does take your hand or touches your elbow, this is just a sign that they are comfortable with you.
- The Vietnamese name is family name, middle name, and then their given or personal name. If the person you are dealing with has a title, then you should address him or her with the title and given name. Their given name is always last. This is similar to the first or Christian name in Western societies.

Appearance/Attire

- It's best to dress modestly for business and social occasions. Tropical-weight clothing is advisable.
- Be careful about displaying too much skin.
- For official programs, more formal dress is appreciated.
- Men will wear conservative suits and ties.
- Women will be in more conservative dresses or business blouses and pants.
- Women should also avoid heavy makeup.
- Shorts should be saved for the beach.

 Gift Giving

- If you're invited to a Vietnamese home, make sure you arrive with a gift, especially for the woman of the family. It is also very nice and considerate to bring gifts to children or elderly parents.
- Present in colorful paper.
- Possible gift ideas could be sweets, fruits, flowers, incense, or even items for daily use. Daily use gifts could include soaps, lamps, or framed pictures.
- Presenting gifts for the home when in the office in front of other employees could be perceived as a bribe. Make sure the gifts are small and inexpensive. A gift with your company logo or from your country is appropriate.
- Gift giving generally occurs at the end of the meeting or during a meal.
- A gift of whisky is a good business choice.
- Flowers are usually exchanged just from men to women. Do not present yellow flowers or chrysanthemums.
- Avoid handkerchiefs (sad farewell) or any black for your gift. They are considered evil or threatening.

 Tipping

- Tipping is not customary but is truly appreciated.
- Government-run restaurants that cater to tourists automatically add a 10 percent service fee to bills. Government-run hotels also automatically add a 10 percent service fee for the hotel maids.
- There are currently no car rentals available, so you will need to look for cabs, which are unmarked and without meters. You can rent these daily and the fee is generally US$30 to US$40. Just make sure you make advance arrangements.
- Large tips are not necessary for cab drivers, but small tips are expected.

Gesture Awareness

- When presenting your business cards, a gift, or even a bill, present with both hands.
- Avoid pointing to anyone. To get their attention or to call a person, use your whole hand with the palm down and moving your fingers in a scratching motion. Beckon only someone that is in a lower class than you or who is in a serving occupation such as a waiter.
- Holding hands or walking hand-in-hand in public is common and fine but avoid any other physical contact.
- The bow is used, especially with the elderly, to show respect.
- Placing your arms on your hips is considered impolite.
- Crossing your arms on your chest is a very rude gesture.
- Do not pass anything over someone's head.
- Avoid touching on the shoulder.
- It's considered barbaric to use a cloth handkerchief and return it to your pocket for future use.

Faux Pas

- Touching a person's head is wrong because it is considered the spiritual center of the person. Only elderly people may touch a child's head.
- Avoid talking about the Vietnam War or any other wars. They want to focus more on their present development and their future.
- Ask permission before taking photos of people or places of worship.
- Be very careful about giving handouts to beggars. Once you do, you could be attacked by a mob of them.
- Do not use loud conversations or too many gestures. It's considered rude.
- Make sure you remove your shoes before you enter Buddhist pagodas.

USEFUL FACTS

President	Nguyen Minh Triet (2006)
Prime Minister	Nguyen Tan Dung (2006)
National Name	Cong Hoa Xa Hoi Chu Nghia Viet Nam Soviet Republic of Vietnam
Size	125,622 square miles (325,361 square km)

Population	86,116,559 (2008)
Capital	Hanoi
Government	Communist state
Currency	Dong
Religion	Buddhist 9%, Catholic 7%, Hoa Hao 2%, Cao Dai 1%, Protestant less than 1%, Islam less than 1%, none 80%
Language	Vietnamese (official language); English (increasingly favored as a second language); some French, Chinese, and Khmer. The mountain languages include Mon-Khmer and Malayo-Polynesian.
Ethnicity	Kinh (Viet) 86%, Tay 2%, Thai 2%, Muong 2%, others 8%
Industry	Agriculture, food processing, garments, shoes, machinery, mining, coal, steel, cement, chemical fertilizer, glass, tires, oil, paper, and tourism
Time Zone	Vietnam is seven hours ahead of Greenwich Mean Time (GMT +7) or 12 hours ahead of Eastern Standard Time (EST +12). Vietnam does not observe daylight saving time.
Telephone Code	International Code: +84 City Code: +4 (Hanoi)
Weather	The weather can vary from wet and cold in one area to dry and warm in another. The best time for their weather is from September to December or from March to April. South Vietnam has a tropical climate and is hot and humid, with rain from May to November and the most rain in June to August.
Voltage/Frequency	220 V; 50 Hz

HOLIDAYS/FESTIVALS

1 January	Solar New Year's Day
Late January/Early February	Vietnamese New Year and Advent of Spring (Tet Nguyen Dan)
3 February	The Foundation of the Communist Party of Vietnam
8 March	Women's Day
30 April	Liberation of South Vietnam (The day when Saigon/Ho Chi Minh City fell to Hanoi in 1975)
1 May	International Labor Day
14 May	Buddha's Birthday
19 May	Ho Chi Minh's Birthday
1 June	Children's Day
27 June	Memorial for War Martyrs
2 September	National Day of the Socialist Republic of Vietnam
6 November	Confucius' Day
20 November	Teacher's Day
22 December	Army Day
25 December	Christmas Day

Most Vietnamese holidays and festivals are based on the lunar calendar, so their celebrations might be on a different date each year by the Gregorian calendar. Even though they prefer the lunar calendar because they can be sure of a full moon the 15th of each month, they use the Gregorian calendar for daily life.

 LANGUAGE TIPS

<u>Vietnamese</u>	<u>Phonetics</u>	<u>English</u>
Xin chao	Sin jow	Hello
Tam biet	Daam bee-uht	Good-bye
Xin	Sin	Please
Cam on	Gaam ern	Thank you
Khong co'gi	Kawn go' zee	You're welcome
Da and vang/Khong	Zaa and vuhng/kawn	Yes/No
Xin loi	Sin loy	Excuse me/Sorry
Toi hieu	Doy hee-oo	I understand

Vietnamese	Phonetics	English
Toi khonghieu	Doy kawm hee-oo	I don't understand
Cho mot lat	Jer mawt laal	One moment, please
Nha ve sinh o dau?	Nyaa ve sing er doh	Where's the toilet?

References

1. Axtell, Roger E. *Do's and Taboos Around the World.* John Wiley & Sons, Inc., 1993.

2. Axtell, Roger E. *The Do's and Taboos of Body Language Around the World.* John Wiley & Sons, Inc., 1997.

3. Bosrock, Mary Murray. *Put Your Best Foot Forward Russia.* International Education Systems, 1995.

4. Centers for Disease Control and Prevention. *CDC Health Information for International Travel 2008.* Elsevier Mosby, 2008.

5. Dresser, Norine. *Multicultural Manners.* John Wiley & Sons, Inc., 1996.

6. Foster, Dean. *The Global Etiquette Guide to Africa and the Middle East.* John Wiley & Sons, Inc., 2002.

7. Foster, Dean. *The Global Etiquette Guide to Asia.* John Wiley & Sons, Inc., 2000.

8. Lewis, Richard D. *When Cultures Colide.* Nicholas Brealey Publishing, 1999.

9. Morrison, Terri and Wayne A. Conway. *Kiss, Bow, or Shake Hands.* Adams Media, 2006.

10. Powell, Michael. *Behave Yourself! The Essential Guide to International Etiquette.* The Globe Pequot Press, 2005.

11. Sabath, Ann Marie. *International Business Etiquette Europe.* Career Press, 1999.

Web sites for Research and Further Information

1. www.101languages.net
2. www.about.com
3. www.acced-i.org/imis_web/staticcontent/1/AC08/Mathias.ppt
4. www.alltrivia.net

5. www.asianinfo.org
6. www.ccrainternational.com
7. www.cia.gov
8. www.consularinformationsheet.com
9. www.cyborlink.com
10. www.ediplomat.com
11. www.eupedia.com
12. www.executiveplanet.com
13. www.friendlyplanet.com
14. www.geoleadership.com
15. www.infoplease.com
16. www.jayp.net/trivia
17. www.kwintessential.co.country
18. www.lonelyplanet.com
19. www.mpiweb.org (CultureActive Tool)
20. www.professionaltravelguide.com
21. www.thomson.co.uk
22. www.timeanddate.com
23. www.tripadvisor.com
24. www.vayama.com
25. www.wikipedia.org
26. www.wikitravel.org
27. www.worldinfozone.com

Maps provided by www.classroomclipart.com.

More Areas You May Want to Explore

Quick and easy seems to be the way our lives have been going over the past few decades, and it is only getting worse—or better—depending on how you look at things. But because we are a lot more rushed, we tend not to bother with the small things. My intent is to provide a guide that will highlight the small things that can make a difference in your interactions with people of other cultures. This book outlines very simply the main details you need to pay attention to for each of the 33 countries covered. I hope it will become a handy reference for you and help you become a better ambassador for your home country.

There are many more points that could be discussed and many more things you may need to learn about. (See the list below.) *Be On Your Best Cultural Behavior* will answer your most immediate needs and concerns when you are dealing with associates from other cultures, but remember, these are only guidelines. Obviously, not every person in a country will do exactly as I've stated. There are variations throughout each country, and individuals have their own ways of doing or saying things. If you have the privilege to work or stay in a country for an extended time, you will pick up on their habits and local customs.

Other areas you may need to explore before traveling:
- Passport/Visa needs and requirements for each country.
- Inoculations if necessary.
- Global health concerns.
  (World Health Organization www.who.int/about/en/)
- Insurance. (Your insurance may not cover you in another country. Check out trip/travel insurance for the various countries.)
- For scheduling purposes, know holidays, festivals, school calendars, bank hours, and work hours.
- Study the political, governmental, economic, legal, demographic, and religious differences of the culture.
- Communication. Most countries are now equipped with every computer or electrical need, but outside the main cities, access may be limited. Check in advance for your specific needs and electrical hook-ups.
- Translators. Prepare in advance and make sure you are dealing with a reputable and dependable company. This can make or break a business deal.

- Transportation. Do you need an international driver's license or will you be able to drive with your existing license? Check before you go and be prepared to drive on a different side of the road. Will you be able to read road signs? It might help to take a class before you get behind the wheel, especially if the wheel is on the other side, or maybe you should hire a driver.
- Be careful when reading the dates and telling time. The clock will be in military time (24 hours) in most countries. Most countries write the day first. January 2, 2009, would be written as 02/01/09. Just to be safe, you might want to write out the month, so you are not confused.
- Embassies/Consultants. Be aware of the location and contact information for your embassy or contact in the country you are visiting. This information is easily accessible online. The U.S. Department of State provides a wealth of information for all countries (www.state.gov/).